RESTART

RESTART

THE LAST CHANCE FOR
THE INDIAN ECONOMY

MIHIR S. SHARMA

RANDOM HOUSE INDIA

Published by Random House India in 2015
1

Copyright © Mihir S. Sharma 2015

Random House Publishers India Private Limited
7th Floor, Infinity Tower C, DLF Cyber City
Gurgaon – 122002, Haryana

Random House Group Limited
20 Vauxhall Bridge Road
London SW1V 2SA
United Kingdom

ISBN 978-81-8400-571-4

Typeset in Sabon by R. Ajith Kumar

Printed and bound in India by Replika Press Private Limited

A PENGUIN RANDOM HOUSE COMPANY

For my father, Prem Swarup Sharma, whose fondness for factory shop-floors is the biggest reason I wrote this book

And my mother, Moneesha Sharma, who suggested I become a journalist long before I had the vaguest idea what journalists did

CONTENTS

CONTENTS

INTRODUCTION

'WHAT IS THE MATTER WITH INDIA?'

When the first plane crashed into the World Trade Center that beautiful September morning, the West changed: it began to look outwards. In the weeks and months after 9/11, the exuberance of the self-obsessed Clinton era became a dim, distant memory. But financial markets feed on exuberance, and on optimism. And so, even as some eyes in the West turned fearfully to the dangerous parts of the outside world, others' eyes turned to seek out those places that offered hope.

One such pair of eyes—bluer and keener than most—belonged to Jim O'Neill, who headed the global economic research division at Goldman Sachs. The vast investment bank was, as usual, quicker to respond to a world in which 'everything had changed'. As the smoke rose from the burning World Trade Center, a trader at Goldman's building—a few blocks downwind—looked up at the papers fluttering through the dusty blue sky, and remarked on 'all the written derivatives contracts that had literally flown out the window'. O'Neill, true to form, saw at once that the energies of the West would turn from the engines of economics to the engines of war. And yet, he pointed out in a report that was to change the world, there was hope for the world economy elsewhere: 'In 2001 and 2002, real GDP growth in large emerging economies would exceed that of the West.'

The large emerging economies O'Neill had in mind were four: Brazil; Russia; India; and, obviously, China. Together, in that 2001 report, he called them BRIC—or, showing the nifty salesmanship that is a large proportion of the skill set of modern finance, 'the BRICs that would build the global economy'. Over the next decade, the four emerging economies would come to dominate global growth.

Twelve years later, O'Neill was a disappointed man. Not in China, of course, which had, in the first decade of the new millennium, come to dominate global manufacturing and trade. Not even that much in Brazil, which grew slower than expected, then faster than expected, then slower than expected again—a sequence clearly Brazil's fault, rather than of those who kept on expecting the wrong thing.

No, O'Neill's biggest problem was India. It was India's apparent failure to match expectations that had caused the whole BRIC idea to be sniggered at on Wall Street; with the financial world's customary sparkling wit, BRIC was now being expanded as 'Bloody Ridiculous Investment Concept'.

O'Neill, stung, said in the middle of 2013 that 'India was the biggest disappointment of the BRIC countries.' His frustration had been growing steadily over the decade-and-some since he had invented the concept. The previous year, when an electricity failure across northern India plunged hundreds of millions of people into darkness in the largest power cut in history, O'Neill wrote in a note to Goldman's investors that it 'highlighted the scale of the challenges'. He ended his note somewhat unusually, by demanding of India: 'What is the matter with you guys?'

What *was* the matter with India?

Superficially, going just by the numbers, we guys hadn't had that bad a decade. Since 2001, the economy had grown manifold. Hundreds of millions of people had been lifted out of abject poverty in a few years, in an achievement unmatched in human history—well, except by China, a couple of decades earlier. Almost every single Indian lived in a better house, ate better food, and had a far higher standard of living than at the beginning of the millennium.

And India had managed solid, sustained real growth in output for many years—not the double-digit miracle that China kept on delivering, but close. Seven per cent growth in gross domestic product adjusted for price inflation—'real GDP growth'—was seen as startlingly fast in 1997. By around 2005–06, that much was being seen as India's birthright. So fast was the economy expanding, in fact, that the amount added to the average Indian's income in the first fourteen years of the twenty-first century was as much as had been added in the entire last half of the twentieth.

Not even the financial crisis of 2008 appeared to have slowed India down that much. Even as America and Europe teetered on the edge of another Great Depression, Indians warmly congratulated each other on their foresight in keeping their financial world detached from that of the West. 'Decoupling' was the in-word that year, a gentle way of saying that emerging economies had happily broken up with the West because the relationship just wasn't working for them any more. Supercharged by the cash being pumped into the arteries of global finance by the world's governments, India's economy finally seemed to be touching double-digit growth at the very moment the industrialized nations seemed to be poised for disaster.

But, then, it all fell apart.

India's economic miracle had been held together by rubber bands and hope, the equivalent of the elderly buses that ply its potholed village roads. It turned out that the early years of this century had all been downhill; the broken-down bus that was the Indian economy had been coasting along, not purring powerfully. Sometime in 2012, it hit the bottom of the slope. And then, when the government pressed the accelerator, the ancient engine stalled.

Month after month, the world's investors looked hopefully at the numbers from New Delhi's statisticians. And, month after month, the numbers were the same, dashing all hopes: manufacturing output was flat. Nobody so much as thought of investing; no company dared to increase production. India's factories had fallen silent, its mines were deserted, its trucks stood parked beside empty highways. Quarter after quarter, GDP growth decreased, and the government seemed powerless to reverse the decline. A noisy, frustrated desperation began to pervade all thinking about India's economic future, both within the country and on trading floors and in boardrooms across the world.

The guys in power then had been, once, feted. They had been called, once, a 'dream team' of economic managers. But their reputations were unequal to the task. They kept their foot on the pedal, but the bus still refused to move. Meanwhile, a crisis seemed to be approaching in the rear-view mirror. India needed dollars to buy petroleum; almost all its fuel has to come from abroad. But Indians simply weren't making enough stuff that they could sell in return for the dollars they needed. And, so, any minute, unless the rest of the world was kind enough to lend us a few billion dollars, India might be stuck without cash to pay its fuel bills.

This was exactly what had happened in 1991, a crisis that became the trigger for India first opening up to the world—and the excuse that Manmohan Singh used to start dismantling socialism as finance minister. Two decades later, Dr Singh was prime minister—and, at the end of his long career in public life, it seemed to be happening again.

Everyone panicked. Senior Indian ministers wandered the cities of the West, caps in hand, begging for investment, for those life-affirming, life-preserving dollars, swearing to anyone who would listen that things would get better soon, that the bus would start moving any minute. Manmohan Singh himself tried, even. But not one member of the Dream Team had much credibility left. The otherwise reticent Dr Singh said, gloomily, when I prodded him with a question about one such stormy session, that when India was growing fast 'everybody was quite happy. Even when there were defects in our policies, they were overlooked. But, when the economy slows down, people try to find fault and excuses.'

Still, India wasn't alone. Brazil and Russia had slowed down, too. Many of the 'tiger' economies of Southeast Asia, too, seemed to be in trouble. But something about the slowdown was very strange: they all seemed to have similar problems.

Here was one: they were short of infrastructure—of roads, of bridges, of working ports. But the vital task of building these was being held up by worries about corruption, by concerns about the environment, or because companies simply didn't seem to be able to find the cash or the expertise. Worse, some of these projects were half built, begun amid great optimism and rosy forecasts in the flush years before the financial crisis.

Here was another: they had governments that seemed unable to take decisions. It seemed that, across the world of emerging markets, democratic leaders had used the go-go years prior to the 2008 financial crisis to buy popularity. Politicians had promised their people free food, or socialized medicine, or cheap housing, or something else that they weren't being able to pay for now that times had turned tough. That meant they were politically weak—and most were further weakened by corruption scandals, too; skeletons from the years of excess being painfully unearthed by various determined investigators. Weakened, frightened, timid, divided, these governments struggled to take the decisions needed to help their economies recover. There seemed no way out.

The emerging-market model, people worried, was broken.

It seemed that there were simply too many things that had to be fixed, and not enough willpower to fix even one. Like a procrastinating student faced with a long to-do list early in the morning, policymakers in developing nations across Asia and Latin America seemed to have groaned and gone back to bed.

And everyone agreed that India was the worst offender.

If Goldman Sachs's O'Neill was the hopeful guiding light behind emerging-market investors, the grumpy yin to O'Neill's ebullient yang was the super-investor Jim Rogers. Rogers cultivates the plain-spoken attitude of a Midwestern farmer; not for him the relatively gentle remarks about 'disappointment' that O'Neill was coming out with. One of the most acerbic voices in the international economic community, he was declaring, bluntly, by 2013 that 'there's nothing good in India'. It was the worst place in the world to do business, he growled. Its politicians made one mistake after another; they made any foreigner who wanted to bring his money into India jump through seventy hoops; and Indian companies were poorly run, unable to be successes without support, open or covert, from politicians.

And Rogers didn't even seem to be the most pessimistic man around. If anything, most clued-in Indians seemed to be even gloomier about India's prospects. Foreigners like Rogers may have been mystified by the 'hoops' that they had to jump through in order to make money in India. But, surely, India's own rich didn't have that problem? Surely they knew who to pay off? Surely they were familiar with little shortcuts that ensured growth and profits?

Turns out they weren't. Throughout 2012 and 2013, India's home-grown capitalists tried desperately to look for investments outside India. They bought steel mills in the West and mines in Africa. Some even set up factories in Southeast Asia—although costs there were much higher than in India. The Indian economy, it seemed, was so difficult to navigate that Indians would rather try to intuit how to make money in a completely new and foreign country.

If the emerging-market model was broken, nowhere looked more broken than India.

All was not lost, however. In India, it sometimes feels like nothing is beyond salvaging. You can always get another call out of a dying phone battery; you can always get another kilometre out of a spluttering car. Somehow, the tired government in New Delhi got its act together a little bit and managed to stave off crisis.

As the gloomy winter of 2013 turned into the spring of 2014, India seemed to have turned a corner. Slowly, it appeared, the pieces of the Indian economy were being reassembled. Fewer voices bemoaned the death of the emerging-market model. A couple of big, prominent companies announced that they were, to their own pleasant surprise, going to make a bit of money. Investors pricked up their ears, hearing that. Money began to flow into India. First a trickle, then a flood—that's how the most brilliant minds in finance work, their totem animal being the brave and individualistic lemming. The big names of Wall Street and the City of London looked around for countries that seemed both stable and recovering, and decided India fit the bill. India's own investors were a little less sanguine about their economy's prospects. A little closer to the economic engine, they could see that it was still spluttering, still held together with wire and safety pins and duct tape. They knew things were broken inside. But when the well-heeled foreigner arrives at your doorstep with money, you ask few questions. Or, at any rate, you take his money first.

And, just like that, in a few short months the mood on India turned. The same country that had been a basket case began to be seen as the hope of the emerging world. The stock market began to hit new highs every week. Indian stockbrokers were puzzled beyond belief, but couldn't believe their luck. Most, with the intellectual and ethical fluidity that is prized in the stockbroking profession, began to predict that the market would rise even higher.

But, oddly, nothing real had changed, yet. All the fancy paper flying around in the financial sector couldn't conceal the fact that India's economy still wasn't growing. Nobody was building new factories, or new bridges, or new ports; nobody was producing more TVs, or ashtrays, or cellphones than they had the previous year. The bus was still stalled. If the model had been broken in 2013, it was still broken in 2014.

When countries feel they're broken, they call in the mechanic. The broad pessimism about India's future pervaded the early part of the election campaign of 2014. But, as it progressed, the pessimism began to dissipate, pushed away by the relentless optimistic promises of the frontrunner, Narendra Modi.

Modi had made a success of several terms as chief minister of the coastal state of Gujarat—economically, at least. His record on inter-religious harmony was, well, considerably less positive. But he was something few Indians had seen before: a natural politician, capable of effortlessly identifying the doubts and concerns of his audience, and of then addressing and minimizing them through a few well-chosen words and an air of indomitable confidence.

Indians had grown tired of worrying about their future. As Modi grew in stature, it seemed they didn't have to. And it was because they didn't want to keep worrying that Modi kept on growing in stature. Investors, foreign and domestic, began to believe again; the markets rose in anticipation of a Modi victory.

But when it came, the victory was even more sweeping than anyone had expected. It was, as we shall see, a sign: an indication of exactly how much India wanted to mend itself, of how much it wanted to stop fretting. Modi's party, the Hindu nationalist and idiosyncratically right-wing Bharatiya Janata Party, swept to a majority in Parliament. A majority meant a government that could act unfettered—something that hadn't been seen for thirty years, for longer than most Indians had been alive.

O'Neill couldn't contain himself. On hearing of Modi's stunning victory, he declared it the most important development for India's economy in those thirty years. At long last, he thought, his prodigal child, his laggard sheep, was returning to the high-growth fold. India, he insisted, was poised to grow at 10 per cent a year for two decades. He did not quite say that all the hard work had already been done, but he seemed to imply that. Once again, O'Neill may be wrong.

By the time Modi was sworn in as prime minister, in May 2014, the mood had completely altered—again. The long years of hesitation and populism, it seemed, had passed. There was a government that had a mandate to take brave decisions, the decisions essential to restore India's economy. Things could change. Which was good, because things had to change.

This book is the story of what has to change.

This book is the story of what has changed in the Indian economy; what needs to change; and this book is about why change is inevitable.

India is broken, but it is going to be mended. It is going to be mended not because any one man wants it, but because a billion people need it to. It is going to be mended because every assumption about its economy is being questioned, and every myth is being seen through.

It is going to be mended not just because it is special, but also because it is not. Every emerging market has similar problems—and every one of those countries is going to fix them. They are going to fix these problems because the same problems have been fixed before, by many other countries on their roads to prosperity.

In fact, this book is about those problems, problems of

infrastructure, of populism, of corruption; this book is about how they are not just problems, but a necessary—even essential—part of an economy's route to maturity. No modern economy can be built without dealing with them. How will people be moved off the land and into factories? How will the poor educate themselves, and feed themselves, and be given the chance to become middle class? How will roads, and bridges, and ports be built? Every industrial nation has had to address these problems—and it's only when these problems are being struggled with that you know a country is progressing, and not stagnating. Each one of these problems is about millions of lives, about a billion tiny decisions—and also about the two or three big decisions that will matter most.

This book is about those decisions; about the steps to maturity that India must take, and the signposts on the road left by those that have gone before.

What's different about today's developing nations is that most of them are doing this as democracies. They have to deal with dissent, and disagreement, and oh-so-democratic vetoes of one kind or another.

Especially in India. India is the most complex country in the world; it has the most layered democracy, the most varied interest groups, the largest number of vetoes. That means there's a lot of noise. The policy machinery isn't well oiled. But the noise it's making isn't that of a crash—it's the noise that accompanies building. It is the noise that accompanies mending.

This book is about that noise; this book is about what we are building.

PART I

DEATH BY LIME REGISTER

India struggles to build anything, whether roads or institutions. It struggles to make things, especially manufactured goods.

In this section, we will find out why we fail; and we will discover just how much that failure damages us.

Thirteen million Indians seek jobs every year. A tiny fraction of them will find them. An even tinier fraction will be satisfied. We will look at why this happens, and we will figure out why we should be very, very scared.

We will ask these three incredibly important questions:

First: How come there are so many people looking for jobs?

Second: Why are there no jobs for them to easily find?

And third: Why aren't they making something of themselves?

And, through the answers, we will learn about Mohandas Gandhi's malign legacy, and we will marvel at what Hindi films tell us about jobs, and we will meet the vicious Lime Register and his mob of fellow murderers, who are responsible for the death of Indian industry.

We will begin to understand just what a hole we're in, and just how much effort it will take to climb out of it.

ROADS AND JUDGES

If you fly into Delhi from somewhere cool and organized, it takes a while to remember where you are. You land, after all, at the freshly built Terminal 3, still too new to have developed the air of overworked decrepitude that is characteristic of our transport system. You drive into town on a shiny elevated toll-road, and you permit yourself to imagine for a moment that China is not, after all, so far ahead of us.

And then you arrive, with minimal warning, at a permanent kilometre-long traffic jam near something called the Rao Tula Ram Road flyover, and reality bangs into your taxi and starts blowing its horn. You roll down your window and gape at the flyover in amazement: it is not so much a bridge, you realize, as it is an ugly concrete summary of India's cussed unwillingness to create sufficient capacity. You don't wish to believe it, but your eyes insist you must: somebody decided that it would be a good idea to create a *single-lane flyover* along—not beside, not across, but along—one of New Delhi's arterial roads. Unsurprisingly, there was an almighty pile-up on the day it opened, and things haven't got better since.

To make it an even more apt metaphor for India's problems, the only solution other than the demolition of the flyover is the widening of the road; but that's being blocked by a powerful coalition of local residents. The flyover was going to be obsolescent from the day it was inaugurated. Even when built, everyone knew it would not be enough.

And there, gaping at the waste and the stupidity, you remember. It's the Indian way, our first commandment, our sole moral imperative: if you have created excess capacity in anything—if you have over-built, or in any way allowed for a crowd—then you have wantonly wasted money.

Indians have learned to live with shortages and delays. Not the shortages of socialism, in which everything nice was rationed; but the shortages of overpopulation, in which every institution, every piece of infrastructure, every square mile is shared by far more people than it was designed for. There are queues for everything, just like in socialist countries; except here, of course, queues usually descend in seconds into disorderly elbow-wrestling matches.

This was not always the creaking country it is today. India was always crowded; but, as old photographs and films of its cities testify, there were times when trams were not always packed, when pavements were wide enough to accommodate pedestrians, and when railway stations were large enough to handle the traffic. When Howrah Station was built in 1905, it had 15 platforms. Today, with 10 times as many trains and 100 times as many passengers, it has 23. India was much poorer in 1905 than it is now. Yet the shortages have been allowed to persist, and grow. London has 13 'A'-category national hub stations; Delhi, with a few million more people to serve, has 5, one of which has only just opened.

It is thus not because India is poor, or has a large number of people, that it suffers a crippling shortage of infrastructure. The people of Bombay are not so poor that they would not pay for slightly better local trains, with a smaller chance of spending one's commute in unwilling communion with their neighbour's armpit.

The reasons for India's infrastructure deficit are deeper than that—born of an enduring belief that anything beyond the basic, any hint of comfort, is sinful and unacceptably expensive. This is a belief with many antecedents: Mahatma Gandhi's tendency to insist on taking third-class train carriages, for one; our deep-rooted socialist ethos, for another.

There are signs that Indians are finally beginning to revolt against this mindset. They may not demand 'world-class' facilities, a ridiculous and imaginary standard that nevertheless much exercises the mind of New Delhi's elite; but they certainly are tired of dealing with non-existent infrastructure. Bihar was once the toughest Indian state to get around—a deeply ironic fact, that, given that it was also the flattest in the country. For fifteen years between 1990 and 2005, it was ruled by Lalu Prasad Yadav, who famously said that his voters walked, they didn't take cars, and so the quality of a road was irrelevant to them. In the years since his successor, Nitish Kumar, took over, the quality of Bihar's roads has improved startlingly—and the voters rewarded him for it. Now, even Lalu talks about roads and bridges.

If there's one thing that unites Indians, it's an impatience with the sub-par facilities that they have to deal with daily. Anything that breaks out of it—the Delhi metro, for example—is regarded with near-superstitious reverence. One of the few places where you can see rambunctious and self-centred north Indians queue up is in the Delhi metro. There is a deep and useful bit of human psychology at work here: something as simple as a shared confidence that there will be place for everyone in the next train leads to civilized behaviour instead of a mad scramble.

It is this bedrock of impatience with the old, the smelly and the crowded that India's politicians have begun to pick up on. Across north India before the last general elections, anecdotes were told about the superb roads of Narendra Modi's Gujarat, about its first-rate infrastructure, about its buses and its electricity. Modi assiduously fed this narrative. In rally after rally in small towns across India, he promised to build infrastructure like China's. For Modi's voters, India's literal incapacity is a national shame. It is not just an inconvenience; it is psychologically troubling, a constant reminder of the country's poverty, and of its weakness.

Naturally, this national inability to build hurts more than just our ego and our pride. In a country with choked highways, strained railways and bottlenecks for ports, it is trade that suffers first. India's long coastline is not a benefit if our vast northern plains can't access it.

Across the Hindi-speaking belt to the north, the biggest problem for manufacturers isn't power supply, or bribery: it's how to get the stuff they've made to the customer who's expecting it. On one occasion, at a conference for exporters in Gurgaon, a man stood up from the floor to say his government had turned him into a liar. The rest of us assumed he was talking about taxes, or regulations, or something of that sort. But no. 'I have to lie to my clients in Europe,' he said. 'Always I have to lie. Because they simply do not believe that their consignment could have left my factory a week ago, but still has not reached Mumbai's port. So I tell them it hasn't left yet.' A murmur of agreement spread through the gathering. Others complained of the same problem; and they all agreed that it took longer to get something made near Delhi on to a ship in Mumbai than it did for it to then sail halfway around the world to Amsterdam, and thence by rail or Rhine to its destination in Europe.

Indeed, the *Financial Times* reported in November 2014 that one French company finds that the cheapest and easiest way to send parts from Bangalore to Hyderabad, a few hundred kilometres apart, is to send them first from Bangalore to Europe, and then back from Europe to Hyderabad. It isn't as if there isn't a decent highway between the two cities; but the moment that a truck hit a state border, it has to stop and wait. According to the World Bank, Indian truck drivers spend a fourth of their time on the road waiting at the tax checkpoints that mark state borders. Factor in the time they spend in queues to pay highway tolls, and they spend less than 40 per cent of their time on the road actually driving. And that's when the roads are *good*. Moving stuff around India costs this country's manufacturers more than they spend paying their workers, the *FT* reports. Even India's lower-than-low wages can't make up for the dent logistics costs make in our competitiveness.

Yes, India has a passion for under-capacity as enduring and inexplicable as its love for cricket. But it is not just the absence of roads that testifies to this. When the manufacturers' trucks arrive at the port in Mumbai, it isn't just that the warehouses there are too crowded, it is that there aren't enough officials to oversee the docks' smooth operations. Sometimes, it takes four or five days just to assign a truck a spot to unload—not because there aren't any spots, but because the port authorities are busy doing other stuff. Other stuff that may be as important, mind you. The simple 'reduce paperwork' prescription hardly works here. Central coordination of where a truck sets down its load, and whether it's close to the place where its container will be loaded on, is pretty essential. It isn't a red-tape problem; it's a capacity-constraint problem. Things are so bad that in 2013 India's largest port was—Colombo. Yes, that's right; that year, the Sri Lankan capital sent more Indian exports abroad than Mumbai did.

As with ports, so with roads and even passport offices: the Indian state consistently fails at creating public facilities to support private individuals.

WHY WE CAN'T BUILD

Why is it that India has this inability to build, whether it is bridges or institutions? Why is it that we can't have nice things?

I think we simply haven't worked on the coordination necessary to produce high-quality public goods that are open to all. Partly that's because we're not a particularly unitary society, and lack the social glue that allows us to treat common property with respect, even when it is crowded. And partly because we have not bothered to invest in increasing the size of the commonwealth. But, again, what is true of ports is true also of roads, of public parks—and of the judicial system.

India's courts are a little like Howrah Station. Once they worked well. But so many people use them now, and they haven't expanded to match the demand. And just like Indian Railways is so unappetizing now that many people choose to just stay at home, the fear of the legal process has taken over our lives. Pretty much any Indian, rich or poor, will pay unaffordable bribes to the police in order to avoid the threat of a malicious lawsuit.

The courts are gloomily aware of their own lack of capacity. A chief justice of the Delhi High Court recently pointed out that although his court settles one case every five minutes, it would still take it almost 500 years to clear its case backlog. And that's if the backlog stays the same, which it probably won't. So far, the number of cases clogging up the plumbing has increased twice as fast as the number of judges.

What happens when a country's legal system turns into its biggest bottleneck? Anarchy, injustice and bullying by the powerful. A recent study by Cornell Law School pointed out that more prosperous Indian states were also those in which more civil cases were filed. This is a vital reminder of the importance of courts: the more prosperous states were also the ones in which people felt that the state was not too overworked to dispense justice. A just order is a prosperous order. But, the Cornell study continued, in recent years even those states found that their judicial backlog had begun to bite: 'India's enormous and growing civil case backlog has discouraged civil case filings in recent years.' Those states with more of a backlog had fewer new cases. India is becoming progressively less just.

The effect on small businesses is particularly stark. The most important thing, if you want to encourage innovation and healthy risk-taking, is fairness in the enforcement of contracts. That's where quick and easy civil cases come in. But a legal system that takes years to pronounce any judgement—and is heavily biased towards the wealthier party—is a disaster when it comes to fairness in contracting. In fact, there's now a phrase to explain India's problems: 'contract instability'. It's a nice way of saying that, in India, people can lie and cheat with impunity. And so they do.

Lying to the government is both an art and a duty in India. Tax evasion is not, morally, considered a crime; neither is insider trading.

This does tend to complicate the business of regulation somewhat. As with a teacher in a schoolroom, the only authority a regulator has is what her charges acknowledge; and in a country with a poor court system and chronic incapacity, a powerful company is that snotty over-tall young boy at the back of the class. It sees no need to acknowledge any authority.

Regulators, meanwhile, don't like to appear powerless. So, although they do not have enough people to do their job, and do not have enormous moral or legal authority over the companies they regulate, they have to pretend. In other words, they too refuse to acknowledge their failures.

But, at least when the inevitable occurs, and they are caught out not doing their jobs, an Indian regulator demonstrates an ability to dredge up excuses of unique quality. The United States Food and Drug Administration censured a series of medicine factories in India earlier this year for various transgressions, poor hygiene among them—one factory was found to have rat droppings in the sanitized area where drugs were produced, another did not have water supply in the bathrooms. All of these plants, naturally, had been certified as safe by Indian regulators. In response, India's chief drug regulator said, huffily, that if American standards were applied to Indian pharmaceutical companies, they'd all have to be locked up.

I'm not singling out the medicine-makers. Tests by Europe's New Car Assessment Programme of five popular Indian cars discovered that none of them met crash safety standards, which didn't concern regulators back home. And the US Federal Aviation Authority (FAA), early in 2014, downgraded India's air safety to the equivalent of 'junk' status. Why? Because in a series of audits, the FAA discovered that the Directorate General of Civil Aviation, the regulator supposed to ensure that Indian airlines met safety standards, simply didn't have enough people to inspect all the planes.

As we shall see, this is a consistent pattern across every sector. It can hardly be argued that proper drug regulation is a luxury. Yet it is something that the Indian government treats as if it were unaffordable. The belief that we are so poor a country that we should never, ever, have slack capacity is very deeply ingrained indeed.

Reversing the mistakes of the past will be complicated and expensive. The drug controllers' office, stung by the outraged criticism that came its way after the rats-in-your-aspirin story, wants to recruit 300 to 400 new regulators a year for the next five years. Admirable. Except it's difficult to see where they are going to get so many all at once. The scars left by decades of systemic indifference aren't easily concealed. People take time to train.

But surely bridges and roads are easier to build overnight than skilled regulators? Well, yes, they are. But so very many of them are needed that the sums quickly reach astronomical levels. Around 2012, the government found a number both astronomical, and nice and round. Before 2017, it announced, India would need $1 trillion to put into infrastructure. That is well more than half India's yearly output. It is also several times what the government collects in taxes in a year. How, precisely, is this big gap to be bridged? The government hopes that business will pitch in—40 per cent of the trillion dollars will come from private investment, according to officials in Delhi.

'But,' you interject in concern, since you've been paying close attention, 'how is that wise? Does India have no regulators worth the name?' And you would be right. India is chronically short of capacity. But it can't build up its physical capacity without building up its human capacity. And that takes time.

THERE IS A TIDE

Time is short.

For every society, there comes a moment that it must seize. That's the moment when it has a bulge in its population—when there are so many very young people in it, as compared to the old, that it takes a giant step towards the future. In the United States, the 'baby boom' saw a vast expansion in its output and productivity—and, equally important, a reconfiguration of its social hierarchies and values.

China is perhaps the best example. It built a world-beating manufacturing sector on its coasts thanks to cheap labour coming in from its interior. It has grown manifold over the past decades, bursting into middle-income status. Now, it grows old, its draconian one-child policy finally beginning to catch up with its demographics. But the working-age population will not start shrinking until 2030, or thereabouts. By that time, hopefully, it will have harnessed the energy of these generations of young people, and propelled itself to wealth.

India is going through that bulge right now, but is completely unprepared for it.

And our ideas are unprepared for it as well. You see, India is unique in history: it needs to go through three transformations at the same time. The first is this demographic transition, the bulge. The second is the disruption that comes with a country building its infrastructure, connecting the dots that are people, drawing itself together. And the third is a social transformation, a turn towards modernity in our attitudes, and preferences, and lives. Each of these is difficult; and we have left them all for the last minute. Other countries have done one and then the other, usually—Britain built infrastructure before it liberalized its society, China was pretty liberal by the time it went through its demographic bulge, and so on. India, as usual, has chosen of its own free will to put its feet up and doze until each of these changes is underway all at the same time.

Oh, and here's the final turn, the one that leaves us well and truly lost: we have to manage these three transitions while being a vibrant and diverse democracy. Who has built infrastructure while being so democratic, for example? The rich countries of the West were oligarchies when they built their roads and railways; the Tigers of the east, authoritarian.

Still, if India doesn't catch the moment, if it doesn't ride the demographic wave, then it will be consigned to poverty and despair forever. Almost every Indian understands this subconsciously. This is why they have expectations of the future, and from their government, that appear so unreasonable. In fact, they are unreasonable—but they will have to be met anyway, or social turmoil is inevitable.

Perhaps you don't believe that. But the urgency, the immediacy, of this need can be felt on any Indian street, if you look for it. It is among the first things any visitor to India senses. She might already know that the median age in India is 25, as opposed to 34 in China, 40 in Britain or 45 in Germany. But no statistic can convey exactly how overwhelmingly young the streets are. Once foreigners might have noted how many people India had; now, they will note in addition how very young most of them are. I too, when I moved back to India from the United States in 2007, reflected morosely that I was moving from a country where I was below the average height to one where I was above the average age.

And young people stand out in another way, too. They are visibly taller and healthier than their parents. Far more of them can read and write. In 1991, when the economy began to open up, India's literacy rate was 43 per cent. Today, it's 74 per cent.

The three-quarters of Indians under 30 do not remember the distant past that shaped the rest of us—the dull, beige India that state socialism had engendered, when incomes barely grew, food was always short, and there was nothing on TV but information for farmers. For the rest of us, the speed of the transformation has been blinding. For them, it is still too slow.

And perhaps it is too slow. One of the most stunning numbers in a country that specializes in mind-numbing numbers is this: 13 million Indians will join the workforce every year from now till 2030. They know their prospects aren't good. Here's why: in the years from 1972 to 1983—not celebrated as a time of overwhelming prosperity—the total number of jobs in the economy nevertheless grew 2.3 per cent a year.[1] In the years between liberalization in 1991 and today, jobs have grown at an average of only 1.6 per cent a year. But, if these young people have to be absorbed, then jobs must grow at least 3 per cent a year—almost twice the rate at which they have since liberalization. This is simply not happening. In other words, one out of every two youngsters who starts looking for a job next year won't find one.

And here's the last, terrifying figure. According to the last Census, 47 million Indians under the age of 25 are *already* looking for regular work, but not finding it. That's right: at this moment there is an army of angry young unemployed in India that numbers as much as the total population of Spain. Or Kenya. Or Ukraine. Or South Korea. And it will grow by six million every year, at least.

That's asking for trouble, no?

THREE BIG QUESTIONS

Go, today, to a small Indian town. There are only three places where you see vibrant activity—queues, discussion, energy. One is the alcohol shop. The second is the newsagent, who will also sell application forms for public-sector jobs. And the third is the guy who sells lottery tickets.

This tells its own story, of desperation and of hope. And it raises three questions.

First: Where did all these young people come from?

Second: Why do they have nowhere to go?

And third: Why aren't they making something of themselves?

Here's the answer to each question.

First: Many of them, perhaps most, came from farms, and they really don't want to go back. Indian agriculture is a dead end—until something changes.

Second: In other countries, at other times, they would have been soaked up by a vibrant manufacturing sector. India hasn't got one—unless something changes.

And third: They don't have the skills for white-collar jobs, or even the few blue-collar jobs that are available—and something will have to change.

Each of these problems needs to be solved individually—and all three of them need to be solved at the same time. Fix two out of three, and it won't be enough.

THE MAHATMA'S MALIGN LEGACY

'If the village perishes,' wrote Mohandas Gandhi, 'India will perish too. India will be no more India. Her own mission in the world will get lost.' Gandhi said many things that the country he helped create has quietly chosen to ignore. But his disdain for urban life, his praise of the farm, is not one of them. Indeed, few countries have as determinedly upheld a conception of rustic, rural purity as has Gandhi's India.

This has been tremendously counterproductive. For one very simple reason: Indian agriculture does not pay enough. Nor will it ever pay enough.

This is one of the few occasions where the statistics are so obvious that they're worth quoting. Here is the most relevant statistic: If farming households were forced to live on their agricultural income alone, then more than 60 per cent of them would be below India's poverty line.

Farmers know this, of course. This is why, at last count, only 17 per cent of them—less than one in five!—subsisted entirely on money from their farm. The remainder all did some extra work, off it.

Another relevant set of numbers: Indian farms are tiny. Over 80 per cent of them are smaller than 2 hectares. Most of them are less than half the size of a football field.

And they are getting ever smaller. They are just over half as big today, on average, as they were in 1970. Everywhere else in the world, farms have gotten bigger in the same time period. Basically, absolutely every part of this country that could be farmed, is; and the number of people in agriculture has just continued to grow.

According to the last Census, in 2011, 55 per cent of India—over half—worked in agriculture. The sector, however, provided less than 15 per cent of India's gross national product. So, in other words, farms employed most of India's people, but produced very little.

And this is exactly where we have tried to help—and exactly where we have made our big mistake.

The problem is that our efforts to fix this have focused on the second number, not the first. Many people have been convinced that if there was just some way to increase agriculture's share of output, some way in which all of agriculture received 'support', things would be better. Most people who think this live in India's cities.

The people who actually work on the land are wiser. They know that they do not earn enough, and are never likely to. Few people born into agricultural families want to work in the fields like their parents did. Few parents want it for their children. Anyone who disbelieves this is welcome to spend a night at any semi-urban railway station in India's vast hinterland. There are few more depressing, and yet uplifting, places. Wander around, and speak to any of the hundreds of young men sleeping on the platforms, waiting for trains. They all have stories to tell, of why they want to leave their villages. If they had money, sure, some would stay back—but by no means all. Most of all, they understand, clear-eyed, that working on the farm will never make them the money they want.

There is an iron link, in any market economy, between how much the market values whatever you produce, and how much you earn.

On India's farms, people don't earn that much because, first, each individual doesn't produce a lot. And second, because the things they produce are not worth as much in terms of, say, televisions and mobile phones, as they'd like.

There are two ways to change this, if you think that it needs fixing. The first is to try and force what they produce—food, mainly—to earn them more TVs and mobile phones. Economists call this rate of exchange the 'terms of trade', and have a long history of advising politicians to manipulate it for one reason or another.

The second way to fix this is by ensuring each person who works on a farm somehow produces more food. This is called 'increasing productivity'—a phrase we're going to keep stumbling across.

India's greatest success in agriculture came from an advance of the second kind. In the Green Revolution of the 1960s and 1970s, high-yielding varieties of grain developed mainly in the United States were introduced across India. The effects were somewhat miraculous. India had long been considered unable to feed itself. It had too many mouths, and didn't grow enough to put in them. It relied on food aid from the West; it was, according to the more sardonic of commentators, 'a ship-to-mouth existence'. But, in barely a decade or so, India was self-sufficient in food. Indeed, in the decades since, India has built up so vast a stockpile of rice and wheat that it is now running out of place to keep it—the paranoid hoarding one associates with a childhood of deprivation.

But the right lessons from this success have never been learned. India's town-dwellers have instead focused on the first kind of intervention—making sure that whatever farmers choose to grow, they can also sell at a high price. (This is the exact opposite of what both Marxist and classical liberal economists have always assumed and recommended. Both those sets of people expected that farmers would have to provide cheap food to a burgeoning urban working class. India's democratic politicians had different ideas.)

21

That's why India has always had a pretty high inflation rate; prices have never really been stable. The government has kept supporting agricultural prices, and at an increasing rate through the first decade of the twenty-first century; that's meant ever-higher prices for wheat and vegetables and milk—and thus quite a bit of grumbling in the towns.

But it's also led to relative prosperity in rural areas. In recent years, incomes have increased for everyone who owns a farm, or works on one, or works near one. So why do people still want to move off them?

Because they recognize that this can't last. Rural distress may have declined, but try telling an Indian farmer that it's the occupation of the future and he will laugh at you mockingly.

And there's one even more important factor: Nowhere in India's vast rural tracts is there a visible ladder to wealth, or the beginnings of affluence—or, truthfully, even to moderate comfort. If you don't inherit land, you are condemned to subsistence. How does a landless labourer use his daily wage to join the middle class? Why would he want his son, who has probably gone to secondary school, to live the same life he has?

This is not an ambition that many of our policies will help him fulfil. For this is an ambition that most of our policymakers would rather a rural worker did not have at all. It upsets too many assumptions.

In India's cities, where policies are set, we have often talked of 'protecting' our farmers. But very few of us know who the farmer we are protecting is. We cannot picture his, or her, face, but we are fairly sure it is weather-beaten. Perhaps it looks to a cloudless sky, hoping for rain. Perhaps not. Either way, it carries 5000 years of history in its eyes. Or in its resigned expression, or something.

The truth is that the millions of Indian farmers are—and this should really not have to be said—all as different from each other as are you and I. And even to the extent that they do the same thing, they labour under vastly different circumstances and with vastly different desires from place to place. There are too many types of Indian farmers to count, not one, and they have as many different interests and demands; and most of them are contradictory. How can you 'protect' them all?

The big farmer in Punjab wants nothing more than his free power and water to continue forever. His daughter is in Jalandhar and his son is in Canada; and what he wants is an end to the rural employment guarantee scheme. There's no controlling these damned Biharis who work on his land now, they are not as desperate as they were earlier.

The smallholder in Telangana wants to know where the canals he was promised are. He knows his counterpart in coastal Andhra has canals; but he, here in the arid upcountry, has to rely on wells he's dug. He paid for them himself, too, where the canals are paid for by the government. And the worst thing is that his wells run dry just when he needs them the most. Where are those canals?

The marginal farmer in Madhya Pradesh is confident. He's confident because he believes he can get his hands on a new variety of vegetable seeds, and the man willing to sell it to him says it will triple his profits. Ah, if only he had a little more cash to invest in it! What a pity he can't mortgage his farm properly. For that kind of returns, he'd be willing to go deeper into debt. One good throw pays for all . . .

The man with 2 hectares near a highway in Gujarat wants to know if you can introduce him to PepsiCo. He thought about it, and he knows it's risky, but he's willing to chance it—he'll turn the entire 2 hectares over to potatoes if PepsiCo agrees to handle the purchasing of fertilizer and comes up with a preferred planting schedule. Apparently someone two villages over got a contract like this, and he wants one too. He's sick and tired of finding a different buyer every year. They fleece you, these traders.

The young man who has inherited land in western Uttar Pradesh has heard a rumour. Is it true that there will be a new road nearby, a six-lane expressway from Delhi to Dehradun? If so, and this is crucial, how close is it to his land? Is it so close that they will acquire it forcibly? That's bad. True, it would be worse if it was so far away that he couldn't sell it for a good price. It's an asset, and surely it is worth more to someone else than it is to him? In any case, he knows a mobile-phone shop in Meerut he could get a share in if he came up with a few lakhs in the next couple of months . . .

The tired-looking man at the Mumbai train station is a farmer. He owns no land and spends most of his time away from his village in Jharkhand, but he insists he is still a farmer. He is going back, isn't he? Twice a year he goes, like clockwork, when his hands are needed on the family's fields. He likes Mumbai, sure. But he only gets really excited when he starts talking about the price of fertilizer, and whether you should grow only rice, or rice and pulses. Of course he's a farmer! He just doesn't live near a farm.

The stocky Bengali from a border district is furious. His paddy crop is struggling; the long-grain varietal he has planted all his life is simply not doing as well as it used to. The sea is rising, he says, and water that once was sweet is now brackish. The rice his grandfather planted in this rich delta could have handled salt, he believes; but 5000 varieties have vanished now. Perhaps one of them would have been perfect. But that's not why he's furious. He's furious because his brother-in-law in the next district, who always had even more saline land, has just built another floor for his house. Because he's stopped planting rice, and turned his field into a big pond, filled it up with saline water, and become a prawn farmer. From the moment the wife heard about the prawns, his own life has become unbearable. The fellow even bought himself a flat-screen TV!

The old couple in Bihar is slightly confused, but pleased. The man at the fertilizer shop always told them that more is better. And that made sense to them, too. But now they're being told by the government to farm their tiny plot more intensively. Look after a small number of seeds and saplings as if they were children; transplant them, one at a time, into your field. Leave space between them, don't crowd them: like a first-class compartment, not general class, the man from the government had said, laughing. Carefully moderate the water. It's a lot of work, sure: but their yield has gone up a lot. And profit has doubled. This is really confusing, but they're not complaining. For the first time in decades, they are enjoying their work.

Does anyone think all these people can be 'protected' by the same policy? The law that prevents the MP farmer from gambling with his land also prevents the young man near Meerut from selling out; mandating intensive farming, as with the Bihar couple, may not help the man in Telangana who really needs a bit more water.

And, in the middle of this, it is wise to remember these two things: that most people in rural areas don't own land; and even those who do survive thanks to money they earn away from it.

Clearly, Indian agriculture is complex enough, and vital enough, to need neither cloying sympathy nor cold contempt. In its cities, the attitude is one or the other. Either you hear that everyone is killing themselves in the countryside, isn't it terrible; or you hear that politicians only care about bloody farmers, who takes care of the cities and the middle class who pay all the taxes? Instead of sympathy or contempt, we can do it the favour of being rational.

And since rationality has come up, let us for a moment consider the twin offences against common sense that come up when Indian agriculture is discussed.

First, genetically modified food. Get over it, people. The Europeans are the richest and most pampered human society in history. India is, to be blunt, not. We cannot exactly adopt their snooty attitude to tomatoes. Is GM food killing us from inside? Probably not. Soyabean has been genetically modified since 1996, corn since about then, and every time we have something from the US that's processed, it's definitely got one or the other. Billions of people have had GM high-fructose corn syrup in their Cokes and their 7Ups and their Dr Peppers, and it's done nothing to them. (Other than ruined their teeth, made them obese, and given them diabetes, but that has nothing to do with GM.) The anti-GM lobby is so powerful and so noisy, however, that they can even pressure the Chinese government into ending its support of GM rice. What chance do India's farmers have? None.

Second, farmer suicides. Yes, people often kill themselves when they are indebted and they see no way out. But, people, stop lying to us with numbers to try and make us feel bad. It is disrespectful to farmers, it is disrespectful to us and it is, worst of all, disrespectful to mathematics and common sense. All you need to know about suicides on the farm is this: that whether or not farmers are killing themselves at a greater rate than other Indians do depends, crucially, on how every state's police and the Census and various household surveys define and categorize 'farmers'. If your emotional pitch for rural distress comes down to this kind of definitional quibbling, find a new pitch. And, ideally, let your new pitch not essentialize and flatten Indian farmers' personalities and motivations, please. After all, it should not run into problems of comparison—in having to explain why 14 of every 1,00,000 middle-class people in Bangalore kill themselves, for example, a number comparable or higher than farmer suicides in most Indian states. Are they in distress? Why do 17 of every 1,00,000 people in famously happy Bhutan kill themselves, a rate higher than Indian farmers in most states? Is there an explanation for the widely different suicide rates among farmers in different states—an explanation more powerful than my Reason for All Seasons, carelessness with the data? Above all, if 20 of every 1,00,000 Japanese kill themselves for an entire complicated set of reasons, many of them to do with cultural views of suicide, why would you imagine they have that three-dimensional inner life—and not the farmers you wish to 'protect'? Basically, what I'm saying is: don't play number games—incompetently!—with suicide. No decision a human being could make is more complex.

And, persisting with rationality for a bit—I promise it will be over soon—just suppose that, indeed, many people kill themselves, and that indicates economic distress and nothing else. Well, then, surely one possible answer to rural distress in a changing world is to ease the transition to towns, a transition so many people want to make, anyway?

People who talk about rural distress—and they are well meaning, certainly, even if and when they are wrong about specifics—are not powerless in this country, though they like to claim that sometimes. They are, in fact, the mainstream. They have parliamentary committees in the palms of their hands. Even 'reformist' finance ministers and prime ministers insist on pardoning all outstanding agricultural loans. Indirect income support to rural areas has risen steadily throughout the past fifteen years. Government-set prices for agricultural goods are higher every year. Rural employment programmes have set a floor for the wages of landless labourers. And, unsurprisingly, rural incomes have soared. Farming may still not be worth your while—but, if you live in rural areas, you are nevertheless earning much, much more than you were earlier. Wages have doubled, or trebled, over a decade for the poorest Indians.

But none of that means they will necessarily want to stay in the place they were born. Some of them might. Many won't. The village has no path to prosperity for those at the bottom of multiple hierarchies—disadvantaged in terms of education, of caste, of profession, and of income. And people who are not from the dominant, landowning castes may have reasons to leave 'home' that are not easily reduced to numbers.

This means that, for all the well meaning and even effective intervention to minimize rural suffering, an age-old historical process of development is working anyway. People, just like in Industrial Revolution Britain, just like in 1990s China, want to move from their dead-end villages to vibrant towns.

But, since 'towns' are a bad word in India—and, a little later, we'll talk about exactly how depressingly true that is—we work instead to keep people tied to villages. And to their low-productivity occupations.

How does the Indian state manage to do this? Through any number of little steps, all of which make it impossible to really move. For example, there's the tyranny of the 'proof of address'. Without this odd little requirement, one can't open a bank account in a city. One can't get a phone. Frequently—and this is one of those Catch-22 frustrations that Indian bureaucrats particularly revel in—one can't get a properly legal rent agreement without a proof of legal address.

Then there are all the little subsidies that are paid out to you in your village: a scholarship, say, or rationed wheat, or the 'employment guarantee scheme', which ensures that you have access to work—as long as you stay exactly where you were born. All these were sold as giving people 'the option' to stay in villages; in actual fact, they force them to stay in villages.

But, even though their loving, coddling government does not want them to leave, many young people will, anyway. Well, if they think they have somewhere to go to—anywhere. Give them a scent of a job in a town, and they will go. One man once asked me, years ago, if I even understood what it felt like to have to remind yourself, yearly, that you don't have the skills to risk moving to a town. It wasn't something you felt good about. But even then, he said, he would move—if he could find someone to live with, a cousin, a friend willing to give him a bit of space on the floor. That seems the biggest constraint for many; not their lack of formal schooling or skills, but the shortage of urban housing.

This is the desperation, the determination engendered by a chronic lack of productivity.

Gandhi did not really approve of poverty—although he chose to appear to approve, usually in order to discomfit some well-dressed Briton. But he did, thoroughly and comprehensively, disapprove of increasing a poor person's productivity. He firmly believed that machinery, like tractors, that made it easier to work on a farm would hurt and not help the poor. 'Machinery has its place; it has come to stay. But it must not be allowed to displace necessary human labour.'

In its slavish but unspoken devotion to this principle, India has really been more Gandhian than it is given credit for. The confusing nature of Indian rural employment—in which work expands to fill the number of mouths to feed—has puzzled generations of economists. The work itself is frequently back-breaking, and produces little of economic value; but those innovations that would make it easier, and free the strength, the intellect and the time of the worker for other pursuits, have never been priorities. India's policymakers had other plans. These are not plans to, say, create enough urban jobs and houses to accommodate those from our villages who want them. No, these are plans to 'strengthen India's villages'.

But these plans force people to stay unproductive—and they force people to stay poor. India's villages are where aspiration goes to die.

A FUTURE UNWOVEN

Most parts of India, even the flatlands of the north, look lovely from the air. Green and rivered most of the time; rocky and dramatic, otherwise. Even the hot, flat, and crowded bits can look quite sepia-toned and lovely from up there, with roofs that blend dustily into the landscape. Closer to towns, you can see roads, and the railway, and bridges—it doesn't really feel like we're short of infrastructure at all.

But look closer. One thing is missing. Fly above the Midwest of the United States, or the Rhineland of Germany, and you see many, many long, rectangular roofs. To Indian eyes they look unfamiliar—strange, even. It takes a little while to realize that they're factories.

This is going to be a bit of a refrain in this book, I'm afraid. It turns out that, once upon a time, we thought we would be a manufacturing economy; and, sometime over the past few decades, we gave up. Oh, we made a ton of excuses—about infrastructure, and globalization, and skills, and so on and so forth. We even tried to sell the absence of a manufacturing sector as a brilliant innovation. Look at us! Everybody else used an industrial sector to get rich, but we are so brilliant and ancient and everything that we have jumped an entire stage, and gone straight to a services-dominated economy, like the US is today! Double Promotion! Service–Led Growth! It's because we are a nation of thinkers, you see. Not like all those others, none of whom has a 5000-year-old intellectual tradition.

Yet without an industrial revival, we don't have a hope in hell of dealing with these masses of young people who want steady jobs.

Note, for a moment, that word 'steady'. To build a solid, prosperous middle class, you don't need just regular jobs—you need security. You need security of location, and you need security of employment—or at least security of income. In other words, you need to be able to offer young people a life, not just one job.

But we've gone about how to give people security all wrong. This has been our approach so far: if you can, through some transcendental miracle, get yourself a full-time job in one of our few factories, good for you: you will never be fired. We have dozens of regulations and legal precedents protecting your employment. You can, in effect, turn up and play games on your iPhone all day, and all your employer can do is sigh and refuse to allow you to charge your phone when it runs out of battery in seven minutes.

Wait a moment, you say. This sounds lovely. In fact, now that you consider it, this is exactly the sort of job that you need. Where, you ask politely, can you find such a job? You can, no doubt, start tomorrow.

Well, here's the bad news: it turns out that employers are terrible people, and don't like being stuck with workers they can't fire. So, cowardly capitalists that they are, they don't hire them in the first place.

Presumably because we are a uniquely generous and altruistic people, we have the most protections on employment in the world. And thus, perhaps because we are also a uniquely self-harming people, we have the fewest people employed in steady jobs.

And it isn't just labour law. Indian employers, like most Indians, will go to considerable lengths to avoid being transfixed by the baleful eye of our government. You really don't want to be noticed. If the fact that you employ more than 100 workers means the government will know your name then, dammit, you will never employ more than 99.

Businesses with less than 10 workers—if you have less than 10 workers, then the government does not deign to notice you at all—employ over 90 per cent of India's workers. These are people in jobs without any benefits or protections whatsoever.

Do pause to consider the magnificence of India's socialist aspirations, and the genius of its policymakers. Attempting to protect workers, they have instead ensured that none exist. Trade unions, in the process of making their own jobs among the most secure in the world, have also made themselves irrelevant. If there was a Darwin Award for public policy, handed out to the ideology most likely to select itself out of the future, then Indira Gandhi-era Indian socialism would sweep the awards.

Or perhaps it wouldn't. Because, after all, even in this so-called Reforms Era, we haven't exactly changed these laws, have we? In fact, they are as restrictive as ever they were—far more confining and repressive than those of our neighbours and competitors. In one study of major economies by the Export-Import Bank of India, only Pakistan and Sri Lanka besides India required the consent of the government before workers were dismissed; only Vietnam, besides India, required the consent of a trade union; and no country besides India required companies to have demonstrated that they had tried all other alternatives before considering dismissal.

It's thanks to our laws that we have smaller and less profitable companies than our peer group. According to UN data, the share of micro and small enterprises in manufacturing employment is 84 per cent for India, versus 27 per cent for Malaysia and 25 per cent for China. The average number of workers in an Indian firm is 75; in China, 191, and in Indonesia, 178.

And the effect of this is stark. Consider textile factories—the cloth and clothing sector is the quickest and best way to expand factory employment, and it always has been. Once, India had textile mills that seemed poised for global success. If you grew up in India long enough ago, you remember when advertisements for cloth brands used to dominate television and magazines—Bombay Dyeing, DCM, Lalimli Dhariwal and Vimal, Only Vimal. Each one of those was a storied mill, and in the vanguard of Indian industry. Vimal itself was, after all, the seed from which grew noble Reliance, the puissant and the mighty.

But all that changed. At a lecture in New Delhi in 2014, my boss, the economic journalist T.N. Ninan pointed out the following disturbing numbers: before the expansion of trade thanks to new international rules in the twenty-first century, India made $10 billion from textile exports, and Bangladesh $8 billion. Today India makes $12 billion—and Bangladesh $21 billion.

That's because the performance of a textile industry is particularly sensitive to how big factories are—a factory needs to be able to fulfil big orders quickly and efficiently. Plus, really long assembly lines still matter in textiles: in some cases, 100 people can sequentially work to make a pair of trousers in the least time. In Bangladesh, the average number of people in a factory is between 300 and 400; in the south Indian textiles hub of Tirupur, it's around 50. The differences in scale are even more stark when you look at the number of machines per factory—in Bangladesh, it's around 450; in Tirupur, 25 to 30.

Bangladesh, in so many ways, does far better than India. Most painful, though, is its performance in textiles and industrial growth. After all, it can hardly be explained by culture—nobody has ever claimed that Bengalis are the most energetic of people. Nor is governance very different the moment the Jessore Road crosses the border. No, the only difference is that they never had our moment

33

of Socialist Glory. And so they don't have the laws that bind us.

Or, to be precise, the laws that bind our poorest to poverty. In a country crying out for jobs, I want you to pause and consider this: Bangladesh, which has not got our oh-so-clever worker protections, employs (proportionally) *five* times as many people in the textile industry as we do.

THE NICE, KINDLY GOVERNMENT INSPECTOR

Labour laws are just one thorny branch in a thicket of regulations meant to prevent Indian companies from doing anything that might make them an honest profit. If you go over a certain size, then that means that the most beloved figure in India, the Government Inspector, will turn up at your door. The Inspector is a kind man. He is a patient man. He is a forgiving man. He wants nothing more than to leave you alone and undisturbed. But what to do, sir, he has children, and they need extra tuition, especially the older one, he can barely add, sir.

Of course, if you have your paperwork in order, then there is nothing to worry about. The Inspector is an honest man. He will not cause you trouble without a valid reason. So he will not trouble you, as long as you have kept the minimal paperwork required by the Factories Act up to date.

All you need to provide that good, kind, patient, forgiving, *honest* Inspector is the following.

Under Rule 3, your application for permission to construct, extend or take into use any building as a factory. Under Rules 4 and 12, your application for Registration and Grant of Amendment of Licence and notice of occupation. Under Rule 3, Subsection 4, your Certificate of Stability. Under Rule 5, your licence to work a factory, which is quite different from your registration of a licence under Rule 4. Under Rule 10, the Overtime Register for workers permitted overtime, as well as a note of which workers are not. Under Rule 12A, your Notice of Change of Manager—which is usually the sole thing you can find in an emergency because only the old manager knew where the other records were kept.

Under Rule 22, your Humidity Register, duly kept dry. Under Rule 15, your Record of Lime Washing and Painting, which must be kept free of white spots. Under Rule 74, the Report of the Examination of Vessels Kept Regularly under Pressure; fortunately, the legal definition of vessels does not include you. Under Rule 103, the Register of Compensatory Holidays. Under Rule 112 and 113, the Register of Child Workers and their Notice as to Periods of Work, as well as the little badge that says 'I Will Burn in Eternal Damnation! Ask me Why?' Under Rules 114 and 115, the Register of Leave with Wages, as well as the Leave Book, which is a completely different animal, nobody knows why.

Under Rule 14, a Health Register, which is completely different from the Reports and Notices required under certain subsections of Rule 123. The latter, after all, pertain to incidents of poisoning, of any diseases suffered by workers, as well as of accidents including Dangerous Occurrences—oh, be sure to keep *two* separate Reports of Dangerous Occurrences, one of those leading to injury, and one of those which don't. It should be obvious that both these Reports are completely different from, and should be filed separately, from the *Register* of accidents, major accidents and Dangerous Occurrences, as required under Rule 131.

Righto. Then you need all Attendance Cards of your workers, under Rule 115, Subsection 3. Also a Muster Roll, under Rule 130, which is actually the same information, as it turns out, so good news there, except it has to be filled in a different format, so bad news in a way.

To the untrained eye, all these look like ways to monitor a working environment. But any factory owner knows this is not true! No working environment is truly monitored until a properly maintained Register Containing Particulars of Monitoring of Working Environment is produced, the layout of which is prescribed by Schedule A of Rule 129, as required under Section 7, Subsection A, Clause 2, Part (e) of the Act.

Please also note that your employee Certificates must be up to date and on file, particularly their Certificate of fitness for employment in hazardous processes/dangerous operations, required under Rule 122; that is to be issued by a Certified (and, apparently, Certifying) government surgeon. This is separate from, and not be filed with, the identical Certificate of fitness for employment in hazardous process and dangerous operations under Rule 81, Schedule A, which is to be issued by a Factory Medical Officer. (What, you don't have a Factory Medical Officer?) For everyone's peace of mind, it's best to not store this close to the form required under Rule 119, which specifies who gets 'wages in lieu of the quantum of leave to which he was entitled in the event of death of worker'. Of course, if the hazardous and life-threatening process in question is driving a crane or such-like, then make sure you also have a certificate from a qualified eye doctor, as is prescribed under Sub-Rule (4) of Rule 81, Schedule G. Naturally, you can have all of these, but if you do not also have the General Certificate of Fitness under Rule 122 for the employee in question, then there may be trouble—and you have only yourself to blame.

Almost done! All you need in addition is the report of examination of any hoists or lifts on the premises, carried out as Rule 72 advises; and, needless to say, the Daily Register of all workers employed on or near a moving machine, as Rule 22, Section 1 so thoughtfully requires. Don't forget a Test Report of your Dust Extraction System, under Rule 122. Or the Register of Examination of any gas containers, under Rule 74, Schedule A, which also demands a separate Report of Examination if a gas container is sealed—presumably as opposed to being open and leaking all over the place, in which case you may have more pressing problems than paperwork.

Oh, and just in case you are drowning in paper and can't find your machines, ensure that you have a folder with Particulars of Rooms in the factory handy, as Rule 133 requires.[2]

If you wish to be exempted from any Rule, all you need to do is submit a request in the form prescribed under Rule 132, and it will, I assume, be duly rejected in three to six months.

If your friendly Inspector, having been fed tea and biscuits and duly plied with the Reports and Notices and Registers and Certificates and Particulars and Rolls that he needs as intellectual stimulation, finds himself satisfied in every respect by virtue of your good citizenship and accurate book-keeping, never fear! You may still be a lawbreaker. Do you have an Abstract of the Factories Act of 1948, as well as your particular state's Rules for that Act, handy? You do, of course, since it is required under Rule 126. Just hand it over to the Inspector and give that good man a moment. He is experienced and intelligent. He *will* find a violation.

This is all you need, happy potential entrepreneur, to be in full compliance with that model of modern legislation, the Factories Act of 1948. There are one or two other such laws, with their associated light paperwork. There's the Industrial Disputes Act of 1946; the Minimum Wages Act of 1948; the Industrial Employment Standing Orders Act of 1946; the Apprentices Act of 1961; the Contract Labour (Regulation & Abolition) Act of 1970, which has completely stamped out contract labour except in 99.8 per cent of factories;

the Child Labour (Prohibition & Regulation Act) of 1986, which has led to the end of child labour; the Payment of Gratuity Act of 1972; the Employees Provident Fund & Miscellaneous Provisions Act of 1952; the Equal Remuneration Act of 1976, so called because 'Equal Pay' is too simple for Indian bureaucrats; the Employees' State Insurance Act of 1948; the Payment of Bonus Act of 1965; the Payment of Wages Act of 1936, which is needed because Indians wouldn't pay people wages otherwise; the Employment Exchanges (Compulsory Notification of Vacancies) Act of 1959; the Trade Unions Act of 1926; the Workmen's Compensation Act of 1923, which is different from the Payment of Wages Act because 'Wages' begins with a 'W' and 'Compensation' with a 'C'; and, of course, the Inter-State Migrant Workmen (Regulation of Employment and Conditions of Service) Act of 1979, which really is a household name these days.

And, naturally, my personal favourite: the 2008 Rules Regarding Prohibition of Smoking in Public Places under the Cigarettes and Other Tobacco Products (Prohibition of Advertisement and Regulation of Trade and Commerce, Production, Supply and Distribution) Act of 2003. The 2008 Rules, among other things, prescribe the exact nature of your no-smoking sign; they include such gems as 'the width of the red band across the cigarette shall equal the width of the red perimeter' of the notice.

But my favourite remains the Lime Register. Every shop, office, and factory in Mumbai has one. You may never have whitewashed your walls, you may have tile or paint or wood, but you better have a Lime Register. Every two-bit bureaucrat in Mumbai can make some lunch money by popping in on any Shop, Establishment or Notified Factory on his way to an Irani restaurant, and demanding to see the Lime Register.

OK, even if you're an unreconstructed socialist, and think all factory owners wear top hats, smoke cigars, and season their lunch with the blood of their workers—even you, Comrade, might be willing to admit that we could trim these requirements a bit and still have a well-regulated manufacturing sector.

That the Indian state is run for its nice, kindly Inspectors, and not for workers or for entrepreneurs, is clearly evident from the fact that we have not, in fact, trimmed these requirements even slightly. Not since the original Acts were passed, in the dim past; not since ever more cumbersome Rules on how to apply those Acts were developed by bureaucrats, through the Nehru and Indira eras; and not, amazingly, at any point in these twenty-some years of unearned growth that we so glibly call the age of economic reform.

And because we have not bothered to dismantle this rusting frame of law and prohibition, there are no jobs—no careers— waiting for all those young people.

THE MANCHESTER OF THE PAST

Drive into Kanpur, and you drive with ghosts. Hours before you hit north India's most industrial town, the ghosts begin gathering by the highway, empty-eyed, decaying, and desolate. Their brick facades tumbling in pieces; their once gleaming roofs rust-red and peeling. By their side, as if to mourn their passing and mark their graves, stand silent lines of elderly trucks.

Once, Kanpur had a thriving managerial and professional class, and a comfortable working class. Once, it was a hotbed of trade unionism, and of capitalism. And what capitalists! It gave to the Constituent Assembly Sir J.P. Srivastava, Knight of the Order of the Star of India, Knight of the Order of the British Empire, member of successive viceroy's privy councils, a man so wealthy, whisky-loving and Churchillian that he set up a party he called the Landowners' Party, and bought the *Pioneer* newspaper, where Churchill had once worked; according to his grandson, the writer Zareer Masani, even his children could not but think of him as an imperialist toady.

And as for industrial workers—there were so many of them, Kanpur even used to have a Communist member of Parliament. Even? I meant 'Usually'. S.M. Banerjee was unbeatable, representing Kanpur from the 1950s to the 1970s, and leaving on his own terms. When he walked down to the magistrate's office at election time to file his nomination, it is said that 50,000 workers followed him. It was said of Banerjee that he lived in Calcutta, but worked in Kanpur's jails. Once an employee of the magnificently named Government Horns and Saddlery Factory—set up, intriguingly, in the house once occupied by the Maratha rebel of 1857, Nana Saheb—he went to jail at least seven times while an MP in the 1950s and 1960s, mostly as moral support for striking workers. In 1953, a quarter of Kanpur's workforce were industrial workers—1,10,000 of them, in 273 factories. Banerjee, it was said, had done something for all of them—even if it was just the signing of a certificate. Paul Brass, writing in the *Economic Weekly* in 1963, says there were a 'wide number of such certificates' a legislator could sign, including 'application forms for student concessions, forms certifying that the man is a member of a Scheduled Caste, attestation certificates for jobs, applications for the allotment of houses and the like'. Banerjee, it was said, had signed 'a prodigious number' of these; this made up for his disadvantages otherwise, such as his campaign having five cars, to the Congress's twelve.

Today, Kanpur is a sad, rusting monument to India's de-industrialization, though it does have a lot more cars. The city where the Communist Party of India was born in 1925 has but a fraction of the industrial workers that walked with Banerjee to the district collectorate. In the centre of town, the traffic-laden streets skirt the vast tracts of land that belong to the mills, their names redolent of the Raj's efforts at supporting local industry: the Elgin Mills, the Cawnpore Woollen Mills, the British India Corporation. The latter's now the Lal Imli Mills, and looks to my eyes like a little slice of Calcutta—red brick and yellow paint, faded red flags and a chain on the gate. Its chimneys soar up above you, barely noticed by townspeople. But it's different for visitors. When I walked, earlier this year, around the city once called the Manchester of the East, it seemed to me like the Lal Imli's chimneys loom everywhere. I wrote, then, that it feels as if they are shadowing you, murmuring, just beyond hearing, of opportunities lost.

The city itself is loud. Loud with traffic, loud with angry voices—but especially loud with the deep bass thump-thump-thump of diesel generators. Everyone has one: the small shopkeeper on the side road in Generalganj, trying to keep his bottles of Coke cool; and the trader in leather, in the pillared and porticoed mansion barely visible behind high walls and the ragged, overcrowded remnant of what was once a pavement; the malls springing up everywhere; even the small plastics 'factory' in a single room in the old 'hatha' districts, where the pre–Independence Kanpur Trust had built low-cost homes for factory workers, housing 42,000 people in just fifteen years.

The air is, naturally, filthy.

The diesel generators kill people; Kanpur has probably the highest rate of respiratory disease in India. But they have also killed the city. The 2000 factories of Kanpur haven't left just because labour relations broke down. They haven't left just because the roads are terrible—after all, it's still a trading town. Above all, they left because there's no power.

Amazingly, 80 per cent of the city steals its electricity. Look out a first-floor window, and you can barely see across the street—and not entirely because the air is heavy with what environmentalists call suspended particulate matter. You can barely see three feet because the view is blocked by thick bunches of wires, electricity wires legal and illegal, tapping into each other, with sparks flying occasionally when the wind blows. The men who do the stealing are local heroes—one, Loha Singh, is also the hero of a 2014 documentary called *Katiyabaaz*, or 'the man who cuts' wires. Writing a few years ago, the movie's makers describe his Robin Hoodesque approach: he 'extorts the rich, cutting off their connections at will and demanding money to "fix" it. To the poor households in his own hatha, he supplies electricity for free.' To those not from Kanpur, and perhaps in possession of the sort of curmudgeonly disposition that finds noble Robin Hoods irritating, this raises a question: are 80 per cent of people in Kanpur really that destitute? Could it be that they are somehow so poor in that benighted city that they cannot pay the very low price for electricity? Somehow, I doubt the chairman of the 'Kanpur Industrial Development Co-op Estate', Vijay Kapoor, who says 'electricity rates in our state are very high when compared with the rates in neighbouring states', actually thinks of them as unaffordable. In Calcutta, the top tariff rate is Rs 8 a unit; in Kanpur, the top tariff rate is well below that—at 4 a unit for the vast majority of consumers. In Calcutta, 12 per cent of power is 'lost' or stolen. In Kanpur, most of it is.

Yes, Kanpur is far away from the sea, and from ports. But it's worth noting that it's still wealthy, the largest city in Uttar Pradesh, the trading hub of the north, the place which pays the most taxes in UP, the place which buys the most luxury cars in that state. The trucks still run; it is the mills that have fallen silent. It is just that the brands being traded in bulk were once better known. But it is difficult to build a reputation for quality when you can rarely deliver on time, thanks to the erratic conditions you operate in. While in Delhi, eight hours to the northwest, the brands we all know of are traded in warehouses in Gurgaon or crowded shopfronts in Chandni Chowk, in Kanpur's Collectorganj, they make their money from deals in Ghari detergent and Jet Knit hosiery, in Rotomac pens and Rupani slippers, in Red Tape shoes and Goldie spices. These are the brands of the north, a consumer area unto itself, isolated not by taste but by its infrastructure.

The men who worked in Kanpur's silent mills have not given up hope. Pass the gates of some of them, and there they are, growing old, sitting under a few flags, demanding that the mill reopen. During the morning, they look for odd jobs, paint a few walls, drive a cycle-rickshaw if they must; in the afternoon, they come and sit in front of the gate they once walked proudly through. The mills have been shut a very long time indeed. You can die waiting, and some have.

But the men who owned Kanpur's silent mills have moved on to other things. Srivastava's New Victoria Mills was taken over by the government long ago. His friend Padampat Singhania's descendants are still, at least, a business family. (Singhania, like Srivastava, was given a knighthood, a KBE. Reading the issue of the *London Gazette*, in 1943, that mentioned this is amusing. There's a long list of Knights of the British Empire, various judges and British general managers of the Railways and Zareer Masani's other grandfather, Rustom, a university vice-chancellor, with their names and accomplishments; and, right at the end, it says, with no pomp whatsoever, 'Lala Padampat Singhania. Of Cawnpore.') The far-flung family now has a branch making toiletries in Maharashtra, and a branch selling paper and paper products in Delhi. The Singhanias left in Kanpur now, apparently, mainly make money from a cement factory in Rajasthan.

In Kanpur, meanwhile, what money there is comes from slightly different industries. From slaughterhouses, from alcohol contracts, and from pan masala. And of these three, the greatest surely is alcohol. Back when alcohol-distribution licences—the exclusive right to sell pick-me-ups to the depressed residents of the Former Manchester—used to be auctioned, Kanpur's went for the most money aside from the four metropolitan cities. Then auctions were dumped and a lottery–based system was instituted which, of course, must have been 100 per cent scrupulously fair and above board and tamper-proof.

And that is what gave us, for example, the wonderful Ponty Chadha. Here's a true industrial success story if ever there was one: man inherits Punjab liquor business; man uses it to get Uttar Pradesh liquor monopoly; man diversifies into real estate, construction and that other bastion of above-board accounting, movie-making; man finally dies in a shootout with his brother over the rights to a hideous suburban villa.

There used to be a word, once, a word that was spoken lovingly by salesmen, through gritted teeth by dyed-in-the-khadi leftists, and hopefully by bankers: 'industrialists'. Once, we called our rich men 'industrialists', not businessmen. In that small semantic change is hidden a vast economic shift.

Shed few tears for those industrialists of old; like as not, they were bandits or cronies or toadies or whatever. But, as the north's industrial economy dies, it is men like Ponty Chadha who are their successors. And the true worry is this: if industry is to be revived, if investment is put in and the thump of the gen-sets is replaced with the squeal of machinery, will the men who now have the money and the networks—Ponty's friends and associates—be willing to do the hard work that's needed?

Consider Ponty's chief rival for the attention of UP's chief ministers, and for the liquor monopoly that he left behind: a man named Jawaharlal Jaiswal. Named, as you can see, in hope. But Jaiswal has, I think it is fair to say, different preoccupations from the other Jawaharlal; it is difficult to see him being turned on by the white heat of an industrial revolution. For this Jawaharlal, the temples of modern India are the corridors of its government. You circle it four times a day, and one day you might be allowed into the inner sanctum where the deity sits, and be granted a boon. He has had, and lost, liquor monopolies; he has won, and lost, elections. He has been in jail and out of it. But he has always grown richer. Can he, and men like him, really be trusted with the task of getting India the jobs it needs?

THE MEN WHO GUARD MACHINES

F ar to Kanpur's east, and far to its north, a couple of days' drive, is Padrauna—the furthest you can go and still be in Uttar Pradesh. Like all the towns of the region, close to the Himalayan foothills, it is infested with mosquitoes the size of bumblebees—mosquitoes that are as dangerous as they look, for they spread a strain of encephalitis that kills 350 children a year in the district, and which nobody has gotten around to synthesizing a vaccine for. Padrauna is a tiny town, as electricity-starved as Kanpur, and as full of quiet desperation.

In the middle of the town stand relics of the past. There's a small palace, for example, a perfect representative of the stained-glass-and-cupola style preferred by the less tasteful sort of pre–Independence industrialist. The stained glass has fallen in, mainly; though a few rooms are kept up, and used as a primary school. (One class, in early 2014, had just done a project on Paris. I am not sure there is anything you are less prepared for on the wall of a battered primary school in a tiny eastern UP town than a caricature of a Frenchman on a bicycle wearing a beret and carrying—I am not making this up—a baguette.) Just outside this decayed splendour, there is a tiny amount of space, and so the good people of Padrauna, being Indian to the core, have arranged for this to become a tea shop.

And here is where we come to the final consequence of India's de-industrialization. Sitting in a tea shop of Padrauna, you can see cause and consequence all at once, history and present and future jumbled depressingly together. Right in front of you is the rambling haveli that, you are excitedly told, belonged—perhaps belongs, the case is in court—to a branch of the Khaitan family. Industrialists, the elderly tea-shop owner told me, one spring morning. 'In business,' the young man with the motorbike agreed.

First, the old man's story: there was a time, he explained, when we had industry here. You will not credit it, but it is true. Look at this mansion!

It turned out that the most shining moment in Padrauna's history was when it was confirmed as being an industrial town, by the arrival, with an entourage, of the Singhanias of Kanpur. They were to marry into the Khaitans, and surely that put Padrauna on the map? The Khaitans, after all, had three sugar mills, a textile mill, a jute mill, and 9000 acres of land on which they grew sugar cane.

But sugar was the first industry to go, a casualty of government policy and confusion. It stands at the border of agriculture and manufacturing, and suffered doubly, therefore, from policies designed to help each. Prices of sugar cane were set by bureaucrats, impossibly high or foolishly low; sugar itself was priced in a similarly confused manner; and the government went from control to decontrol in a manner that must have given everyone whiplash, as well as causing them to lose large amounts of money. Sanjaya Baru, who wrote his doctoral dissertation in the 1970s on why sugar needed real price decontrol (it hasn't yet happened), traced the problem to the fact that there are so very many competing, politically powerful interests at hand: the cane-growers, sugar consumers, the landowners who dominate the big cooperatives, and the mill-owners. Everyone was using someone to defraud anyone.

Anyway, here is the consequence of this crazed sugar policy: the Khaitan mill is now defunct, and has been sold to real-estate developers. But it wasn't the only mill in the area. The only house in Padrauna larger than the Khaitans' was the one belonging to the family that had once ruled the princedom. Right next to it is their gift to the town, the largest sugar mill in that part of the world— now a dark cavernous space where the rustle of your feet and the soft cooing of pigeons nesting somewhere high above echo eerily off long, tall banks of metal.

Outside, in another mirror of Kanpur, sits a contingent of the men who once worked the mill. On a twisted-rope bed, with a single light-bulb above them, they sit and sip tea; there has been a watch, they say, kept on the mill day and night. It is not hope, or not entirely hope. It is fear: will the machinery, expensive and relatively new, be stolen? The fear that the company's majority owner will strip it bare of its assets runs deep in the Indian worker, and is often justified. They took their fear to Atal Bihari Vajpayee, they said—the local ex-royal is a politician, and so they could get in to see the former prime minister. They fell at his feet, they say, and told him of their mill. But Vajpayee said nothing. Perhaps Vajpayee had learned; in Kanpur they still speak, with derision, of a speech in 1996 when he had come to that town and said that, if he became prime minister, smoke would once again billow from its chimneys.

The men who met Vajpayee haven't been paid for years, but they come every day; that day may be the one the machines are resurrected. Those machines are new; they are quite unlike those in the one sugar mill that remains in Khaitan hands in far-off Bengal, which are driven by steam engines from the 1930s.

This mill has not been handed over to the real-estate strippers and the scrap merchants yet. But perhaps it will be, soon. After absurd government pricing rendered it unprofitable, it was taken over by the state and further ruined. And then, one day, the state announced it would be revived, by a rich man from outside. That man would pump in money, get it working again, smoke would once again spiral from its chimney. For some reason that didn't work, and now the workers, unsleeping, guard its gates. I, at least, was not left wondering why. Walking through the mill, I picked up a piece of paper, a faded yellow receipt from an earlier decade, bearing an overseer's signature. Right on top were the initials and name of the man the government had chosen to try and revive the pride of Padrauna: Jawaharlal Jaiswal.

TEA-SHOP TRUTHS

As you sit at the tea shop by the Khaitans' brokedown palace, you can see right into the tube-lit dingy room, with two pitted desks, that is the Padrauna office of the UP Sugar Co-operative Limited, trusted with the task of restoring unprofitable mills to rude capitalist health. Through the window, you see towers of dusty files darkly framing the slight old man as he tells you about Padrauna's industrial past; they provide a touch of realism, of context, to his hopes.

Behind you, however, is the tea shop's final gift, its window to the future: a more sardonic voice, a voice less experienced but more angry. The young man with an Enfield Bullet who asked for extra cardamom in his tea couldn't be poor, surely. But it is he who brings this story full circle. 'Without power, there will be no factories,' he says, cutting off the old man. And it is true; at night Padrauna is plunged into the dark of hours-long power cuts, with no fans to keep away the water-buffalo-sized mosquitoes.

And without factories, he does not need to say, there will be no jobs. He does say: 'Only jobs matter.' Travel across any part of north India, and you will hear the same thing. People are anxious to have alternatives to the farm. After all, the work is back-breaking—who would work on an unmechanized farm if you didn't have to?

The service sector—small retail, odd jobs of this or that kind—is picking up the slack. But they know it's chancy, and not the kind of thing that gives you security, a steady income. True, what you really want is a government job. That, after all, is the perfect sort of employment: you are un-fire-able. Stable and secure. But even the most populist of politicians in the most backward of states now realizes that, awe-inspiring though the Indian state's capabilities may be, even it may struggle to find public-sector jobs for 13 million more people a year.

But I do wonder: When these brash young men want jobs, do they know exactly what jobs they want? Which factory job could satisfy a guy who already drives a Bullet and wears a Manchester United T-shirt?

Yes, you need a manufacturing sector. No country has risen to prosperity, and comfort, and even to a shared public civility and trust, without one. But you can't wish away the young people you have, either.

It is too easy to say that a demand for jobs means also that they approve of the policies that would deliver jobs. Politicians understand this better than policymakers. When people say 'give us jobs', they do not mean 'give us job-creating policy', they mean 'give *me* a job'. Nor does it mean that they are willing and eager to take any job that's offered.

This returns us to the cardinal error of Indian policy. It tried to protect workers instead of work; and it failed. It tries to protect farmers, instead of farming; and it fails.

India failed, because its rulers apparently didn't quite understand who the worker was, and who the farmer was. And it might repeat that mistake with the millions of young and aspirational people who have today replaced workers and farmers as the obsession of India's government.

THE DANGEROUS INDIAN DREAM

Prakash arrived in the big city in 2011, from the small town of Bareilly in central Uttar Pradesh. Over the few years that I have known him, he has picked up a characteristic Delhi veneer: his phones have gotten smarter, his shirts have gotten shinier. He started off as a delivery boy for a small kabab shop, riding a battered second-hand cycle that he'd bought with money his grandmother back home had saved from her pension. He still does that, but now has a dazzling number of other balls in the air. He drives kids from a local primary school home; during wedding season, he works as a waiter; he stands occasional shifts as a salesperson at a mobile-phone showroom; and, also, he 'helps out Imtiaz'. He was very cagey for a while about this Imtiaz, and the nature of his own 'help'. Eventually, I learned that Imtiaz is a slumlord of dubious reputation, and Prakash is part of his extended retinue. His duties involve hanging about and having tea—and, through these strenuous activities, adding to Imtiaz's immense air of consequence.

The reason I've singled out Prakash to talk about is not because his experience is unique. If anything, it's the opposite—many young men have made similar journeys, and found equally diverse and unsatisfying sets of jobs. No, the reason I mention Prakash is that, when I asked him what he wants of his future, he had an answer ready, and it was one that resonated. 'I want a lot, but actually quite little,' he said. He added: 'I have desire, but no ambition.'[3] (Prakash had the unmistakable air, once he delivered himself of this epigrammatic answer, of someone who had thought a great deal about how to phrase this very point and was now pausing for applause.)

Prakash had unerringly put his finger on a problem that he shared with many other young men. He wanted material advancement—a new phone every year, a bit more money to spend on snacks at a mall. But he had no idea how he could ensure a steady climb up a ladder of status and income. One of his friends had become a partner in a shop that sold cheap covers for mobile phones; but he, Prakash told me, was the exception. It was too much of a risk. Another friend, from Bareilly, was working in Rajasthan's industrial belt. Too arduous, Prakash explained, for too little money and too little advancement.

It was this denial of his options that Prakash called a lack of ambition. But he was being too hard on himself, I thought. It wasn't that he was unambitious; he saw, clear-eyed, that the economy offered him little. He could read and write, but with effort; he had few other skills beyond bike-riding, arithmetic, and an encyclopedic knowledge of every mobile phone on the market. Once, I asked him whether he thought of going off and picking up a skill or two. He rolled his eyes and asked: 'And then what?'

His concern was, again, bang on. Had he gone to college, he would have earned a third more than if he just finished high school. But college is a four-year, expensive proposition. Yet, if he'd just learned a skill instead, as I was suggesting, it wouldn't have been as valuable. Skilled machine operators, in 2010, were paid just 14 per cent more than unskilled workers.[4] That isn't the sort of money that's likely to get people rushing to apprenticeships or night schools, or borrowing relatives' savings in order to take a course at a polytechnic. It's the oldest truth in economics: if the material returns to some action aren't high enough to make up for the psychological effort of doing it, it doesn't get done.

What Prakash really hoped for was one big deal that he could be a little part of. If he helped Imtiaz with some shady real-estate manoeuvre, for example, and got a tiny sliver of the profit, that might be enough for him to set up as part of the rent-seeking economy himself. A little space with a chair and a TV, people to call on the phone, a second deal on the horizon perhaps, and the prospect one day of air-conditioning and a retinue of his own. That's the Indian Dream. We have created a country where there is no clear path to advancement other than becoming a rentier. Should it surprise us that this is the highest hope of our hopeful?

Failing this dream, at the very least he would want a 'sitting-down job'. His counterparts in the countries that trod this path before India might well have been looking for a shop-floor job that provided them with a bit of security and a bit of camaraderie. But, for a complex set of reasons, Indians are going to be harder to please.

Here, in my opinion, is the biggest reason: there may be a social stigma in India attached to working with your hands that's higher than most anywhere else in the world. And there's social prestige attached to sitting behind a desk that's correspondingly high, too. Not one IIT engineer in the past ten years has taken a shop-floor job.

And when I say 'social', I am of course tiptoeing, like we all do these days, around the unpalatable truth. These young urban Indians may not mention caste in the context of their career choices. But they are shaped by it, anyway, whether they will it consciously or not.

Perhaps this will change in time. There is an entertaining story that is told about western Uttar Pradesh. Once the upper castes owned the land, and the landless Dalits tilled it, rented by the day.

Some upper castes have now sold their land, and some of it has been bought by Dalits. Meanwhile, the elite can also afford to buy farm machinery—tractors, harvesters, and so on. And, to make a bit of money, they might rent out its services, along with their own as operator, to local farms. So, now, one might see an odd role reversal in UP's countryside: of an upper-caste man sweating in the sun, hired to plough a Dalit's fields.

But the attitudinal change that such reversals could engender is not here yet. What remains is an ancient heritage of looking down on manual labour. For what it's worth, the word that north Indians speaking Hindustani use for 'sweat' is from an Urdu root; the word for 'knowledge', from Sanskrit. Make of that what you will.

Now, economic theory would suggest that the presence of such non-market–based discrimination would be counteracted by the invisible hand of the price mechanism. Or, in other words, if there's work that a lot of people don't want to do, then the wages you'd get paid for doing it keep on going up. And perhaps that's exactly what's happened with how much agricultural labourers get paid.

But the problem is that there are other barriers too. By the logic of the market, an untrained receptionist or salesperson and an untrained factory worker should be paid approximately the same amount; if most untrained people would far rather be receptionists, then they should be paid correspondingly less than if they became factory workers. Yet the average monthly gross salary of a machine operator in a major automobile manufacturer in Delhi is Rs 7700—while a receptionist is paid Rs 11,700, half as much again. This means that the invisible hand isn't working properly. What we've missed, in thinking this through so far, is that the stigma against manual labour can go deep enough to affect salary offers; and, in addition, that there are unspoken barriers of caste and class and upbringing that can prevent job-seekers from leaping straight into the sort of service jobs that they'd find ideal.

THE WRONG SCHOOLS, THE WRONG SKILLS

So here's what we're left with. Not everybody wants to pick up a skill if it involves manual labour. And, in addition, the returns to picking up a skill aren't great—as I said, a mere 14 per cent increase in your salary is not the sort of money that attracts even the avaricious. And that's why we wind up with this strange and disturbing gap: 13 million people join the job hunt every year; only half get jobs. And yet, by 2022, there will be a shortfall of nearly 350 million people—more than the entire population of the United States—in the 20 quickest-growing sectors of India's economy.[5]

Bridging that gap is the job of the educational system. Yet that's another public good that the government has, by and large, failed to provide. Since independence, the government has focused on the kind of higher education that the ruling elite loves—highly subsidized engineering colleges, for example—while ignoring what the vast majority of Indians need. Education in India today, particularly high school, vocational and college education, performs a totally different function from what we need it to perform: it's a form of social and intellectual screening, not a way to pass on useful skills. We need to know someone has gone to college to know they're from the right sort of background, and have the right level of potential. It's never what you learn in a school or college that matters; it's that you got in.

Since 2000, the government has tried to make up for this criminal lack of focus through a solid expansion in primary and secondary education. But the jump from that to cheap, accessible, and useful vocational training has simply not been made. Without that leap, the skills gap will continue to separate young men like Prakash from the futures they want.

What's the problem with Indian vocational training? Well, consider some of the requirements for, say, the construction industry.

Remember, construction isn't the most skilled job anywhere in the world; in India, it's often the sector that those displaced from the agricultural sector try first. But only one out of every ten Indian workers in construction is considered 'skilled' by her employer. Indian builders frequently bring in construction workers from China and the Philippines to complete projects, because they're more productive. By one reasonable estimate, over 7 million skilled construction workers will be needed by 2022.

But will the system be able to create them? Hardly. For one, there's that old problem of capacity again. Altogether, even if every single training institute filled every single seat with a building-industry trainee, that wouldn't even meet half the demand. And, in addition, there are onerous requirements for admission: you need to have passed the Class X board examination, for example, with science as one of your subjects. Really, you need Class X science to pick up the basic skills required for a construction site? I suspect whoever designed this course and picked this requirement has never been near a building site in his life. Meanwhile, the courses can be between one and three years long; but most construction workers are migrants, in cities for six to nine months of the year only.

Not that anyone in the system cares that much. This army of the unskilled is supposed to march up the skills ladder by joining, en masse, the 8000 Industrial Training Institutes or ITIs. These are the places with the ridiculous entry qualifications, and the too-few seats, and the overlong courses. But here's the kicker: they're unlikely to change, because they don't really care about their students. Now that's a pretty grand statement, isn't it? How can I make a claim so sweeping? As a simple deduction from the following fact, revealed by an ITI head to *Business Standard*'s Aman Sethi: not one ITI in India has a full-time placement officer. It isn't the job trainers' job to get their trainees jobs.

HONESTY ALWAYS FLOPS

Hindi movies have noisily and dramatically psychoanalysed this country for seventy years. Through them, we get a sense of how we feel about ourselves, our government, our cities, and our economy. In the 1950s, with the hot breath of freedom on our necks, we barrelled forward optimistically on the road to good fortune, singing along with Raj Kapoor. By the 1970s, we had lost enthusiasm. We had turned angry and distrustful, and the hero wasn't a lovable wanderer, but a lone young warrior against the injustice of the powerful. And, in what should have been an early warning of dissatisfaction about the overpowering statism of the Indira Gandhi years, the villains were cronyist businessmen, smugglers, and corrupt government officials. But then, things turned. Liberalization made us optimistic again; our heroes got younger, wore clothes with prominent, if misspelled, labels; and pretended to be as comfortable in Piccadilly as in Patiala. My old boss, Shekhar Gupta, always said that a watershed for Indian society was the success of 2001's *Dil Chahta Hai*—a story about three rich young slackers trying very hard not to grow up, and eventually failing. That was the first movie, he insisted, in which the heroes were rich—and untroubled by their wealth.

But there's one thing that's been missing throughout. There's been distrust of wealth, as in Raj Kapoor's *Shree 420*, where a migrant to 1950s Mumbai is seduced into dishonesty. There's been rejection of wealth, as when Shashi Kapoor faces down Amitabh Bachchan in *Deewar*, and reminds him with infuriating sanctimony that a house, a car, and a bank balance are nothing when weighed against a mother's love. And there's been embrace of wealth, as in 2010's *Aisha*, starring a series of brand names worn by Sonam Kapoor.

But what we haven't really had is the road to wealth. In Indian movies, you inherit wealth, or you marry wealth, or you spurn wealth. You don't earn it. If you believe that our movies reflect our national psychoses, then this has to be one of the fundamental facts about how we view our futures: you can't get rich through trying.

The occasional exceptions to this rule are, if anything, even more revelatory. I can think of two movies in the past decade which have been about material success. One is *Guru*, a fictionalized biography of Dhirubhai Ambani. When Ambani died, he had gone from nothing to building the second-largest corporate empire in the country; but everyone believed, even his most devoted worshippers, that he had cut a few corners on the way.[6] That he had not been entirely scrupulous did not make him worthy of condemnation; it deserved celebration, instead. It was, in fact, so central to his legend that the climactic scene in *Guru* features the Ambani character defending his decision to do so.

The other movie I can think of has an even sadder and more revealing conclusion. *Rocket Singh: Salesman of the Year* was released in 2009, and did everything right. It showed a man making his way through honesty and hard work, and ended with him opening his own business. Wonderful. So what's the sad conclusion? Just this: it was a terrible flop. Audiences, apparently, didn't think the premise was in the slightest bit believable. Remember, these are audiences who otherwise demand 40-year-olds in college and badminton-playing Pomeranians.

We simply don't believe, as a people, that investing in yourself and then working hard and honestly at your chosen profession will get you anywhere. And perhaps we're right. Or, perhaps, this is a self-fulfilling prophecy.

Nandan Nilekani, the billionaire-turned-technocrat-turned-politician, has often quoted something that Raghuram Rajan—now the governor of India's central bank—told him over a decade ago. Rajan worried that 'the Horatio Alger story is not yet part of India's popular imagination'. In the Victorian era, Alger's novels were everywhere—cheap, accessible, and as addictive as candy, they told and retold the same story. Of a young man who dealt bravely with poverty and difficult circumstances, 'improved himself', worked hard and honestly, and who ended the story successful, respected, and middle class. They didn't wind up extravagantly wealthy; just secure and comfortably-off.

For the red-hot socialists of the Depression, a half-century on, the Alger stories were the founding myths of predatory capitalism and of an oppressive American Dream. But they're not just moral examples. Societies where such stories are popular are societies where such stories become possible. The Indian Dream, of one big deal and then joining the rentier class, is a danger to those who believe it, and to everyone else. A Dream—American, or capitalist, or what you will—that can be shared by even the poorest, in which there exists an ethical and accessible stairway to security, is not a danger but a blessing. The presence of Horatio Alger stories—like *Rocket Singh*—would be, as Raghuram Rajan said, 'a sign that the sentiment around India has truly transformed'. Somehow, India needs to make Indians think *Rocket Singh* is more likely than *Guru*.

PART II

THE STAINS OF PAST SINS

India has altered beyond imagining in the years since 1991. But the changes have been half-hearted. India has shied away from real change, for fear of pain. But, as tends to happen, this avoidance means that we have hurt ourselves all the more.

In this section, we'll look at turning points, at opportunities seized and missed, at the moments that have together brought us here.

We'll look at the Great Reform Moment of 1991. We'll wonder together if it was all that great. And we'll look at when reforms ran out of steam.

We'll explore how Indian politicians have, in crises, taken the right decisions. And we'll explore how they have too often taken the path of least resistance, and how that has hurt us.

We'll discover the danger of short-term thinking. We'll look at the moment that Indira Gandhi turned India sharply to the left, and discover how it was less strategy, and more short-sighted political manoeuvring.

We'll see how we tried to build up a sense of solidarity; an industrial working class; a belief in our own cities. And we'll see how we failed. We'll look at how Bombay was once India's hope, and why Mumbai should not be India's future.

We'll wonder at how we have tried, over and over again, to build more things—to close India's yawning infrastructure deficit. And we'll see how we've come up short, again and again—and the price in blood and treasure and anger that we've paid for our attempts.

India hasn't stood still for the seven decades since Independence. Far from it. We've tried self-improvement, we really have. Until we learn when and where we failed, how can we know what we'll get right?

'INDIA IS WIDE AWAKE'

On the 24th of July, 1991, Manmohan Singh famously misquoted Victor Hugo: 'There is no power on earth that can stop an idea whose time has come,'[7] he said. 'I suggest to this august House that the emergence of India as a major economic power in the world happens to be one such idea. Let the whole world hear it loud and clear. India is now wide awake. We shall prevail. We shall overcome.'

It is likely that most of the august House was unimpressed. Here we were in the midst of an economic crisis, and this technocrat was mumbling on about destiny? But there were enough, inside and outside Parliament, who heard that speech—a fire-fighting Budget that also, incredibly, managed to discern glory in the dim future—and felt a bit of a thrill. Not for nothing is there that subtle echo of Nehru's Freedom at Midnight speech: 'India is wide awake.'

Reading that speech today is an odd experience indeed. There is a sense of purpose to it, a sense of direction and destiny, that was notably absent in Dr Singh's last years as prime minister. The agenda he outlines sounds, at first, strangely contemporary: 'The thrust of the reform process would be to increase the efficiency and international competitiveness of industrial production, to utilize for this purpose foreign investment and foreign technology to a much greater degree than we have done in the past, to increase the productivity of investment.'

What Dr Singh was saying then was that forty-plus years of being closed off from the outside world had failed to create a sufficiently dynamic industrial sector. India had striven to protect its manufacturers from the world; but in protecting them from imagined predators outside our borders, we taught them to see Indian consumers as prey. By opening up to the world—to foreign investment, to foreign competition, to foreign *ideas*—Dr Singh expected that Indian companies would smarten up, serve their consumers better, and take on the world.

As it happens, Manmohan Singh was proven completely wrong.

We all know that, in 1991, India launched Reforms. And we know Indians' lives changed irreparably after that, and overwhelmingly for the better. But here's what tends to be forgotten. The aims that the reforms process purported to serve—to make Indian industry more dynamic and stronger, and to make India globally competitive—were never achieved. In fact, Manmohan Singh failed in 1991, if we were to judge him by his stated aims.

He failed because Indian manufacturing never recovered from that day in 1991 when Singh whipped away its protections and exposed it to global competition. For many of the largest states in India, like Maharashtra and Uttar Pradesh, industrialization peaked in the 1980s or the early 1990s.

He failed, as it happens, because the reforms that he so stirringly outlined that hot July day did not go far enough.

On that July evening in 1991 when India changed forever, I was a schoolboy; and, like most schoolboys I was completely uninterested in such things as Budgets. I do, however, remember exactly where I was that evening.[8] I remember because I was utterly spellbound by Dr Singh. Not, I hasten to add, because of anything he was *saying*, but because the grainy, indistinct television broadcast was being played for me on a computer monitor. Since this was the first time I had ever seen anything but text or clunky images on one of those ever-so-slightly curved screens PCs had back in 1991, it was pretty unforgettable.

Naturally, this was a demonstration—at an exhibition of next-generation electronics in Calcutta. (As it then was, and as I firmly intend to keep on calling it until I die, whether of natural causes or stubbornness.) The memory, however, resonates strongly all these years later. For one, it serves to remind me that those years before 1991 were not years of unrelieved desolation. As with Europe in the Middle Ages, there was always steady improvement; it was just that the true explosion of creativity had yet to arrive.

The other reason it resonates is because it fits in so neatly with what I know that speech achieved—both the good it led to and the harm it did. We are, after all, insufferably proud of our 'techies'; in the past few decades, India's software engineers, supposedly world-beating, have been a notable economic success and an equally notable source of national pride. I was staring longingly at that computer screen because, at that point, all I wanted to be was a techie.

But that image reminds me, also, of the harm that was done. The experimental graphics circuitry that I was so impressed by was being shown off by some young fellow hoping to get backing for his plan to manufacture it in India. (My fellow 1990s geeks will wonder, so I'd better answer: I can't remember for certain, but I think the computer was a Commodore Amiga.)

I am fairly certain that, even if that young fellow did scrape up a few investors in tight-fisted Calcutta, his company went bust shortly thereafter—thanks, paradoxically, to the reforms that Manmohan Singh was outlining at that doubly hopeful moment.

What happened? Two things. First, India's currency drastically lost value alongside Dr Singh's Budget—meaning that crucial foreign inputs, such as the integrated circuits that make graphics cards work, became suddenly expensive. And second, foreign goods flooded the Indian market much faster than most entrepreneurs—including that hopeful hardware guy—could set up genuinely world-class factories.

Why did the architects of liberalization allow this to happen? Why did they let the rupee crash? Dr Singh was fairly explicit about what he expected from Indian industry: 'The time has come to expose Indian industry to competition from abroad in a phased manner . . . Our entrepreneurs are second to none. Our industry has come of age.' Oops. So why couldn't Indian industry respond the way that Dr Singh exhorted them to in his Budget speech?

THE FIRES OF '91

The rupee crashed because it had to. The mistakes of decades had caught up with us. In fact, the rupee had to crash for the same reason that Dr Singh was being allowed to open up India in the first place—that we were bankrupt. OK, technically, no; but effectively, yes. Certainly, we didn't have any dollars left in our vaults; and that was both what spurred the 1991 reforms and what required the 1991 liberalization.

India needed dollars. Then, as now, we had a rapacious appetite for things from abroad: oil, gold, the various glittering building-blocks of consumerism. Under Rajiv Gandhi in the 1980s, the middle class—and the government—was encouraged to spend; we were, after all, being taken to the twenty-first century by our dynamic prime minister, weren't we? Unfortunately, neither the middle class nor the government was encouraged to earn.

Rajiv certainly caught everyone's imagination, and his death at a tragically young age means his time in office has been retrospectively Camelot-ed, and given a glow of sainthood with undertones of tragedy and of vision. Naturally, this is enormously undeserved—and not just because his career in office began with riots in Delhi in which thousands of Sikhs were murdered, though that should really have been enough, especially given that he never displayed any real remorse for the killings. That indifference does not, of course, stop all accounts of his life from descending into saccharine hagiography. (Only a cynic, surely, would believe that this lack of objectivity might also have something to do with Rajiv's wife being India's most powerful person for a decade.)

Among the many disasters of Rajiv's term—from 1984 to 1989—was that he let the government deficit leap up from a steady 6 per cent of gross domestic product in 1983 to well over 8 per cent—and even 10 per cent at times. Think of this as the government happily borrowing from the future, like an improvident young wastrel. Rajiv, like many young men in a hurry, wanted nice things; unfortunately, since he was PM, the nice things he wanted were, for example, colour television and submarines and foreign military adventures. Rajiv stepped up defence spending in particular. The *New York Times* reported in 1988: 'The increase in military spending has been dramatic since Prime Minister Gandhi took office in late 1984, rising nearly 50 per cent over what was spent two years ago to about $12 billion. That represents 5 per cent of the gross national product.' In retrospect, given these enormous sums, and given the cesspool of cynical depravity that is the arms industry, it shouldn't surprise anyone that allegations of corruption began to be thrown around.

Nice things need to be paid for. Submarines and colour TV and the like needed to be brought in from abroad. But we didn't make enough stuff that we could trade for these little luxuries. And so we kept on borrowing from the rest of the world, in addition to borrowing from the future. The deficit on the current account, a measure of how much India was being forced to borrow to cover its overspending, went up sharply from around 1 or 1.5 per cent of GDP before Rajiv took over to 3 per cent of GDP towards the end of his term.

Economics has very few real laws. In fact, it only has one, but that one is of iron: you cannot spend more than you earn forever.

By the end of Rajiv's term, India's finances were showing the strain. His bureaucrats urged him to go to the West for help, for a loan or two to tide India over. But Rajiv's government was tottering as much as India's finances, and he determined that being bailed out by the International Monetary Fund would be a political disaster. At that moment, a crisis became inevitable.[9]

When the crisis hit, in 1991, national pride was the first casualty. To finance its overspending, India had been borrowing vast sums. In 1985, India's external debt was Rs 25,800 crore; by 1989, Rajiv had taken it up to Rs 70,000 crore. The amount it had to pay in interest on these loans ballooned, inevitably—and the improvident young wastrel suddenly discovered credit-card debt. By the end of June 1991, India stood very close to defaulting on its loan payments. It simply didn't have enough dollars.

Nor would anyone lend India any more money—not, at least, without actual security. India's word was no longer good enough; only gold would do. Indians may not have cared a great deal about government profligacy. But news that 67 tonnes of your gold is being flown from India's vaults to banks in Europe does serve to jolt you into an awareness of crisis.

And more: it makes you feel conscious that you're in danger of losing your dignity.

Prime Minister P.V. Narasimha Rao was not a decisive man. As we will see, he was not exactly an ideological reformist, either. But he had spent a life in politics, and he knew in his bones that national honour was at stake in the crisis. In fact, he always said that his hand was forced by the threat of national disgrace: 'Once you become a defaulter your entire economy, your honour, your place in the comity of nations, everything goes haywire,' he said in a 2004 talk with Shekhar Gupta.

It was at that moment, when national pride was at its lowest, that Manmohan Singh told his boss what needed to be done: the rupee had to be drastically 'devalued'—or one rupee had to become a lot less valuable, in dollar terms. That would do two things: first, it would help rebuild the dollar reserves India needed to pay off its various obligations to the rest of the world. And second, it would mean that all the foreign stuff India was hooked on would get more expensive—and so we would hopefully buy less of it.

This devaluation of the rupee was the essential first step, if a catastrophic and humiliating default was to be avoided. It was also to prove fateful for Indian industry.

WHERE RAO WENT WRONG

There is a reason that it is the Budget speech of 1991 that is remembered. It had a self-confidence and an assurance visible in precious few other acts of those tumultuous weeks. There was, later, a price to be paid for that diffidence.

Consider the act of devaluation. The first step was taken on the 1st of July. Dr Singh had told Rao it was necessary; but everyone was being very circumspect about it, partly because the new government hadn't even demonstrated its majority in Parliament yet.

It was kept hush-hush. Every now and then, economists have occasion to behave like secret agents, and this was one of those times. There was even a code name for the operation: 'Hop, Skip and Jump'. The 'hop' was that first step: a 9 per cent decrease in the rupee's value, to 'test the waters', as one participant subsequently recalled. That wasn't as much as was needed. What was hoped was that people would object, but not excessively. The Reserve Bank of India went so far as to claim that it was 'a normal process of adjustment'.

Nobody was fooled. Pandemonium broke out. The government was accused in Parliament and out—one can only imagine the aneurysm today's news anchors would have had—of dutifully following orders from the International Monetary Fund. This accusation had the dubious virtue of being necessarily true, since the only thing that India could do was to devalue its currency. That was an unexceptionable fact that any economics graduate anywhere, including the IMF, could, would and did tell them. Worse, however, various socialist firebrands darkly hinted that orders from Washington were much more extensive, and that India would have to sign the nuclear non-proliferation treaty, for example, or cut defence spending which would leave it helpless in the face of the United States' military might. (As if it wasn't already.)

Unsurprisingly, Rao got cold feet. According to most reports, he called Dr Singh telling him to postpone the 'jump', the additional 11 per cent decrease in the rupee's value. Perhaps the instruction came too late, which is what Dr Singh seems to have told Rao. Or perhaps the finance minister ignored his boss completely; perhaps he even indulged in a bit of misdirection, claiming that the deed had already been done and it would look terrible to reverse it now. Whatever trick he pulled, the fact is that Dr Singh had indicated to his man in Bombay—the central banker C. Rangarajan—that the Reserve Bank should go ahead.

I suppose only three people knew for sure what happened. Rangarajan and Rao said things about this incident that appear to contradict each other. And Dr Singh is—shocker!—discreetly silent. Reform in India started without parliamentary sanction—the government didn't have a majority, and Parliament hadn't met yet. It started in spite of the doubts of the man in charge—Rao actually tried to pull the rupee devaluation back. It started with no road map, no explanation, no destination, no plan.

Except in the Budget speech, at no point did anyone in government suggest that a fundamental change was underway. Indeed, every step in the 1991 liberalization was justified only in terms of the crisis that had preceded it, not in terms of the future that might follow. In his Independence Day speech six weeks later, Rao would refer to the devaluation, the first step in India's reforms, thus: 'We have paved the way for increasing our exports by slightly changing the exchange rate of the rupee.'

Some now claim that this half-heartedness was only tactical. Just words. We'll examine, later on, why that's not really true—and the heavy price that India has paid for politicians unable to talk openly about how economic reform is not just necessary, but beneficial; and not just beneficial, but right.

But, for now, what we really need to know is this: the prime minister who launched reforms never had an overarching idea of what he intended to do, and where he intended to go. He just wanted to address a temporary problem, fight a blazing fire. When the fire was out, he stopped caring.

That is where everything went wrong.

That is why those expectations from Indian industry in the 1991 Budget speech remained unfulfilled; this is why that techie I met must have failed to set up his graphics-card factory in time to fight Intel and ATI and Nvidia.

Because 1991's reformers were unconvinced about the virtues of reform, they left it incomplete. And because they left it incomplete, reform failed to do everything they said it would.

Worse, their half-measures and timidity have set the template for all our efforts at reform since. Had they just been a little braver, it would not have been so widely, and mistakenly, accepted today that good economics is bad politics. That fatal misapprehension, which cripples even the strongest and most reformist of India's politicians, is Rao's legacy. To push forward the reforms that Rao started, we have to first accept that Rao was no reformer.

AN AGENDA UNFINISHED

For most of the twenty-three years since 1991, it was not really obvious exactly how half-baked the reforms process had been. Once can understand that, in a way: what was done was so very vast that it seemed quite impossible that what was *needed* to be done was even vaster.

And yet, if you really looked, whichever angle you chose, the same truth was visible: India's reforms had stopped halfway. Somehow, that is deeply typical. After all, doing a haphazard, half-assed job is practically the only thing that unites us as a country. 'Giving up halfway' could be our national sport. (In fact, it is—except we call it 'Indian cricket'.)

These are just some of the ways that India stopped short that we're going to be looking at in the following pages:

India reformed product markets, freeing up the prices at which products are sold to consumers. But it neither created nor reformed markets for land and labour, the things that go into making those products in the first place.

India opened up to external markets, removing restrictions on the movement of goods across international boundaries. But it did not open up internal markets; goods still couldn't move easily across the borders between our states.

India let the rupee lose just enough value to put a lot of imports-hungry manufacturers out of business. But it didn't get the rupee to lose enough value as was needed to get manufacturers exporting instead.

India got its government to stop doing some things it should never have been doing, like running hotels. But it didn't get its government to start doing the things it should instead—like regulating how natural resources are used.

India allowed new companies to set up easily in all sorts of industries where they had previously been prohibited. We let new companies be born; but we didn't arrange to let dying companies die.

India tried to create a globalized and productive manufacturing sector, but didn't try to create a globalized and productive workforce.

India tried to create new jobs that ex-farmers could go to, since farming could not be kept profitable. But it tried to keep farming profitable anyway, through high state-set prices for farm products, and through subsidizing fertilizers.

Each one of these is a different angle. There are others. But they all add up to the same thing: the 1991 reforms just didn't go all the way.

THE ORIGINAL, STINKING SIN

Manmohan Singh's stoic willingness to endure what, to outsiders, looks like epic humiliation has long excited wonder, admiration and derision.[10] This endurance is not a recent phenomenon. In fact, it was visible early on—the humiliation began the moment his political career did.

In his two decades as a politician Dr Singh embodied, as did nobody else, the contradictions of the Indian reform process: silent, usually, with only the occasional sharp outburst; diffident, usually, with the occasional bold step forward; subject to a barrage of withering criticism, yet somehow still standing at the end of it all.

And it began almost immediately after he was sworn in as minister in 1991, when he departed decisively from the Congress party's election manifesto. That manifesto—now the subject of some epic myth and misinformation—was, in fact, a truly extraordinary document. It was, as it happens, a backward-looking document in which Rajiv's Congress refused to acknowledge Rajiv's mistakes. Indeed, it was the very opposite of rational and reformist.

The manifesto had ended with a stirring pledge: to roll prices back to the levels they had been in July 1990. In particular, the prices of diesel and salt and edible oils—but also 'postcards, inland letters and envelopes' and 'cotton sarees and dhotis of 40s count or below'. (In case you're wondering: '40s count' is coarser cotton. Also: Why only dhotis? Why not lungis or pyjamas? Let the conspiracy theorizing begin.)

Dr Singh, early on, flatly said this promise was impossible to keep. He even told his Congress colleagues that the rollbacks were 'imaginary'—which led to some of them throwing a bit of a hissy fit, and to the first of many, many demands for his resignation. At his first press conference, he was equally sharp on India's subsidies: 'There are no free lunches,' he said—the title of a famous book by Milton Friedman about economic policies' hidden costs.

But it was Dr Singh's Budget of 26th July, so very revolutionary, such a statement of intent, that nevertheless set up Indian reform's original sin.

Since India was overspending so massively, Dr Singh had to cut back. It was a new world, Dr Singh said, and India had better square up to its harsh realities. Some things were just unaffordable—such as subsidies for fertilizers. These may not have broken the bank when they were first introduced. But, even before Iraq invaded Kuwait and the world's supply of oil and gas began to be seriously disrupted by the build-up to war, they had become nearly unaffordable. Over the 1980s, these subsidies had grown tenfold: from Rs 340 crore before Congress was re-elected in 1980 to Rs 4400 crore in 1990–91.

Dr Singh was fairly sharp on the subject of fertilizer subsidies in the 1991 Budget. 'Insofar as fertilizer subsidies are concerned,' he had said, without even a perfunctory attempt at a calming preamble, 'with effect from this evening . . . there will be an increase of 40 per cent, on an average, in price.' Into a no doubt stunned Lok Sabha, he further dropped the following withering remark: 'The economic rationale for an increase in the price of fertilizers is so obvious that it does not need to be stated.' This line always reminded me of another—the scariest line in any economics textbook, the one that you would read just as things got tough: 'The remainder of this proof is trivial, and is left as an exercise to the reader.'

Fortunately for the MPs, and unlike those horrible textbook-writers, Dr Singh decided to state the rationale anyway: 'Nevertheless, I would like to draw the attention of the House to the fact that there has been no increase in fertilizer prices since July 1981. In these ten years, there has been a continuous increase in the procurement prices of paddy and wheat, as also in the market prices of other crops.'

Perfectly reasonable, you'd think. But the canny finance minister hadn't survived in Delhi for decades without picking up a sense of the cover you need for something like this. The decision, he was to say later, had been cleared by the Cabinet's subcommittee that dealt with political affairs; he'd even gone so far as to get Narasimha Rao's consent *in writing*.

But none of that helped. The hellish noise that had followed the devaluations of the rupee were nothing compared to the pandemonium that now broke out. Hindi heartland MPs threatened to resign. Farmers' organizations marched in protest—though, since this was also peak sowing time, I think we can be a little sceptical about whether the 'farmers' organization' marchers were in fact farmers and not, well, organizers.

The government, remember, was in a minority in the Lok Sabha; and the prime minister himself was far from being unchallenged. Thus, when 40 Congress MPs signed a 'farmers' parliamentary memorandum' that took the decision to task, Rao called a meeting of the parliamentary party.

Even Rao was taken aback, perhaps, by the stridency of their objections; and he accepted the recommendation of a panel of Congressmen that the decision be withdrawn. He told Manmohan Singh as much—according to legend, not directly, but through a senior bureaucrat.

Manmohan Singh offered his resignation—the first of many times *that* was to happen.[11]

Eventually, a compromise was hammered out. Prices would increase 30 per cent, not 40 per cent; and 'small farmers' would be exempted.

This was, really, not a compromise at all. It had the form of countless such half-measures in the years to come: occasions when 'pro-poor' loopholes would be built into reform measures that, in effect, would help the rich instead. Enough people understood this even at the time. *India Today* quoted a farmer in rural Uttar Pradesh as saying, 'The price difference now will make big farmers corner government-controlled stocks through *benami* [false] names.'

The reasons that Rao chose to betray Dr Singh were important, and revealing. They were fourfold.

First, the new prime minister faced outrage from the antediluvian relics that peopled (and people) the Congress party, all of whom were quite unprepared to see the sacred legacy of the Nehru–Gandhis called into question. Rao refused to face them down and do some plain talking about precisely where the sacred legacy of the Nehru–Gandhis had left their unhappy country. In failing to be open about the disasters of the past, he instead set the tone for India's reforms: apologetic, and stressing a quite imaginary continuity. It is a continuing amazement to me, as it must be to all rational observers, that this cowardly and patronizing attitude has not just become mainstream among India's politicians, but that it is universally praised as being wise and far-seeing.

Second, the new prime minister faced outrage from agrarian, Hindi-heartland MPs. He could have faced them down and insisted that the Congress would protect agriculture, but not coddle it. Rao had the opportunity to remake the Indian political economy, turn it into a locomotive that pointed forward instead of back; but, not for the first time, a politician refused to take the plunge. The fear that political setbacks in the heartland would inevitably follow from economic reform and that such political reverses would be irreversible was first articulated in this confrontation. Just to set in context exactly how wrong Rao was in his fear: the Congress had just five MPs in Uttar Pradesh in the 1991 election, down from 15 in 1989 and almost all 85 in 1984. In 1996, it again won five. In 1998, zero. Clearly, if UP's farmers wanted a party to protect their subsidies, they had other more credible alternatives to the Congress. Still, Rao's fear of the farmer, like his embrace of stealth, also became a hallmark of post–reform India—and with as little justification.

Third, the new prime minister faced outrage on the floor of Parliament. It had just won a vote that allowed it to stay in office; but now various wild-eyed socialists were threatening to move amendments to the Budget that, if passed, would require the government to resign. Rao had a great opportunity to call the Opposition out on its hypocrisy. After all, for the vast majority of MPs, the outrage was feigned. They had no intention of going back to the people a few short weeks after the last election—polls are time-consuming and expensive, and voters have a tendency to throw out any MP who imprudently chooses to bother them more than once in a year. The leader of the Opposition, L.K. Advani, explicitly said 'there is no immediate threat to the government'. The former prime minister V.P. Singh was busy planning those farmers' protests, but his support for the reform measures was 'well known' in Delhi, according to *India Today*. Rao refused to tackle this doublespeak head-on. What appeared and appears a quite irrational fear of the consequences for his government's survival became, in the years to come, routine: a government, even if confident in its numbers, would never ever submit to a challenge on the floor of the House on a matter of economic reform.[12]

And finally, the new prime minister faced outrage from the anti-American left. In fact, the most-used word in the newspapers and in Parliament that hot long-ago summer was 'conditionalities'—standing in for the theory that absolutely everything in the Budget had, in fact, been written by the International Monetary Fund as a condition for lending India money. The most wild-eyed representative of these brave warriors of the radical left, the firebrand trade-unionist George Fernandes,[13] had already openly accused the government of taking the IMF's dictation on the matter of subsidies. In fact, he'd raised the issue in the Lok Sabha well before the Budget; and even at that point, the prime minister had very visibly shied away from answering the accusation. Here's Rao, from the Lok Sabha's proceedings a fortnight before the Budget: 'I will reply to your second point [from Fernandes, about subsidies and the IMF] later. [Interruptions] . . . It does not mean that we are owning it. The only thing is I will take time to answer you in detail.' No answer came, naturally.

In refusing to make the eminently sensible point that the IMF's recommendations were not really recommendations, but a reasonable reminder of the only possible way forward, Rao would set another template for future reformers: a paranoid fear of appearing treasonous. After all, Gandhi had won us freedom from the British while implying that those who wore foreign cloth were traitors; and Nehru had kept us free while his acolytes muttered similar imprecations about those who shared 'Western' views that socialism was counterproductive. Reform was weakness, reform was submission to the West, reform was ever-so-slightly treasonous. That pattern, too, was set in stone a few short weeks after the reform process started.

Faced with this betrayal, and with Rao's offer of a compromise, Dr Singh gave in. Here is both the tragedy and the glory of Indian reforms—and, for that matter, of Manmohan Singh's career. What was implemented was always a little short of what could have been done. But something got done anyway.

When Dr Singh stood up to defend his Budget months later, he also had to announce the rollback of his decision on fertilizer subsidies. What was revealing was how much, even then, he chose to conceal about the true nature of the decision. Dr Singh decided to make his bending to Rao's dictates a virtue; following him, India has decided to make 'gradualism' in reform a virtue.

He began by admitting that 'strong views have been expressed on both sides of this august House'—that, in other words, he had been stabbed in the back by his own party, and not just the Opposition. After that meaningful beginning, Dr Singh again laid out his theory that higher procurement prices would compensate farmers for higher fertilizer costs; but then added: 'It has also been argued that the increase in procurement prices would not compensate those small and marginal farmers who have little marketable surplus and produce mostly for their own consumption. I see considerable force in this argument.' Or perhaps he didn't completely. Who can know for sure?

You see where the capitulation begins? He followed it up thus: 'I am, therefore, convinced that consistent with the basic philosophy of my Budget, in particular the importance our government attaches to an adjustment programme which is both growth-oriented and is imbued with a genuine concern for social justice, it is necessary to modify my proposal . . . I, therefore, now propose to fully exempt the small and marginal farmers from the 40 per cent increase in fertilizer prices announced on 24th July, 1991.'

In that paragraph is visible all you need to know about India's reforms not just in 1991, but in the quarter-century that followed. Pragmatic; politically expedient; deceptive; insufficient; better than nothing; disappointing; hopeful.

HALF-REFORMS HALF WORK

A lot did get done in those frantic weeks and months in 1991 and 1992. Industry and foreign trade were both largely freed from the horrific Licence Raj. Taxes were rationalized, and financiers made money. External investment poured in, as confidence in India recovered. New products appeared on India's shelves.

But the process remained incomplete—because, as I said, it was always half-hearted. This matters. It matters because it is precisely what did *not* get done in that first flush of crisis that we continue to struggle with. For one thing, nobody has been able to end fertilizer subsidies yet. In fact, in 2014, they cost us about as much as they did in 1991, proportionately—and they're even more politically untouchable, having survived all these years.

Here are just some of the things that hold us back today:

Markets for labour, land, and capital that are restricted, even though the markets for the stuff you create with them have been freed up.

Taxes and hold-ups at state borders that are often even more onerous than those between India and the rest of the world.

A rupee that's artificially valuable, which means we think we can afford more than we really can, and produce less stuff than we should.

And, most of all, a government machinery that is set up for the Licence Raj of the 1970s, not the half-free market of today.

Each one of those things is, in essence, the leftover agenda of the 1990s. Amazingly, you can read reports that Finance Minister Manmohan Singh commissioned in the early 1990s on possible reforms to these areas that sound like they were submitted to Prime Minister Manmohan Singh in 2014.

Even that first burst of activity in reforms that began in June 1991 was brought to an abrupt end. Oddly, it wasn't because the minority government lost the confidence of the Lok Sabha, something that Narasimha Rao clearly feared when he advised caution to Dr Singh on fertilizer subsidies. No; halfway through its term in office, Rao's government was, in fact, no longer even in a minority in the Lok Sabha. And yet Rao called a halt to reforms. This was because the Congress lost two state elections—in Andhra Pradesh and Karnataka—and Rao, from Andhra himself, decided this was the electorate whispering gently into his ear. It is a pity he did not read it as the electorate gently whispering 'not enough', though this is a misreading he shares with most post–reform politicians.

This, the Rao Inversion, is the primary characteristic of Indian politics since 1991. From Rao all politicians have inherited the ability to attribute every electoral reversal to economic reforms, while being convinced that every electoral success is because The Masses are in awe of your empathy for their poverty.

The reason that the agenda was left incomplete is that, at the time, no destination was specified by the government. Even what I am calling an 'agenda' is an imposition of basic logic after the fact; at the time, most in government would have run a mile from the suggestion that their actions represented anything but continuity, only perhaps with a little extra energy because we were on the brink of a national humiliation to rival Miandad's last-ball six.

It wasn't as if the government stood up and said: look, we have failed you for years; and now we are changing course. Dr Singh, at least, did say at several points early on that there was no going back to the past; A.K. Bhattacharya recalls that the new finance minister spoke sharply at his stormy first press conference about transcending the act of begging the Aid India Consortium in Paris, every summer, for dollars—a task he himself had performed as a civil servant in the 1970s.

But the idea of changing course was, itself, suspicious. It was suspicious because it looked like a betrayal of Rajiv Gandhi, dead so young; and it was suspicious because of the repeated accusations that it was happening on the instructions of various nefarious sorts in Washington, DC. The allegation about IMF 'conditionalities' that many, including Fernandes, had made, could be very sharp indeed. Fernandes frequently accused the government of something close to outright treachery: 'The Council of the IMF is not much concerned with the conditionalities it has put before the government, but certainly the hands which control it are very concerned about this as they want our signatures on the Non-Proliferation Treaty.' Even Yashwant Sinha, who had been finance minister in the short-lived government before Rao's and is still an active politician—though somehow one with a reformist reputation—wrote in his newspaper column: '[The reduction of defence expenditure] has obviously been done under pressure of the International Monetary Fund (IMF) and other donor countries . . . I think in doing so, the finance minister has sacrificed the national interest at the altar of IMF.' The *Indian Express* front-paged a story that Dr Singh had 'given away Budget secrets to the World Bank'.

There was an opportunity here: an opportunity to declare, as Murli Deora vaguely urged the government, to defend its choice of actions. 'If they [the World Bank and the IMF] have come to our rescue, there is nothing wrong in it. If some of the measures suggested by them are good for our economy, we must accept them. If they are not good for us, we must reject them.'

Indeed, there was an opportunity to declare a shift in orientation. But all the energy of the government in 1991—save Dr Singh—was directed instead towards insisting that no change had been made.

Narasimha Rao, for example, shoved the responsibility anywhere else he could. He first insisted in Parliament that he was just implementing things that everyone else had already decided: 'All the other measures which were really written about in newspapers times without number. For months and months they were being discussed. Panel discussions took place. So, it is not as if the measures which we have taken just dropped from the heaven overnight. We were not even three–four days old, how could we prepare all those papers? The papers were ready.'

Then he said it was just a matter of honour: 'We know that there are no alternatives to what we have done. We have only salvaged the prestige of this country . . . I do not say that our economy has been booming or is going to boom immediately.'

And finally, this supreme bit of waffling, in which he seems to indicate that he himself is nothing, but that his finance minister was merely implementing the vision of a long line of dead people named Gandhi: 'These decisions are not unqualified decisions and I cannot say, I cannot guarantee that these decisions will not bring their own distress and their own disadvantage. But that is where the Congress manifesto and the history of the Congress, the party that runs the government, comes into the picture. It is not Manmohan Singh. It is Manmohan Singh plus Mahatma Gandhi, Jawaharlal Nehru, Indira Gandhi, Rajiv Gandhi and we, the small people on whom the mantle has fallen, this is a combination. Here is a person who knows what is to be done and here we are who know what the people want. There will be a marriage between the two. There is absolutely no doubt about it. We will not pursue anything which will be against the national interest or against the programmes of the Congress meant for the poor. This is the guarantee that I can give to this House. We go by the manifesto.'

Ah yes, the manifesto, the one that promised prices would be rolled back. In all the myth-making about the 1991 manifesto, few people have bothered to read it. Among other things, it promises 'effective import substitution'; and it praises India being largely cut off from the world economy, saying that the economy was largely 'insulated from the adverse effects of recession or inflation in other parts of the world'. It is difficult to see what is particularly reformist about a manifesto in which the 'Planning' section is as large as the 'Economy' section, and says, quite explicitly: 'The Congress reaffirms to the path of planning for development, the seeds of which were sown during the freedom struggle . . . The Congress will restore the planning process immediately.' And as for those prices which it promised to roll back, the manifesto was explicit on how they'd been caused: by a reckless increase in 'administered prices'. Or, in other words, by the government doing its job, being responsible, and trying to keep from overspending. 'When prices of particular commodities rose' under the Congress in the 1980s, the manifesto wistfully reminded its credulous readers, 'the highest priority was immediately given to taking the steps required to curtail or roll back the rise, using both fiscal policies as well as the public distribution system'. There was even a little paean to the wonderfulness of nationalized banks. This is not, by any means, a recognizably reformist document.

The Manmohan Singh of 1991 felt no need to be hobbled by untruths. Perhaps he thought he didn't have all that long: 'The life of a finance minister is notoriously short,' he said after his first Budget. But, by the next year, even he had learned. In the debate over his second Budget, in 1992, he quoted various bits of the manifesto out of context to claim he was merely implementing them. Rao's prevarication in this, as in so much else, set the pattern for the post–1991 years. The truth—that the crisis of 1991 was caused by Jawaharlal Nehru's Plans together with Indira Gandhi's statism, and topped off by Rajiv Gandhi's profligacy—was dangerous. It could not be said. Instead, Rajiv had to be converted into a prophet of reform, and the 1991 manifesto his gospel. The truth was so dangerous that, like the Shah Commission on the Emergency, it is almost impossible to find an original copy of the 1991 manifesto.

Change was bad; continuity was good. But this meant that, essentially, the people of India, and their Parliament, were never told the truth about the direction that the reforms process was supposed to go. If everything was a momentary response, or an interpretation of the manifesto; if nothing was different; then how could a failure to follow through on reform ever be recognized? This was the fatal genius of Rao. He never wished to be locked into any path; he would always maintain ambiguity as long as he dared. By never committing explicitly to an entire roadmap for economic reform, he could escape the need to do anything more than the minimum.

And that's why, after the losses in the state elections of 1994, Rao only talked about economic populism, not reform. He had decided not to make any more 'mistakes', said *India Today*, reporting on the 1996 election campaign: 'At that time [in 1994], he had criticised [Andhra chief minister] N.T. Rama Rao for resorting to populism. But now he is not averse to telling the electorate that his government had set aside Rs 30,000 crore in the Eighth Plan for poverty-alleviation programmes and is planning to treble the figure in the next Plan.'

Rao's worry—that elections were lost because of reform—became part of the baseline assumptions of Indian politics. When N.T. Rama Rao's pro-market successor, Chandrababu Naidu, was voted out in 2004, it was assumed it was because of 'reforms'. When the Vajpayee government was voted out that same year, it was again assumed it was because of 'reforms'. In both cases—as with Rao's own defeat in 1996—it was probably because the government failed to act quickly enough against rural distress, especially in drought years. Somehow that gets blamed on 'reforms'.

In fact, Rao's initial worry, that economic reform is the opposite of rural welfarism, has not just infected those doubtful about the market economy in general, but even those who are fans of it. Even today, the tiny sums spent on the rural guarantee programme are somehow seen as the insupportable burdens that destroyed the Indian economy, a pathology that makes very little economic sense.

It is not as if some people did not catch on that the government was not committing to a course of action. As so often happens, it was the people who didn't want a change in India's orientation who also wanted to force Rao to admit that change had taken place.

Here is the communist Indrajit Gupta: 'For the first time since independence . . . the government and the Congress Party is abandoning the ideological framework of the Nehru-Gandhi line of development within which it had sought to function all these years. This is my most serious charge against the Congress Party. I have to assume it largely from what we are trying to understand and study, because the Prime Minister never said a single word about it . . . The rationale behind it has to be explained to the House and through the House to the people. I think Mr Gorbachev, whatever his errors or mistakes or failings may be, he never hesitated to explain to his people and the Soviet Union what were those errors, what were those deviations, what were those mistakes committed under the old system which led their economy to a severe crisis. But here we are not told anything . . . I am saying here, that a major departure is taking place. You may deny it. But I think in the weeks to come and sooner than later, it will be quite clear that under this government a major departure is being carried out by the Congress Party to depart from the framework which it has followed from the time of Jawaharlal Nehru . . . In a kind of hush-hush way, in a backdoor way, this whole framework and ideology is proposed to be given up. You are free to do it, if you can convince the country and the people that without it we cannot survive . . . But please tell us what is your rationale.'

Here's Somnath Chatterjee, another communist, a few months later, just before the Opposition walked out rather than vote on the 1991 Budget: 'Not one word has been said as to what is the objective of the economic policy of this country. For whose benefit is this policy? . . . I found that my friends on the Congress side were very strongly and enthusiastically thumping their desks when the finance minister was criticizing the functioning of their own previous governments. They had supported the policies and the Budgets which are repudiated by the finance minister today. You had supported the Budgets during Mrs Indira Gandhi's time and during Rajiv Gandhi's time, and now you are also thumping the desk when those Budgets are being repudiated. This is the consistency of your policy. I am, therefore, not enamoured of your policy.'

To listen to the reforms' discontented, one would think it had gone much further than it had. To listen to those carrying it out, one would think that it had never even been imagined.

Thanks to Rao, India's turn to the market didn't go all the way. We didn't specify a destination; we didn't even admit that we were on a different road.

And thanks to this, the reform programme stayed incomplete. And here's the amazing thing: nobody cared. In the mid- to late-1990s, voices urging the government to keep on with the reforms progress were notably thin on the ground.

Nobody was worrying, because the half-hearted reforms were half working.

Each of the half-done reforms worked to do the same thing. They gave people access to a bit more to spend on; but they didn't make them more 'productive'. People, especially the middle class, began to feel far richer than they should have.

Take that product market–factor market asymmetry I mentioned earlier. When product markets are decontrolled, then pretty much anyone can set up factories selling, say, candy. This is *awesome*. Earlier perhaps Indians had to eat candy from the same few elderly private companies, or from the public sector ('Kisan Mithas', I imagine, sold in grey recycled-paper wrapping with a picture of Gandhiji sucking a sweet); but now a lot more candy was available and the competition would force the private sector to improve quality.

But, alas! This happy feeling won't last. Because, to ensure that people continually get improved candy, the ingredients that go into candy also need to be made continually cheaper, or easier to buy and sell. Land must be available for new candy factories, instead of being occupied by the same old candy factories—factories that only make the kinds of candy we no longer like. Labour must be allowed to move into those new candy factories. And capital must be allowed to stop financing the old factories, and encouraged to start financing the new. Just saying 'we're now allowing you to set up a factory' doesn't go far enough if you also say 'but we won't let you have any of the things you need to do so'.

But, even if you don't do all that, for a while you do get some decent candy. That, in a nutshell, was the 1990s and the early years of the 2000s.

THAT FALSE FEEL-GOOD

Reforms weren't rolled back. Nor did they completely stop after 1993. Both the governments that succeeded Rao's—the United Front government, a coalition of 15 mainly left-wing parties, including some Communist parties, and the National Democratic Alliance, led by the Hindu nationalist BJP—were broadly reformist. But they did shy away from saying so, and from doing anything that looked dramatic. The momentum of 1991 was allowed to wither away.

What they did do, however, was keep that feel-good feeling going. In a way, that was part of the problem; it took the pressure off. It didn't just postpone the inevitable; it made many of us imagine that the inevitable was, well, evitable.

Indeed, Indian reformers became experts at creating a feel-good atmosphere without actually doing all that much. P. Chidambaram, thrice finance minister, is the leading proponent of this art. Even the things he did were carefully chosen for maximum feel-good impact: for example, when he was finance minister for the United Front in 1997, his Budget reduced the complexities in personal income tax law as well as in taxes on companies. Naturally, this was called a Dream Budget, since we all dream about taxes on a regular basis.

(Wait, say this book's innumerable readers who remember nothing from the 1990s except Kajol's hairstyle from *Kuch Kuch Hota Hai*: did you say Chidambaram was in the United Front, and not the Congress?

I did. Let me explain. It may take some time. This parenthesis will just have to stay open in the meantime.

Chidambaram had left the Congress the previous year, to protest an electoral alliance with one of the two dominant parties in Tamil Nadu, the AIADMK.

Then his party, the Tamil Maanila Congress, shortly after he presented the 1997 Budget, left the United Front to protest the denial of the prime minister's post to its leader. And then, in 2001, Chidambaram's party—which remember, had left the Congress because it objected to an alliance with the AIADMK—formally allied with the AIADMK. Chidambaram, at that point, left the party—which merged into the Congress in 2002. Then, in 2004, Chidambaram joined the Congress. Indian soap operas are frequently less inventive than its politics.

Incidentally, as of November 2014, the Tamil Maanila Congress exists again—although Chidambaram has not yet closed a circle by jumping back to it.

Chidambaram is not trained as an economist—he is a well-known lawyer—but has been finance minister thrice, and is one of the 'faces' of Indian economic reforms. He started off, however, as a draconian minister of internal security in the Rajiv Gandhi government, and it is amusing to read one MP's response, in a 1991 Lok Sabha debate, to Chidambaram's first economics-related appointment, as a commerce minister who quickly liberalized trade policy: 'Mr Chidambaram who was the Minister in the Home Ministry looking after the portfolio of Internal Security, Public Grievances and Pension, he has become a Minister of Commerce. Now how does he know everything that in a hurry he declared a policy?')

So tax codes might be slightly simplified; and consumers might get their paws on cheaper imported goods, something the BJP–led government started allowing in 1999. But the central issues were considered too difficult to tackle.

That is why the very sectors that boomed in the new post–reforms India were the ones which didn't need the government to spend any political capital on moving reforms further forward.

The holy trinity of Indian growth is the following: finance, telecommunications, and information technology. Each one of these grew *around* the government's inaction as much as through its action. Each one of these took advantage of technological progress that rendered pre–reform regulation irrelevant. The seeds for each of these were sown in the early 1990s; very little effort was required thereafter.

Information technology is the most obvious example: after all, the software industry barely existed during the high noon of the Licence Raj, and Indira Gandhi would have had to be clairvoyant to have set up regulations choking its growth. Several onerous labour laws did not apply to it; it didn't need much land; it didn't produce anything material, which inspectors could inspect and declare sub-standard till you paid up; it didn't need vast amounts of start-up capital—Infosys, India's most celebrated software company, was founded with Rs 10,000 that Narayana Murthy borrowed from his wife.

As the political scientist Devesh Kapur has noted, various Indian politicians figured out early that this is why IT was flourishing. The law minister in the first NDA government, Arun Jaitley, pointed out that India 'did not traditionally have any laws on IT and, as a result, the industry was able to flourish in a largely unregulated environment'. His colleague in charge of the sector, Pramod Mahajan, put this a little more pithily, saying that Indians won in 'IT and beauty contests, the two areas that the government has stayed out of'.

Telecom is perhaps a less obvious example. But it shows a great deal of the same characteristics. Most clearly, the extraordinary rate of improvement in cellphone technology reduced the need for high-cost land and difficult-to-find capital. It is true that successive government 'policies'—the National Telecom Policy of 1994, and the New Telecom Policy of 1999, both confusingly abbreviated 'NTP'—helped the telecom explosion. But it's important to note that the crucial aspect of both NTPs is that they clarified that the government would not consider off-limits to private enterprise a wireless sector that was never formally off-limits to private enterprise.

Incidentally, one policy worked better than the other—the 1999 policy worked to expand the sector in a way that the 1994 policy didn't. The only real difference? After 1999, private operators didn't have to pay the government up front for all the radio spectrum their services would be using. Instead, they could share revenue with the government. This meant getting into the business was cheaper, and so cellphone charges were, too. Another factor that made call rates cheaper was that after 1999 spectrum wasn't required to be auctioned, the way it was between 1994 and 1999. Auctions led to overbidding; overbidding led to default, or to high charges. These questions would have an ironic resonance more than a decade later, when corruption scandals related to radio spectrum broke.

Indeed, all the various changes to telecom regulation were not precisely the product of government initiative. Even at the time, they were seen as a *response*. In particular, they were a response to how the vast and influential company Reliance had been permitted to expand into services that it had not, in fact, paid the licence fee to enter—no doubt purely through oversight, because absolutely no other reason presents itself as likely to me, nope sirree not at all.

The minister in charge, Arun Shourie, was characteristically open in admitting this: 'By exceeding the limits which restrictions sought to impose upon them', he has been quoted as saying, companies such as Reliance 'helped create the case for scrapping . . . regulations'.[14] It is difficult to see this as a product of policy reform, therefore, and not as good old-fashioned lobbying, which happened on this occasion to have a positive fallout.

In other words, after the mid-1990s, successive governments were never really interested in completing the 1991 agenda. It seemed that the 1991 reforms were working away; and a little tinkering here and there at the margin would keep the Indian economy growing.

WE MAKE NOTHING. NOTHING!

Indians, when life gives them lemons, will not make lemonade. No. They will instead put up a large sign over the lemons, saying 'DEHYDRATED SUGARLESS LEMONADE. GOOD FOR DIABETICS.' They will then write several books praising dehydrated sugarless lemonade as a unique Indian development, well suited to our climate and traditions. US–based management professors will declare this an example of frugal innovation. Indian entrepreneurs, they will say, have found a way around the constraints of their environment.

This is pretty much what happened with India's legacy of reforms after 1991.

All products of circumstance were declared to be products of design. All the consequences of fear or error were declared to be consequences of wisdom. All deviations from global best practice were declared to be necessary for the unique Indian environment.

'Gradualism', for example—coined to describe how China's pro-market reforms were different from the 'shock therapy' that the former Soviet bloc underwent—was considered appropriate for India. 'Gradualism' was a colossal fraud; but few bothered to join their voices to that of Montek Singh Ahluwalia, who, in a much-read piece in 2002, tore into the notion that the reforms were purposefully gradual—saying that the record suggested instead they were 'not so much gradualist as fitful and opportunistic'.

Reform 'by stealth' was considered indispensable, given that voters in India were supposed to be unable to understand that more money in their pockets was a good thing. (You will note I assume that enough voters had more money in their pockets during the post–1991 period in the first place. This assumption is based on many studies, large amounts of data, as well as on extreme and complete obviousness. Even the Communist Party of India [Marxist], on the subject of decreased poverty after twenty-three years of reforms, has been constrained to tone down its opposition. Its 2014 election manifesto says merely that 'the reforms have not made a significant impact on the depth and severity as well as the wide spread of poverty'. When India's beloved and indispensable Left is reduced to questioning only whether the reduction of poverty thanks to 'neoliberal policy' is significant or insignificant—instead of loudly complaining that poverty has increased massively—you can be fairly sure that poverty has *decreased* massively.)

Narasimha Rao, in later interviews, would even brag about what a good job he did of concealing what his government was up to, describing 1991 as 'a complete U-turn without seeming to be a U-turn', because 'you cannot afford U-turns in this country'.[15] He seemed so proud of his political management, one would think he had *won* the 1996 elections.

But even where the reform process had clearly failed—in its destruction of the existing Indian manufacturing sector, and its failure to build a new one—standard analysis didn't even try to explain or excuse it. Instead, we gave the failure a lick of paint and tried to sell it on eBay. It was a 'services-driven' development model! We *meant* to keep our share of industry low, honest! We were leapfrogging conventional industrialization and going straight to a mature Western-style economy with a big and diverse services sector! Those factories might work for the Chinese but they are too boring for us! Because we are all descended from ancient Vedic mathematicians, and we will all be Software Professionals, Six-Figure Salary, Green Card Applied For![16]

And so we return to that central failure. Even as, through the late 1990s and early 2000s, it became harder and harder for pre–1991 factories to stay open, nobody seemed to care—because of 'gradualism', and services, and IT, and leapfrogging, and because everything was being made cheaper in China anyway. For too long, nobody paused to ask *why* it was cheaper in China, a country richer than India. And so, entire shop-floors were mothballed, and then fell into disuse, their unions fighting desperate and misguided rear-guard battles, nobody defending the idea of manufacturing but an isolated and discredited Left, politicians and businessmen alike looking at the pre–1991 factories dotting India's towns and thinking only about the real-estate fortunes they represented, and not of the magic of manufacturing. We just stopped *making* stuff.

This is a familiar refrain, you'll say. Don't I hear it from the Americans all the time? Blah-blah-blah, Rust Belt, US Steel, blue-collar, Andrew Carnegie spinning in his grave, jobs to China, NAFTA, plaid-shirt values, etc., etc.? Yes, except for one big difference: the average US worker was way too rich for factories to make money in an era of free trade. He expected to be paid way too much.[17] There was absolutely no way that the average Indian worker would have expected to be paid too much.

It's only now that the economy has slowed, now that the middle class is hurting, now that we once again import far too much and export too little, that we've woken up to the fact that we make practically nothing in this country. If you're sitting in India, look around you. Look at the little things—your coffee cup, your teaspoon, your ashtray if you have one,[18] your snazzy smartphone, your television, your ball-point pen. Too few of them will have been made in India. Now imagine what you, yourself do. Chances are that, whatever it is you do to earn a living, it's worth something to Indians—but very little to outsiders. That, right there, is what leads to a current-account crisis. And it's the consequence of a de-industrialization that was not stealthy at all—but that still made far less noise than you'd expect.

Go back to that techie, the one on whose computer monitor I saw Manmohan Singh launch the brave new world we live in. As I said, he must have failed. I don't know why his business failed—partly, I'm sure, because the rupee was devalued, and he couldn't afford expensive inputs for the graphics cards he was going to build. Or perhaps he failed because he struggled with land for his factory; because the power kept on going out; because he needed a dozen environmental permissions and didn't know how to go about it; because two dozen people asked him for bribes, and wasted his ready cash; because nobody in the banking sector gave him a loan at the interest rates he was willing to pay; because he couldn't find skilled workers, and if he did, he would be subject to ruinous regulation. And if he managed to survive that obstacle course, perhaps his delicate chip-boards were damaged on India's terrible roads; or perhaps they were delayed so long at the port, he lost his contract.

But he must have failed. So many entrepreneurs did. We have no way to measure their silent desperation, or the years and creativity that they wasted. We can only listen to the silence where there should have been the music of manufacturing.

MY FATHER, THE BELIEVER

The boy who stood there watching Dr Singh's Budget didn't know the speech would change his world sooner than he could imagine. That was mid-1991; less than two years later, my father was looking for a new job, and I sadly had to abandon my beloved Calcutta. Dr Singh had put my dad out of work.

My father believed in India's factories. He would tell me later that he knew early on, as an undergraduate at IIT, that he wanted to be on a shop-floor, surrounded by machines. His first job was in a tiny town called Kumardhubi in Dhanbad district, in a factory that—among other things—supplied cast iron underground tracks to local mines. The factory had been set up before Independence, managed out of Calcutta by the boxwallahs at Bird and Company. (Who I thus always imagined as Most Superior Beings—till I learned that Amitabh Bachchan had been one of them.)

The years that my father was hired, however, were troubled ones. The troubles would probably have been above his pay grade at the time; but I've dug out the numbers, and it seems that the factory, formerly extremely profitable, had begun making large losses starting from 1967. Costs had risen sharply, it turns out. As it happens, when in 1966 a desperate Indira Gandhi devalued the rupee by 40 per cent, it had hit all sorts of little factories hard, and Kumardhubi Engineering Works was one of them.

What's worth noting, however, is that the company recovered its health. It cut costs, it became more efficient, and it got back into the black in four years. It stayed healthy for years after my father left it to go to the public-sector engineering behemoth Bharat Heavy Electricals Limited; what eventually brought it down was, naturally, labour trouble. Its later history was sadly typical: decline, strike, lockout, bankruptcy, nationalization, lease, revival, profits, greed, over-reach, strike, and a lengthy legal battle that ended in liquidation. The last you hear of it is a 2013 court order that says: 'It appears that in the properties of the Company, namely M/s Kumardhubi Metal Casting and Engineering Limited, some illegal construction work is going on. There is a vast open land [*sic*] with the aforesaid Company.' These are the mills that were to be the temples of modern India; they are nothing now. Nothing but hosts for the parasitical organism that is India's construction mafia.

My father would not have been surprised by how the Kumardhubi story turned out. Though it is interesting that it survived that earlier devaluation, because the division he was working for in 1991 did not. By then, he had to pay closer attention to things like currency risk, since he ran the 'switchgear' division of the Indian subsidiary of GEC Alsthom, an Anglo-French engineering firm. I'm still a little confused about what switchgear are; my father explained them to me as 'fuses and switches, but bigger'. What's relevant, however, is that they were big metal things with lots of imported parts that were tinkered with and assembled in two factories, one near Allahabad in Uttar Pradesh and one outside Calcutta. And in the years after 1991, the spike in the price of the imported parts essentially put his division out of business.

My father spent the last third of his career working in one loss-making manufacturing company after another. It wasn't as if he complained about it—he was an engineer, was he not? What else should he do? The economy for which he had trained was one of increasing industrialization, in which the corrugated iron roofs of factories would spread out till they covered the entire country. But it was an economy that was not to be; the dream fell apart in legal battles and lockouts, in asset-stripping by rapacious capitalists and in maximalist demands by greedy labour leaders.

Kumardhubi Engineering, which had recovered from an earlier devaluation, could not survive this one. It might have, if it were allowed to be efficiently managed, if it could pay off its old workforce, and start afresh. But that was never an option. It shut down in 1995. That was also the year that industry's share in India's economy peaked, at 22 per cent. I had just started college, studying economics and not engineering. I suspect that my father, nine years away from retiring, never quite understood why I wasn't as enthusiastic about big metal machines as he was. If more of us had been as starry-eyed about India's factories as he was, we wouldn't be in this mess today.

THE GREAT LEAP LEFT

So that year, 1995, is one possible turning point, a point of inversion, a moment at which India resolutely and visibly takes one path and not another. It's my preferred one, the point at which both the headlines and the statistics suggest that the reforms of 1991 lose steam.

There are others, of course. For some people, 1991 itself. For others, 1984, when the assassination of Indira Gandhi and the Congress–led riots that followed traumatized a generation, and when the horrific Union Carbide gas leak in December legitimized a distrust of multinationals that has continued long into the reforms era.

Many others pick 1977, the year the Congress party's long post–Independence hegemony was finally punctured at the Centre, bringing in the Janata coalition, and 'Firebrand' George Fernandes, who demanded that Coca-Cola give up its Secret Formula or leave India—but, more importantly, the year that the Left Front rose to power in Calcutta, speeding up the decline of the East, the natural location for India's factories and mines and steel mills.

But the most persuasive of these earlier dates is 1969. India began that year a pragmatic, 'mixed' economy with a ruling party in which many starkly different shades of thought were in healthy contention. It ended that year a make-believe socialist economy, and a government in lock-step behind a single leader.

The tragedy of the Great Leap Left of 1969 is how very avoidable it was. It was born not out of ideology, not even out of strategy, but out of the most petty of tactics. Indira Gandhi is often excoriated for being the worst of India's many socialists. This is unfair and unjust. Mrs Gandhi was many things, but never a real socialist, a socialist of conviction. She was that far worse creature: a politician capable of finding an 'ism' for any occasion.

In what is now generally accepted to be the canonical example of sexist overconfidence, the Congress's Old Guard of regional leaders[19] had decided in 1966 that Indira Gandhi, who had few distinctive qualities at that time other than being Jawaharlal Nehru's daughter, was just the person to become India's prime minister, because she would be silent and demure and easily controlled because women are like that, aren't they?

Naturally, in a few short years Mrs Gandhi was locked in a titanic struggle for control of the Congress with the regional leaders, who were collectively known as the Syndicate (a word that echoes the Mafia—unintentional, but I suppose strangely accurate).

Mrs Gandhi's preferred form of warfare was the style that, in later years, has come to be associated with the Pakistani Army. She preferred to build up and use proxies against her enemies, people she could deny controlling, and whose excesses she could deplore in a leaderly and moderate fashion. Many contend, for example, that the Sikh separatist Jarnail Singh Bhindranwale began as one of Mrs Gandhi's proxies, in the Congress's political battle against the Akali Dal in Punjab. The Pakistani Army seems to have forgotten how that story played out for Mrs Gandhi.

In the 1960s, Mrs Gandhi's chosen proxies in New Delhi were a brigade of left-wing Congressmen who were called the 'Young

Turks'. (I wonder what it says about us that the most famous terms in our political history invariable reference events in other countries' political histories.) And the ground on which she chose to fight the Syndicate was the concentration of economic power.

You see, Mrs Gandhi suspected the old Indian capitalist class was funding her opponents in the party such as her deputy and finance minister, Morarji Desai. The Syndicate had originally chosen her as prime minister to keep out Desai, as they had chosen Lal Bahadur Shastri before her—after an ugly spat in the very room in which the dead Nehru lay, according to Krishna Menon. Once they had a chance to observe Mrs Gandhi with greater concentration, the Syndicate unsurprisingly decided they preferred Desai.

So complete was Mrs Gandhi's subsequent victory that it seems inevitable to us now. But it hardly seemed so at the time. One can only speculate how differently our history would have turned out had Mrs Gandhi chosen a different field of battle than India's economic orientation. Mrs Gandhi chose the battleground; the Syndicate obliged, and met her on it. In a 1968 Congress session— back in those days, party meetings were venues for disagreement, not sycophancy—the party's president, a grandee from Karnataka, launched into Mrs Gandhi's economic policy. It was increasingly clear, he said, that the public sector was grossly inefficient. Its failure to make profits was 'stark'.

Mrs Gandhi fired back. Such criticism was 'puerile'; the public sector wasn't meant to be profitable or efficient or any of those vile baniya things, but to 'preserve and promote national self-reliance'. (Always run a mile from any policymaker who thinks 'self-reliance' is an economic principle.)

It is tantalizing to imagine how close India came to taking a Sharp Turn Right instead of Indira's Great Leap Left. Had the Syndicate been a shade more united, had Mrs Gandhi been a shade less compelling, we would have been talking of the Reforms of 1969, and we would have had a nine-year head start on China.

But Mrs Gandhi was too clever, and her country too unlucky. Soon her plan was out in the open: to use the Young Turks against the Syndicate, and leave them isolated.

The Young Turks had, for years, been hammering away at India's banks, insisting they lent only to the wealthy. They had a point; the penetration of formal finance was pitiful, and many banks had become noticeably close to the great Indian corporate families: UCO Bank was considered to be the Birlas' bailiwick, the Oriental Bank of Commerce was the Thapars', and the Tatas had connections to the Central Bank of India.

As late as April 1969, Mrs Gandhi had chosen to remain above the fray, indicating there might be other ways to control the banks, while retaining the threat of nationalization. She hoped, thereby, to split the Syndicate, and bring some of the more socialist members over to her own side.

But circumstances forced an end to her equivocation. In May 1969, India's third President, Zakir Hussain, died in office.[20] Mrs Gandhi saw the consequent presidential election as an opportunity to exert her will on the party. The Syndicate defied her; she received word, in June, that they had secretly picked a candidate for President of whom she didn't approve.

Defy Mrs Gandhi and she always, always, upped the stakes. The choice of nominee was to be made, officially, at the annual meeting of the Congress, in July. On the first day of the meeting, Mrs Gandhi pretended to be unwell, and instead sent a note to be read out. She called it her 'Stray Thoughts', which elegantly demonstrates that title-giving is a far more delicate art than prime minister-ing. The note made a clear, stark threat: do what I say, or I will eviscerate your backers, and divide you in the bargain. Mrs Gandhi's political brilliance lay in her ability to cynically use the ideologies in which other, better people believed, to manipulate them into giving her more power; here, she effortlessly transformed the struggle for control of the Congress into an ideological battle.

But the party elders were in no mood to be thus bullied. In a closed-door meeting to select the President, Mrs Gandhi was decisively outvoted—with her senior Cabinet colleagues, such as her home minister and finance minister Desai, voting against her.

She flew back to Delhi and wrote an exquisitely polite note to the finance minister.[21] Morarji Desai was told that, given he had been an opponent of bank nationalization, he couldn't possibly implement the policy. So she was sacking him and taking the finance portfolio for herself. The next morning she called the economic affairs secretary, a legendary economist named I.G. Patel,[22] and told him to nationalize the banks. It was done in a few hours; and public response was ecstatic. People cheered on the streets. Desai's sacking was forgotten; Mrs Gandhi was the hero of the hour. By December, the Congress had formally split.

Mrs Gandhi learned this lesson: always, always outflank your opponents ideologically. If necessary, say one thing, do another. In public, she took her Great Leap Left; in private, she was urging Henry Kissinger to get Union Carbide to India. She followed up bank nationalization with various other policy changes that she said were meant to build a socialist state, but were actually meant to batter her opponents into submission. By 1971, she had invented the 'garibi hatao' slogan, and got 44 per cent of the vote in the elections, enough for a landslide. Her opponents, the Syndicate, got 10 per cent of the vote, and 16 of 543 seats.

Nineteen sixty-nine was the year that India's lost decade began; it was the year that 'hurting the rich' began to be seen as identical to 'helping the poor'. Yes, it deserves, perhaps, to be remembered as the point at which independent India lost its way.

But, in many ways, the real battle for the soul of India in 1969 was not being fought in the corridors of Delhi. It was being fought on the streets of Bombay.

VILLAGE OF MILLS

Bombay, in 1969, was an industrial city. There were hundreds of mills and factories, their chimneys delineating the city's skyline the way that skyscrapers do today; when Bombayites moved away, they missed the sound of the morning sirens as much as the sound of waves lapping at the shore. The blocks of one-room apartments built at the turn of the twentieth century for migrant mill-workers, called chawls, had given birth to a vibrant working-class society; almost half the city's workforce worked in a cotton mill. The day that bonuses were handed out, the shops and the restaurants and the bars stayed open all night.

As with every industrial working class in the world, there was an expectation of ever-increasing prosperity, the sense of security that gives rise to entrepreneurship and education and, eventually, a sizeable middle class. Of course, the sharp divisions that are the defining characteristics of Indian society did not disappear—Muslims and Hindus gravitated to different roles within the mills, frequently, as did men and women—but there is considerable evidence that these differences were becoming less powerful. Yes, upper-caste Maratha weavers refused to work with Dalits, because in some older mills, yarn had to be actually sucked by the worker on to the machine; but, on the other hand, there is evidence that the proportion of Dalits employed in mills went up steadily—from well below their proportion in the city as a whole in the early 1900s to well *above* the larger proportion by the 1940s. And while the backbone of working-class culture was of the various Marathi-speaking ethnicities, Marathas were actually barely more than half of all mill-workers. But, it appeared, a certain homogeneity, based on shared experience and class solidarity, was emerging.[23]

It was this that, in 1969, was threatened. It was the solidarity of a possible industrial *middle* class that was in the process of being destroyed.

There were mills all across the islands of Bombay, but the greatest concentration, of 130 of them, was in a few square kilometres that came to be known as the 'mill village', or Girangaon. Marathi writers and playwrights examined—and, in some cases, consciously created—the differences between Girangaon and the wider world. Girangaon differed from not just the Konkan belt from where many of its workers had come; in its ability to build alliances across caste, it differed from the rest of Bombay, too. One such writer, Mama Warerkar, who died in 1964, used the name 'Girangaon' to great effect—contrasting it to Girgaon, an affluent and upper-caste neighbourhood far to the south, where a mill's managers might live. Girangaon built solidarity; Girgaon did not.

And Girangaon was, politically, Red. It voted solidly for the Communists; indeed, in India's first election in 1952, the strength of the Communist Party in Girangaon was such that the candidate who lost the Central Bombay seat to the Congress blamed Girangaon for his defeat. That candidate was B.R. Ambedkar; the Communists' decision to defeat him instead of allying with him was, in many ways, the first grievous injury to the solidarity they had been supposedly championing.

But the death-blow to Girangaon was not to come from Dalit

parties. It would come from Balasaheb Thackeray. Balasaheb's writer father, Keshav, had been one of the leading lights of the divisive movement in the 1950s to create a Maharashtra state out of the old Bombay Presidency, a movement that essentially insisted that the city of Bombay itself was a Marathi-speaker's patrimony, and that others—particularly Gujaratis, so commercially dominant—had less of a claim to it. Balasaheb took this heritage and ran with it.

It is one of India's greatest tragedies that it has had very few natural politicians, and that those it has had have rarely been centrist pragmatists. This is perhaps because the political centre is usually being squatted upon by some member of the Nehru–Gandhi family—some of whom have been expert intriguers or profoundly charismatic, but none of whom has been a really natural politician.

Thackeray was, in contrast, among India's greatest practitioners of politics' darkest arts. The Sith Lord of Dadar, surveying the political landscape in the 1960s, determined that to rule in Mumbai he would have to break the Red fortress of Girangaon; and, over the 1960s, he did so in a relentless campaign of promises, populism, intimidation, violence—and Culture.

The cultural battle has resonated down the years. Girangaon had long been home to communist-inspired theatre productions, and to community festivals that the Communist Party of India helped organize. In fact, the CPI's national office was in the middle of Girangaon, in what was called the 'Dalvi Building'. But Bal Thackeray and his Shiv Sena chose to take the CPI head-on, organizing instead through clubs of wrestlers or cricketers or kho-kho players. Most particularly, he took away from the CPI the organization of the local Ganesh festivals; by 1969, the communists did not run even one of them, according to the historian Raj Chandravarkar.

(Communists in India have not just been willing to compromise with organized religion, they have been eager to help organize

115

religion. The CPI in Bombay, like the Congress in an earlier era and the Shiv Sena in a later one, used the Ganesh festivals as an opportunity to raise funds and project power. In Calcutta, Durga Puja celebrations were closely linked in most cases to the local Party office. Often, through the 1980s and 1990s, the communists would set up a stall right by the *pandal* happily hawking translations of Marx and Engels and Lenin. Sometimes Marxism's bearded trinity would even feature inside the pandal, which no doubt confused the average socialist bhadralok—which graven image should be bowed to first?)

The Shiv Sena grew increasingly bold; they had to demonstrate to their cadre that they, and not the Communist unions or the Congress government, ruled the streets. The Congress was happy to use the Sena to attack the Communists, as well as other undesirables—yes, that brilliant 'proxy' idea again. In 1967, Nehru's friend and minister, the socialist Krishna Menon,[24] stood as an independent in the North Bombay constituency, with Communist support; the Sena was happy to attack the commie-loving 'outsider', and the Congress chief minister was happy to allow them to do so. Rallies were disrupted, organizers were beaten up and all that, but to understand exactly how fine a man Thackeray was, you need to look at the cartoons he drew during Menon's campaign. One, published the day before the election, showed Menon with his arm around two young white girls, with the caption: 'This is why Menon wants to be defence minister.' Menon lost; emboldened, in December of that year the Sena led an audacious attack on the CPI's headquarters of Dalvi Building, set fire to it, and almost destroyed it.

And, in 1969, Bal Thackeray demonstrated that he now ruled Bombay, not the Congress, and not the Communists.

The provocation was typical: a demand that Karnataka cede to Maharashtra the district of Belgaum, in which a Marathi-speaking town was surrounded by Kannada-speaking countryside. Delhi,

Thackeray thundered—Thackeray always 'thundered'—had betrayed Bombay. Not one leader from Delhi would sully Bombay's sacred soil. Particularly not traitors like Morarji Desai, still finance minister at the time.

Desai was, for Thackeray, the easiest of men to vilify. Had he not, as chief minister, suggested that Bombay become a Union Territory, and not the patrimony of proud Maratha men? Was he not a Gujarati, and yet dared lay claim to being the most powerful man from Bombay?

Thus, when Desai came visiting in February 1969, the Sena attacked his motorcade. The police fought back; the Sena escalated the violence, and the entire city shut down for four days. It only ended when Thackeray called off his men.

And he did so only after his overlordship of the city had been accepted by the Congress government. They had to go, hat in hand, to him, begging him to write an appeal for peace. Fortunately, they knew where to find him, since at that time they had put him in jail. He had shown that, from his cell, he could shut down the city. This meant he was immune forever; he was never thrown in jail again. From 1969, Thackeray ruled with absolute power, and with absolute impunity.

In June 1970, the Sena's freedom to act was established. The Communists' leader in Girangaon, and the area's representative in the Maharashtra Assembly, was Krishna Desai—a man drawn from one mill family among many, a man who lived in a one-room flat like all of them, and who spent his evenings in their social and sporting clubs. In June 1970, he was murdered by a group of men; almost all of those convicted of the murder had ties to the Sena, according to the historian Gyan Prakash. The killing created a vacancy in the Assembly, and to drive home the point that there was a new sheriff in town, Thackeray ensured that the Shiv Sena defeated Desai's widow in the by-election. This was the Sena's first state lawmaker.[25]

In Thackeray's long battles for Marathi pride, it is his many social victories that are often emphasized: his destruction of a certain upper-crust cosmopolitanism, his transformation of the open-minded port of Bombay into the closed provincial city of Mumbai. But there is an additional, and even more momentous way in which the street battles of 1969 changed Bombay's—and India's—destiny. They were instrumental in making India a rentier state—a place in which politics became about claims on state patronage rather than about discovering and creating alliances and solidarities.

I'm not claiming that a Bombay in which the Left had absolute power would have succeeded. The example of Bengal, where the communists' ascent to power paralleled the state's industrial decline, is a more than sufficient reminder not to romanticize the power of the unions. A Left dependent on corrupt union leadership can be as parasitical as any other political force. I shed no tears for the Left. After all, in 1969, they remained powerful in Delhi, where they were busy propping up Mrs Gandhi's minority government, and they were never the most responsible of stewards.

But, nevertheless, it is important to see the distinction between what the old order in the mill village had sought to create and what their replacements willed into existence. The Left had sought power to labour, and mills that were working and fair and profitable, in which people's old identities slowly dissolved. The Marathi-pride Right demanded the perpetuation of those identities. First call on resources should go to Mumbai's firstborn, the Marathi-speakers. The men whose patrimony Mumbai was should get a cut of the profits that outsiders were making. Girangaon's old rulers wished to be weavers; the men who came after wished, indeed, to be the lilies of the field, for they would toil not, and neither would they spin.[26]

Raj Chandravarkar put it best: 'The Shiv Sena's capacity to fulfil the expectations it had generated, to find jobs for its boys, to resolve disputes in the neighbourhood and to do favours for its clients depended on acquiring political power.' The fatal link between identity and violence on the one hand and power and patronage on the other was established.

A citizen's occupation as an industrial worker was no longer to be her primary political identity; it was replaced instead by her ethnic origin. This displaced the focus of state policy away from ensuring a favourable climate for Bombay's mills. They became, increasingly, locations of disputation and violence. Finally, in 1982, 2,50,000 mill-workers went on strike in Bombay, led by a man named Datta Samant, a doctor who had little to no experience of the textile industry. Samant kept them away from work and refused to negotiate. But technology and the law both conspired to defeat him. Mill-owners, struggling with onerous labour legislation discovered that it profited them little to keep the mills open, anyway—for powermills, which could be set up in small-scale units, could take up the slack. Instead of running big textile factories, it made more sense for the owners to subcontract to a dozen small powermill operators—none of whom was regulated, and few of whom paid taxes. The mill-workers found that, in the year they were on strike, their entire industry shut down around them.

As the textile industry died, how could it continue to pay for patronage, for the competing, expensive machineries of violence that the Congress and the Shiv Sena had built?

Fortunately there were other plans afoot. The purest way in which political power can be turned into wealth has always been the same: control of revenue from the land. And, in 1969, Maharashtra's politicians were in the process of discovering how the commercial possibilities of Bombay's real estate, and its infrastructure, were as addictive as any drug.

RECLAIMING BOMBAY

Mumbai is the only city in the world with 15 million people and one road.

To an outsider's eye, the city's layout is mildly insane. It is almost completely linear. When driving from the old town at the southern tip of the island to pretty much any of the other districts you're likely to go, you have no options—you're on the same road as anyone else. This has led to monumental traffic; today, Mumbai is not so much one city as a series of neighbourhoods, divided by hours of commuting time that are barriers as effective as any wall.

It was not supposed to be like this. Even as the Shiv Sena was rising to power fifty years ago, this problem was foreseen, and the solution was known: to expand the city.

Not northward, along that one road; but eastward, to the mainland, with road and rail links across the estuary that divided it from an increasingly crowded old city. There was space for an impressive DC-style Capitol for the state of Maharashtra, a centrepiece for the new business district; it would shine against the foothills of the Western Ghats when visitors approached the new town across the water, their backs to the old. Just shifting Bombay's centre of gravity would reorient the city's public transport away from overcrowded roads to rail—and, crucially, to boat and ferry.[27] That would help it overcome its unique disadvantages—a city centre more isolated, and with less land than anywhere. (Two-thirds of the land in a 25-kilometre radius of Bombay's downtown is under water. Compare that with 22 per cent for Jakarta, and 5 per cent for Seoul.)

Bombay, instead of being a straight line bursting at its single seam, would then fan out three-dimensionally, like every other city in the known universe.

As we know, this didn't happen. The reasons it didn't are very important. They reveal three things. First, how the politics of the states they're in can hold back India's cities. Second, why the focus away from production (the mills) and towards division (the Sena) is what needs to be reversed. And third, why infrastructure just does not get built.

You see, the creation of a new twin to Bombay across the water had a policy rival. And that was the way that Bombay's seven islands had become one to start off with: reclamation. It is odd, as many have pointed out, that the process of creating land where none was before is known as 'reclaiming land from the sea'. This tells you all you need to know about the English language, and its ability through apparently harmless words to effectively justify your right to take pretty much anything you want.

As Gyan Prakash has pointed out with sad sarcasm, it is extremely ironic that the crusading lawyer, Khurshed Nariman, who managed to have reclamation stopped in the 1920s because of his accusations of 'colonial high-handedness and secret payoffs', gave his name to the piece of land—Nariman Point—that became the focus of restarted reclamation efforts in the 1960s.

And, it turns out, everyone in power preferred reclaiming expensive parcels of land in South Bombay to building a city across the bay. Why not? You could, after all, make money off it: you reclaimed land, and then allotted it on the cheap to your builder friends.

The idea of a capital—and a Capitol—for Maharashtra on the mainland instead of the islands would have been doubly troubling. After all, hadn't the Shiv Sena and the various Maratha supremacists within the Congress just fought a battle to ensure that Marathi-speakers did not lose Bombay? If the seat of government moved off the island and on to the mainland, could Bombay Gujarati politicians, the local successors of Morarji Desai, not argue, once again, that the multi-ethnic island be made a Union Territory, freed from Maharashtra politicians?

This too: Was it not essential to what Maharashtra politics was becoming that Bombay not be lost, and that projects like the Backbay Reclamation go ahead? Because it was such projects that could finance the politics of patronage that the state was devolving into—a politics of competition over the fruits of success, and not over differing ideas for the future. Without the builder mafia, you could have no ethnic-supremacist politicians. And without the strongmen, you would have had no builder mafia. The state of Maharashtra needed Bombay not just for its identity, but to finance the particular identity politics, the politics of primacy, that it had developed.

And the politics of Maharashtra would choke Bombay to death. Today, it's nearly impossible to buy a house in Mumbai. In 2012, Bloomberg calculated that the city was the most unaffordable real-estate market in the world. The average citizen would have to work for three centuries to be able to buy a nice house in the city—since the cost of the average good home was 308 times the median income. This isn't an accident, or a product purely of Mumbai's odd geography. No, it is born of design. We have chosen to kill this city.

Consider just two things that keep houses scarce. One is rent control. Drive down Marine Drive, and look up at the glorious Art Deco facades of one of the world's great sea-faces, built in that first reckless rush of reclamation before Independence. Then look closer, at the rain stains and the crumbling arches. Marine Drive is collapsing before our eyes; largely because the law requires rents to remain at the levels they were in 1940. When Suraiya, a singer and actress who personified Bollywood's most refined era, died in 2004, there was a ruckus at her Marine Drive apartment. She'd lived there for seventy-one years, paying Rs 400 a month for a 2000-square-foot apartment worth tens of crores. Suraiya died alone; but the moment she did, a dozen heirs to her rent-controlled apartment popped wailing out of the woodwork.

Thanks to rent control, there are 19,000 buildings in Mumbai that should be condemned, but people are living in. Every year, people are killed when their roof falls on them. Landlords don't bother to fix the ceilings or the short-circuiting wiring—why should they, for the pittance they're receiving? Nor can they redevelop the buildings so that more apartments go on the market.

And the second way in which real estate has been choked off is through floor-space regulations. Mumbai may look like the only Indian city with skyscrapers—but the truth is it isn't supposed to. It isn't supposed to because the government for years imposed a 'floor-space index', or FSI, of 1 on most of the island.[28] That meant that, if you were building on a plot of 100 square metres, your new building couldn't have a built-up area of more than 100 square metres. Building more—going higher, in other words—was illegal. Yes, I know. For a city chronically short of housing, this is nothing short of insane. Every major island city—Manhattan, Singapore, Hong Kong—has skyscrapers. Just to compare: the permissible FSI in Shanghai, or in New York, or in Hong Kong, is between 10 and 15. It is only plains cities that are flat.

Thanks to this insanity—born of an attempt to appear green, and keep building to a minimum—Mumbai actually has only 1.1 square metres of open space per person. Just to be clear, that is less than New York. That is less than Hong Kong. It is even less than Tokyo, the gold standard for urban density.

Here's the best part: when the FSI regulation was introduced, in the mid-1960s, the permitted FSI was 4. Yes, it's actually gone down since then, although the space crunch has increased manifold. That's because, in the interim, everyone figured out exactly how much money there was to be made by only allowing skyscrapers one by one, with each having to ask for permission and an exemption from the rule. There's a solid lobby of builders in Mumbai who want FSI to stay low. And politicians.

Through the 1970s, as Bombay's ganglords began to figure out that construction was more lucrative than drug smuggling, they shifted focus—to intimidating tenants, 'protecting' slum residents, and serving as middlemen between builders and politicians. The chain-smoking, chain-wearing Haji Mastan would give interviews saying that he was reformed, and now he just financed films and real estate. Except, of course, he seemed more ashamed of saying 'financed' than he was of his past, because finance is un-Islamic.

The second rung of the Shiv Sena's leadership changed to reflect this over the 1970s: from businessmen such as the successful Thane mayor Satish Pradhan, or ex-Marxists to out-and-out 'dadas' or local toughs. The Congress too chose its own local champions. So did communities like Muslims and South Indians. By the time the late 1980s rolled around, it was difficult to tell the difference between a builder, a film-maker, a community organizer, a politician, and a trigger-happy gang leader, a confusion that continues to scar Bombay to this day—and, worse, has completely ruined Hindi movies' plots.

To imagine a Mumbai, today, without the Shiv Sena—and the politics it pioneered, for after the 1970s every major party in Maharashtra has become a clone of the original Sena—is difficult. But do it, anyway. It would be a Mumbai, perhaps, where textile companies are seen as possible employers and taxpayers, not as owners of land. It would be a Mumbai unafraid of its mixed heritage, and willing to share power with satellite towns.

Fifty years on, the 'Marathi manoos' whose primacy the Sena and its offshoots seek to protect is imagined above all as an aggrieved petty government official, not a trader, nor an entrepreneur, nor a mill-worker. Traders are Gujarati; vendors and shopkeepers are from Uttar Pradesh or south India; mill-workers were leftists. Oddly, as Delhi moves away from being the sort of place where the government's the only game in town, Mumbai has moved further into the crushing embrace of a regulating, thieving state.

The old Mumbai of mills has vanished; some of what remains is memory, some is anger, and some is greed. It is memory and anger that drive the nostalgic agitprop of *Cotton 56 Polyester 84*, one of the finest plays of recent years, in which two laid-off textile workers sit at a newsagent's stall and talk about their past. The play was directed by Sunil Shanbag, the son of communists who met and fell in love and married in the CPI's Dalvi Building. (His sister, Anuradha Ghandy, was perhaps the best-known woman in the Maoist rebel leadership.) The title comes from the game the two old men play, counting how many of those who pass by are wearing shirts of cotton, and how many are wearing shirts of the materials that took their jobs. The play was released in 2007; in July 2008, the Dalvi Building, empty for two years, finally came crashing down. Its death did warrant a mention in the papers—but only because of the heroism of an office worker who went into the collapsing building to rescue a street dog and her puppies.

Today's Mumbai is best summed up, perhaps, by what Girangaon, the village of mills, has become. On the very parcels of land where, once, India's first multi-ethnic, multi-caste industrial community was beginning to evolve, skyscrapers of dubious legality have climbed taller than any chimney. In the late 1990s, when the 'redevelopment' of mill land started, you could still walk into Phoenix Mills, now the beating heart of a new shopping district, and walk past the evening shift of mill-workers on your way to a brand-new bowling alley.[29] Today, even that is gone, and Phoenix's iconic chimney has been painted with bright banks of colour as if to emphasize that it doesn't believe in work any more. What has arisen from the ashes of Girangaon is a strange beast indeed.

BRIDGES TO NOWHERE

The long bridge to Bombay-across-the-water never did get built. But others did. The Western Express Highway, for example, is usually one long traffic jam partly because a bridge is being built to help unclog a bottleneck. Not just does the construction create another bottleneck, but once it's done, the flyover will immediately create another bottleneck. This is what happens when you try to patch a system, instead of decongesting it.

As we saw with the reclamation-versus-township story, the politics of primacy, as opposed to the politics of solidarity, became irreconcilably bound up with power over a city's rules and administration. And that, in turn, was irreconcilably bound up with how its infrastructure got built.

An unusual, but vicious circle developed: the death of manufacturing created a rentier state; the rentier state built poor infrastructure; poor infrastructure killed manufacturing.

And, again, it's the stories of Mumbai's infrastructure that need to be told to see how this vicious circle operates.

Look, for example, at the grand plans to take pressure off the Western Express Highway. As Murphy warned, everything that can go wrong, will: patronage battles; political turf wars; confusing environmental laws; powerful lobbies who want things just the way they are; and, even, sibling rivalry. Seriously.

The idea is that Mumbai's Only Road needs alternatives. One option is what has been imaginatively called the Western Freeway, in order to effectively and completely distinguish it from the Western Express Highway, the existing Only Road. You see, Mumbai doesn't really care very much about ensuring that things have distinctive names—frankly, I hope we get to keep both Western Freeway *and* Western Express Highway, just for the novelty of having at least some big things in that city that aren't named for Shivaji.

The Western Freeway is a lovely little concept, with various bridges linking promontories and even a little tunnel to round it off. Very First World. It was so very exciting that the first bit of it even got built. The Bandra–Worli Sea Link, as it is grandly called, cuts travel time by an hour between those two bits of the city. Wonderful. Of course, you exit the Sea Link and land up at a traffic jam at a badly planned U-turn. And the traffic just keeps on piling up.

That's because, as usual, the plan hasn't been taken to its logical conclusion. The rest of the Western Freeway hasn't been built, meaning that the current Sea Link now really should have the title of Only Bridge, to go with Only Road.

Why hasn't the rest been built? Well, the plans called for two more sea links, this time from Worli to Haji Ali and from Bandra to Versova, the next two links in the chain northward and southward. And here's where the politics got involved. Overseeing the bridge-building were the good folk of the Maharashtra State Road Development Corporation Limited, controlled by the fine upstanding people at the Nationalist Congress Party. They handed out contracts and such, with due attention to process, I'm sure, and absolutely no funny stuff, not at all, no sirree.

Then along came the Congress Party, not to be confused with the Nationalist Congress Party. The two Congresses were nominally fraternal allies, but, like most brothers, they hate each other. The Congress controlled another state government organization, the nice fellows of the Mumbai Metropolitan Regional Development Authority. The MMRDA decided it wanted a *third* project—a coastal road, hugging the shoreline all the way from south to north. This idea was chosen purely because it was intriguing, and absolutely not because the two parties were competing for patronage and for funds from possible developers, not at all, no sirree.

Both sides claimed that, under India's byzantine environmental laws, their preferred project was less harmful. The government in Delhi seemed to worry that *both* were too harmful. Of course, the idea that many cities elsewhere manage to build more than one road and more than one bridge without running afoul of environmental legislation supposedly much stricter than in India has occurred to nobody—and particularly not to successive Union ministers in charge of the environment.

And it wasn't just political siblings who were fighting. Two actual brothers, who were not too fond of each other either, were fighting too. The man who got the contract to build the additional Sea Links was Anil Ambani. The man expressing interest in the coast road that would take away the Sea Links' tolls was his brother, Mukesh. Many infrastructure projects have been shut down in India when corporate rivals have complained. When the two warring sons of India's richest man are the ones complaining about each other, then things don't just get shut down, they get buried.

And, finally, as the icing on the cake: couldn't some stop-gap arrangement be constructed, at least, maybe a flyover or two on land to minimize the impact of all the traffic coming racing off the Only Bridge? Sure. A plan had been in place for a few decades. But it might mean—I am not kidding here—that a couple of well-known residents whose luxurious apartments abut the Only Road might lose their sea view, or possibly their sea breeze. They petitioned successfully against the flyover. It is worth noting that, had they been poor farmers instead of Lata Mangeshkar, and petitioning against losing their land as opposed to losing their sea views, they might not have been as successful.

In case you think I'm exaggerating, or that what happened to the Western Freeway couldn't possibly be true of anything else, gather round, ye innocent ones, and hear tell of the Mumbai Trans Harbour Link. A grand idea, children, and one that we heard tell of last as a bridge connecting the old town with a grand new Capitol for Maharashtra across the sea. Well, good ideas never die; they just stay in the Planning Stage. Fifty years on, that bridge is still being discussed.

What's holding it up? Well, the good folk of the Maharashtra State Road Development Corporation tried to hand out the contract several times, and ran into a familiar set of problems and accusations. The winning bid came in, eventually, from Anil Ambani. But it seemed, even to the good folk of the MSRDC, to be too low. He may just possibly have had an incentive to keep it extra low, if he wanted to ensure that the winning bid wasn't that of his main competitor for the contract, a fellow apparently named Mahesh—no, sorry, *Mukesh* Ambani. (What a coincidence!)

Then the 2008 crash arrived, everyone ran short of cash, and Anil's company said it could no longer build the bridge. Remember, he would have spent a lot of money just to make the biggest landowner in Navi Mumbai, at the other end of the bridge, very wealthy. And that was a chap named Manish—sorry, *Mukesh* Ambani. (Funny, the name sounds familiar.)

Anyway, the nice fellows at the Mumbai Metropolitan Regional Development Authority— that's the one run by the Congress, not the Nationalist Congress—seized this moment to take away from their allies the right to oversee the bridge. They did this purely because they could do a better job, and not for any other reason, no sirree.

The bridge was then delayed further because—and I am not kidding here, people—the MSRDC, one wing of the government, refused to hand over the blueprints, plans, and feasibility studies to the MMRDA, another wing of the government, until Rs 25 crore was paid. It's so refreshing when blackmail is done openly, don't you think?

The MMRDA, stung, responded with largeness of heart and greatness of spirit; it refused to let the MSRDC add additional lanes to the existing connection between Mumbai and Navi Mumbai.[30] They complained—and this is also true, I am not making this up; I couldn't if I tried—that they didn't want to make things easier for commuters, because then fewer of them might take the new bridge. Yes, the new bridge that hadn't been built yet.

Mumbai's troubles have not ended there. It hasn't just been two allied parties, and two estranged brothers, trying to trip each other up and watching the city collapse at their feet instead. Even the central and state governments—run for a decade by the same political alliance!—were quarrelling.

Take the saga of Mumbai's second airport. Just as there were to be two docks, one serving the island city and one for the new city across the estuary, there were to be two airports. But the Navi Mumbai airport stayed on hold for years. Why? Because the Union environment ministry was worried about 160 acres of mangroves— the gloomiest plant known to man, even if you include the weeping willow.

Are mangroves perhaps endangered? Nope. They're being depleted, but are not endangered. Some would imagine the species could survive the minimal depredations required to build an airport for India's commercial capital. In fact, just to be clear, there are 14,400 acres of mangroves around Mumbai alone. There are at least 64,250 acres of mangroves along Maharashtra's coastline.

In other words, the Union ministry was arguing, apparently in all seriousness, that Maharashtra's government—run by, remember, the same party—could not spare 0.24 per cent of its mangroves to build an airport. This is exactly the sort of maximalism that gives environmentalism a bad name, and leads people to imagine that environmental regulations are merely obstructions to be avoided, rather than laws necessary to protect future generations.

FOREVER SECOND

Bombay has always been India's second city. Once Calcutta led, in terms of innovation and industry and excitement; and today it is Delhi. The primary cause of this also-ran status is that Bombay, and now Mumbai, has consistently been the biggest and most visible playground for all that has gone wrong with the Indian economy.

Here it is again, the roll of dishonour:

The politics of primacy, which seeks to win through communal polarization and ethnic strife, rather than through the construction of solidarity. Mumbai saw its purest form in the politics that the Shiv Sena pioneered and all the city's other parties adopted.

The patronage that is the fuel this politics needs to burn—the rent-seeking and the skewed policies that allow party workers to be whole-time toughs. In Mumbai, this too took its purest form, as the powerful turned to manipulating the world's most overpriced real estate.

The infrastructure deficit that is born of these skewed policies—especially in endlessly bottlenecked Mumbai, with its Only Road and its dead dreams of a twin across the water.

The comfortable elite that wants nothing to change. Mumbai's powerful are more puissant than most, and can block a flyover or a road expansion with ease.

The arbitrariness and caprice and contradiction of India's environmental laws. Mumbai is subject to coastal restrictions, mangrove-protection requirements, and even environment-related controls on the height of skyscrapers, presumably to avoid skyline pollution.

And the crippling fear of getting voters to pay for what they use, most visible in the failure to get the Mumbai suburban rail to pay for itself.

Mumbai, more than most parts of India, is locked into a downward spiral. There will come a time when the energy and optimism of the average person on Mumbai's streets and in its boardrooms will simply collapse under the stress placed on them by their crumbling, creaking city. It is and was said of Calcutta that what that great city thinks today, the country thinks tomorrow. Here is what they should say of Mumbai: that what it suffers today, India will suffer tomorrow.

FOR WHOM THE TOLL PAYS

That gleaming imaginary arc across the sea that Charles Correa and his fellow-architects dreamed up for Bombay in the 1960s might still get built. The contractor-politicians of the 1980s put it on the back-burner; the rioter-politicians of the 1990s didn't care; and the warring brothers of the 2000s delayed it. But the Maharashtra government is still hopeful it will get built.

Back in 2005, when the state government first bid it out, to be built in partnership with the private sector, it was to cost Rs 4000 crore. The two Ambani brothers bid; each probably bid too low, because even if they lost money on the deal they really didn't want the other to *make* money on it. Naturally, that plan didn't work. Then, in 2008, the state government bid it out as a building contract, not as a partnership agreement; now, it was to cost Rs 6000 crore. Fine. Except this was Financial Crisis year. And nobody bid. When it was bid out for the third time, in 2011—again as a partnership—it was to cost Rs 8800; when the bids were formalized, in 2012, it was to cost Rs 9630. Amazingly, after all this confusion, we wound up in early 2014 with nobody willing to build it.

That's when the state government decided to do it themselves. By then, of course, it was to cost Rs 11,000 crore. It's one of those things that only contractors really understand: imaginary bridges just get more expensive the longer you don't build them. Now, it appears the Japanese might give the state 80 per cent of the money for it. The government's going to take that money, and use it to pay a private company to build it. This is the fifth or sixth possible way in which to finance Mumbai's dream bridge; it may just be the best.

You see, this really is the crux of the problem. Everyone agrees that India's short of infrastructure. Politicians say so; commuters say so; foreigners say so; investors say so; even environmentalists are willing to admit it, if you catch them in a truthful mood. But absolutely nobody agrees on how to pay for all the infrastructure India needs.

Today, the countries of the West, and the Chinese, can build many enormous and expensive things without straining their exchequers. But that wasn't always the case—just like it isn't true for India today.

And this question of payment is one of those things that everyone in history tried to solve. And, as it happens, everyone in history got it wrong.

The Roman Republic built its first aqueducts primarily by going to war, taking other people's money, and turning them into slaves.

Georgian Britain, in the 1830s, had 8000 tollgates (in a pretty small island) to finance improvements and maintenance for each little stretch of road. They all had different tolls, confusing and delaying long-distance travellers; and were the cause of intermittent riots.

The Americans paid for their railways by handing out public land—usually land stolen by the American public from the Native Americans, who don't count as having a public—to the railway barons, saying that once the railways were built, the land would increase in value.

Of these three, only the first, the building of Rome, happened without large-scale corruption and cronyism. This should serve to remind a large number of Indians that yes, there *are* things worse than corruption.

In any case, let's just say that not all of these innovations travel well.

Indeed, American railway financing couldn't even manage the trip a few hundred kilometres north to Canada. Turns out railway financiers are happy to be given vast stretches of the American prairie in the expectation that it will become more valuable, but aren't quite that happy if you try to give them a nice peak or two in the Canadian Rockies. So potent was the ensuing scandal that it caused Canada's first prime minister to resign, which must have been a nice way to start off Home Rule.

As we saw with Bombay's bridge, there are really only four ways to pay for big, useful things.

First: the government builds it, and pays for it out of taxes.

Second: the government pays the private sector to build it. The government then either absorbs the cost, or tries to charge people using it.

Third: the government makes the private sector pay to build it; and, in return, they get to charge people using it.

Fourth: the government makes the private sector pay to build it; and, in return, they get concessions on other things, like land.

Everything else is basically a combination of these four options. The problem is working out which one is least likely to defraud vast numbers of people, or to create a permanent oligarchy, or require ruinous taxation, or leave most public works half-built.

In India, we've tried various combinations. In the Vajpayee era, between 1998 and 2004, there was a clear focus area: roads. The railways were struggling, as were ports—but Vajpayee's real interest was roads. Not just the big highways, but the little rural roads that can change people's lives. He pushed two major programmes, one that built rural roads and another that repaired the highways linking India's four largest cities. How did Vajpayee pay for this? He set up a fund that put a one-rupee tax on every litre of petrol or diesel sold. This was back in 1998, when petrol and diesel were pretty cheap—it worked out to between 5 and 11 per cent of fuel spending. As with the equivalent road tax in the United States, it was a mistake to not use it as a proportion of the cost of petrol instead of an absolute amount. Today, the road tax is around 2 per cent of fuel costs.

The government took this money, put it in a central road fund, and distributed it to states for rural roads, to the National Highways Authority for highways, and so on and so forth. Road-building ran into trouble in a lot of places—but it looked like they were getting built.

Not fast enough, however, for the new government that came into power in 2004.

When Manmohan Singh took over as prime minister, he had two major priorities. The first was administrative reform, the subject of his first speech; the second was infrastructure, which he said would be sorted out by a high-level committee that he'd chair himself.

The irony is overwhelming. A failure to overhaul administrative procedures and an inability to manage infrastructure are probably the two biggest reasons why Dr Singh's party was voted out ten years later.

The problem that Dr Singh had to deal with, however, was that the National Democratic Alliance years had not exactly been frugal. Few governments ever are. (That the NDA was no exception to the rule bears repeating, because in the UPA years it tended to be forgotten, and a halo of virtue was tacked on the NDA in death that it never wore in life.)

The Economist, writing on how to pay for Indian infrastructure, said at the time the NDA left office: 'If both state and central governments are counted, the country's fiscal deficit hovers around

10% of GDP. Increasing it would be difficult. Spending—committed to civil-service wages, defence and, above all, interest payments—is hard to cut. So where is the money to come from?'

The new government had a bunch of ideas. One was to use all the dollars that the Reserve Bank of India—which the events of 1991 had turned into the kind of paranoid hoarder that holds on to old toothbrushes forever—had accumulated. They were just sitting there doing nothing—and so Montek Singh Ahluwalia suggested they had better just go into building infrastructure projects, not into buying US government debt. This was a bad idea for various reasons, and thus it wasn't tried in the end; but it does go to illustrate exactly how desperate the government was for funds. *The Economist*'s own answer was, as it happens, perhaps the most sensible. It quoted someone on the only real answer for India: 'The government should raise taxes and spend it.'

But that wasn't what the government had in mind. Nobody wanted to raise taxes. Nobody ever does. Instead, the government turned to the private sector, entreated it, begged it, and finally bribed it into promising to build the infrastructure we needed—the roads, the power plants, the telecom towers, the ports and the bridges.

Trouble ensued.

PART III

SEVEN YEARS OF PLENTY

The Book of Genesis is not exactly known for its economic theory. But, had Prime Minister Manmohan Singh, in 2004, read its forty-first chapter with sufficient attention, the course of his government might have been different.

In Genesis 41, the story is told of how an Egyptian pharaoh was troubled with dreams. The dreams were of seven fat cows, and seven thin cows; and of seven rich heads of grain, and seven withered, wasted heads of grain. The monarch sought to have his dream interpreted. His court magicians could give him no answer that satisfied him; but Joseph, the hero of that section of Genesis, gives the pharaoh a convincing explanation, even though Joseph was not even a part of the Planning Commission. The seven fat cows and good ears of corn, says Joseph, represented seven years of plenty with abundant harvests; the seven lean cows and the withered ears of corn represented the seven years of famine that would follow—a famine so harsh that the years of plenty would be forgotten. And so, Joseph advises, the pharaoh should 'look out for a man discreet and wise, and set him over the land of Egypt'; and this man should be in charge of taking a fifth of the harvest during the seven good years, and setting it aside for the bad years to follow. Naturally, Joseph gets the job, which shows you that this story must be a legend, since in real life such jobs go only to duly empanelled members of the Indian Administrative Service.

Dr Singh's government took office in 2004. From then till 2011, India had seven years of plenty. Growth in gross domestic product *averaged 8.1 per cent. In the middle of 2011, growth began to slow sharply. It fell to 6.5 per cent in 2011–12. And then below 6. And then below 5. As Dr Singh now knows, Joseph was being optimistic. The memory of seven years of plenty can be wiped out by far less than seven years of want. Had Dr Singh and his government stored up more in the good years—whether in terms of being a little more frugal with government spending, or in terms of doing a little more reform when they had the opportunity—then perhaps they wouldn't have spent their last few years in office watching their reputations wither on the vine, to continue with the Biblical metaphors.*

What went wrong?

You will have been given various reasons, of varying degrees of silliness. Things didn't go wrong because of corruption, or because Dr Singh was a weak man, or because his boss Sonia Gandhi believed too much in subsidies, or because of inflation. At best, these are all half true. And even if half true, they are entirely wrong—as explanations.

In this section, we will look at the real reasons.

We will see how Dr Singh, and a number of the first-generation reformers around him, thought that growth would tick along with or without more reform. They'd done the hard work already, surely? And now we could manage 8 per cent without breaking a sweat. Maintaining high growth was the least of their worries.

Dr Singh, as he stared at another crisis in the middle of 2013, or as his government was humiliatingly voted out in 2014, must have regretted that overconfidence, at least a little.

After all, had he retired at the end of the Seven Years of Plenty, in 2011, he would not have had to worry about how much his legacy shone. His story would be one hard to beat: a man who, entirely thanks to his own effort and with no help from his background, worked his way from a small village in the Punjab to Cambridge; a man who became Chief Economic Advisor at 40, governor of the central bank at 50, and finance minister before 60; and, finally, the first prime minister to be re-elected after a full term since Nehru. Instead, he found that the very middle class that had once adored him, convinced he was the only honest man in politics, now cheered as the courts pushed the cops towards finding evidence that would declare him corrupt. In 2004, it was difficult to find someone who didn't respect him and his soft-spoken integrity; in 2014, those very people would compose nasty SMS jokes questioning an apparent unwillingness to speak.

Dr Singh could survive all that, perhaps. You don't get to where he has without a certain degree of confidence.

But he's also an economist. And the numbers would have spoken to him far harsher than any words. Growth rates almost halved from the 8 per cent he thought he had given us forever. Meanwhile, inflation had doubled; prices increased 5 per cent a year in 2004, but over 10 per cent a year a decade later.

The Seven Years of Plenty ended, and they had been wasted. Sonia had found a man 'discreet and wise', and set him over the land of India. But he had not seen the years of plenty for what they were, and so he does not end his career as Joseph did. He fell short of being a prophet.

IT'S ALL ABOUT GROWTH

So what did Dr Singh's government do wrong? Were they sins of commission, as everyone assumes? Or perhaps they were sins of omission, so much harder to detect and diagnose?

One grave error, certainly, was that the government seemed to think that 'fiscal responsibility' was something that happened to other people. The NDA government that preceded Dr Singh's United Progressive Alliance was not, as *The Economist* pointed out at the time, the most restrained of spenders. In fact, it was considerably less restrained than was the UPA. (This is not the sort of thing people generally believe easily, so here are the numbers: The Centre's fiscal deficit, the amount it spent more than it received, averaged 5.5 per cent of GDP under the NDA. It has averaged only 4.7 per cent of GDP under the UPA. Both alliances hit the danger mark, 6 per cent of GDP, once; both crossed that mark once. That's in spite of the fact that the NDA had fewer years than the UPA.)

But it did at least produce a law that was supposed to restrict government spending. It was right there in the name: the Fiscal Responsibility and Budget Management Act, 2003. The UPA came into power, took one look at the terrifying phrase 'Fiscal

Responsibility', and threw the Act out the window. One of the first things that the new finance minister P. Chidambaram did in 2004 was to postpone the targets the fiscal-responsibility law had set for the government. No Act was going to constrain Chidambaram's Budget Management.

Economic theory is an art more than a science. It fails at prediction half the time—or at just under half the time, which it feels is a defensible definition of 'success'. It is a particular joy, therefore, when economic theory gets things right. Here's what economic theory says high fiscal deficits are likely to cause: high interest rates (yup), a balance of payments problem (yup), and high inflation (oh definitely).

In other words: economists tell governments not to overspend because of *precisely* the bad things that happened to the Indian economy when its government consistently overspent.

'Did you not tell me,' I hear you say, 'that we shouldn't blame Sonia Gandhi and her ruinous populism? Then what is this overspending thing?'

OK, good question. Well done, imaginary reader.

Look, for a moment, at some of these famously ruinous schemes. The National Rural Employment Guarantee Scheme, for example. It got Rs 33,000 crore in the Budget for 2013–14—just 6 per cent of the fiscal deficit for the year. That simply didn't break the bank, no matter how loudly people insist it did. You might object to it for other, perfectly valid, reasons. But you can't blame it for emptying the treasury.

Perhaps it wasn't sins of commission at all, but sins of omission. The government failed to take the tough calls to cut spending that it should have. It spent far too long trying to protect Indians from high fuel prices. It spent far too long giving Indian industry—pretending to be panicked about the financial crisis—tax breaks. Instead, if it had been spending a little less, would there have been more money with Indian companies—and thus more investment, and less of a slowdown? Perhaps.

But the real answers are tougher and more complicated. Nor, really, is it easy to blame any one person for it this time.

The fiscal deficit was higher as a proportion of GDP, *because GDP wasn't as high as it should be*—that is, because growth slowed.

The government spent more than it should partly because it found it difficult, politically, to raise fuel prices even though the price of importing petroleum skyrocketed. Why was the politics of raising fuel prices so complicated? Partly because people just weren't feeling as wealthy as they could have been, and so they weren't as willing to deal with the higher prices. And why weren't they feeling as wealthy? Because growth had slowed.

Overspending wasn't a cause of India's slowdown. It was a symptom.

'BUILD THE PLANTS, AND GROWTH WILL COME'

G rowth wasn't supposed to slow down.
Nobody really expected it to. Investors didn't: when the Manmohan Singh government was re-elected in 2009, the stock market soared. The government hadn't: it kept on assuring people the 'Indian growth story was intact' and the 'fundamentals' that had delivered 8 per cent growth still existed.

There's a distinction drawn, often, between the first term of the Singh government, from 2004 to 2009, and the second term, from 2009 to 2014. Between 2004 and 2009 the numbers were good; between 2009 and 2014, not really. And, for many of his last years in office, the numbers were pretty disastrous for a bit, though they recovered by the end.

But to pretend that, somehow, things went wrong after 2009 is a particularly odd thing to say. It wasn't as if it was a different government, with different aims, different capabilities, and different policies.

Indeed, to pretend that the troubles in UPA-II, as Dr Singh's second term as prime minister was called, weren't a product of decisions already taken, is downright, well, stupid. Even the various corruption scandals of UPA-II were, in fact, over decisions taken in UPA-I. The 'expensive' welfare schemes of UPA-II were, in fact, set into place in UPA-I. And so on and so forth.

Here's a helpful hint: the usual reason people claim that the troubles of UPA-II were not born of the wonderful days of UPA-I is because they're looking for an alibi for being overenthusiastic supporters of UPA-I, and hysterical critics of UPA-II. Indeed, such swings of opinion—of 'sentiment', to use a word of which stock-market analysts are over-fond—are actually part of what has gone wrong in the past ten years.

To return to the problem: we know that most of the trouble arose because growth had slowed. But why did growth slow? There are a million fancy reasons that people tell you, usually because they have chosen someone or something to blame. Don't listen to these people. Listen to the numbers.

The numbers tell you the one big reason that growth slowed: the private sector stopped investing. Investment, as a proportion of gross domestic product, had averaged 24 per cent between 1996, when Narasimha Rao was voted out, and 2004, when Manmohan Singh was voted in. By 2008, just before the financial crisis, investment as a percentage of GDP had gone up by ten whole percentage points, to 34 per cent. It was this ratio that dropped sharply, to 30 per cent in 2011–12.

Growth had slowed because the investment environment had become poisonous. Nobody wanted to put their money into anything—because too much cash was already locked up in unproductive investment. That 34 per cent investment rate? Turned out it was too high. The investments that had been made in that flush of excited heavy breathing before the 2008 crisis weren't really paying off.

Let me tell you a few numbers, so you know I'm right. And then

I'll tell you what really happened.

Here's one number: towards the end of UPA-I, the total value of newly announced investment projects every year was between 10 and 14 per cent of GDP. That's a big amount; new investment projects were being announced worth around as much as the total taxes the government collects. The big change? By 2013, that number had dropped to 1 per cent. Yes, it was a *tenth* of what it was earlier.

Here's another number, a number that shows you why big-value investment wasn't happening any more. In 2006, the value of stalled projects—where a part-investment had been made, but which had been held up for some reason—was negligible. By 2012, almost 3 per cent of GDP was stuck in one project or another. These were places where capital had gone to die. They couldn't go forward; and you couldn't get your capital out, either. With those examples in front of them, is it any wonder people had stopped investing?

And what really happened? Why was 2 to 3 per cent of India's GDP stuck in these projects?

For one, too many expectations of profit turned into fears of losses at the last minute, because the project owners had not expected regulators to be as strict as they were. Their optimism had been misplaced.

What else?

Pipelines full of gas that plant planners had assumed would arrive didn't get built, and even if they had, there was no gas to fill them; the electricity that was supposed to allow new factories to start working somehow went missing, too. Again, optimism had been misplaced.

Here is the truth, however unpalatable: the sudden turn to pessimism in India's slowdown was a direct product of the overexcitement that marked India's boom. Blame Manmohan Singh for feeding that over-optimism. When he first came to power, plans were hatched; India would become a 'power-surplus country' by 2015, for example. We'd have more electricity than we would know what to do with. But such plans need a vast amount of investment in power-plant capacity. And they need vast amounts of fuel.

Time was short. Coal would be provided. Gas would arrive. Build plants, and it would come.

How wrong that was.

As I said earlier, the plan to build India's infrastructure in double-quick time was Dr Singh's call in 2004. But the government didn't have the money—or, in Dr Singh's opinion, the ability—to build as much infrastructure as was needed. And thus, the government begged the private sector to do it. Instead of being reformists, Dr Singh and his cabinet turned into investment managers. They thought that speeding up India's growth was simply a matter of getting more private-sector investment going. And the private sector responded.

That, in a nutshell, is exactly why the investment rate spiked up in Dr Singh's first term. And the failure of this 'public–private partnership' model is exactly why the investment rate crashed after 2010.

The failure of these partnerships cut deep. 'PPP' had become the second-most common three-letter acronym in the UPA era. The public sector provided inputs and permissions; the private sector provided expertise and capital; and the result was supposed to build a new India.

Everyone failed to live up to the inflated expectations. Government departments, for example, still had vast numbers of regulations on the books that they could choose to enforce. So they would enforce them arbitrarily—with no thought of how they might monetize that arbitrariness, no sirree!

Or perhaps, if and when they feared they might get into trouble for colluding with the private sector, they'd enforce all of these regulations simultaneously, no matter how contradictory their demands. Naturally, delayed permissions meant delayed projects.

The private sector, meanwhile, had treated requirements and contracts as an initial negotiating position, not a strict requirement. A government stuffed with supposedly brilliant lawyers couldn't write even one decent contract. Companies would try and wriggle out of contracts they'd sign—and they'd usually succeed.

Meanwhile, the government had promised enormous amounts of natural resources—land, coal mines, natural gas, radio spectrum—to companies. They'd promised it cheap, or free. The cheaper it was, they argued, the more likely that the private sector would get infrastructure or manufacturing built. But, whenever the government assigns things cheap, or free, middlemen and the politically connected make money off the process.

The policy call that Dr Singh took in 2004 to rely on partnering with the private sector—remember, few objected at the time; it, in fact, seemed entirely reasonable—failed to deliver the infrastructure it promised. Today, some of us look at the problems of the past ten years, and imagine that we can treat the symptoms—scare or coax bureaucrats into handing out more permissions, say, or, promising more coal mines to the private sector.

Yes, each one of these problems seems temporary. But each one of these is actually deeper, a product of India's unfinished business of reform. Until we fix the causes of these three problems, and not just the symptoms, India won't pull itself out of trouble.

LOOKING THE OTHER WAY

One of the most overused phrases over the past few years when writing about India has been 'policy paralysis'. Like all overused phrases, it is, in fact, a misused phrase. When people talk about paralysis in 'policy', they are not actually talking about 'policy' at all. They aren't, usually, grumbling about the fact that major legislative reforms have long been stalled—since 1994, in fact. Nope. They're talking about *administrative* paralysis. They're talking about delays in the permissions that private sector 'partners' were promised. They're talking about arbitrariness in what permissions are needed when. And when businessmen talk about 'policy paralysis', they don't actually want a change in policy; they want to make sure the policies aren't going to be applied.

The 1991 reforms process stopped short, and abruptly. Back in the Licence Raj, the Indian government never heard a regulation that it didn't think was needed; much of this structure has survived to the present day. They are complicated. They are exhaustive. They are prohibitively expensive to follow in every detail. And the details are usually contradictory.

This means that the only way you can run a business in India is by breaking some rule or the other. I suspect that the deep thinkers of the Licence Raj assumed that all businessmen were likely up to no good anyway—so why not turn them formally into criminals?

The reason that businesses nevertheless got built the way they have is because most ingenuity went not into the quality or uniqueness of what they were selling, but into managing the government. You wanted to make sure that you wouldn't be arrested for any of the various regulations you were being forced to break. And the government, if it was 'pro-growth', basically implicitly promised not to enforce the rules that were on the books.

The problem is, of course, that governments aren't single beasts, with a single, simple thought. The Indian hydra has more heads than any other. There's a confusing multitude of departments, all with overlapping domains—the roads ministry may promise an investor she won't be put in chains if she tries building a road, but the environment ministry may haul her away in handcuffs anyway. Or the Centre may promise to sign on the dotted line of every single permission a project requires, only to discover that the state government the project is under has no intention of doing the same thing. Or, most confusing of all, one bureaucrat within a ministry may make a promise the next bureaucrat thinks is unkeepable.

The other problem with this is that, sometimes, people want to enforce the rules. Or are forced to, even if they know the rules are outdated and counterproductive. The man in charge of implementing the government's promise may be a fanatical ideological opponent of the private sector, or simply an austere upper-class bureaucrat with a patrician disdain for money-grubbing businessmen. He may turn his disdain for such compromises into an assertion of his moral authority: Look at me! I am so honest! I must follow the rules! My hands are tied!

Or the man in charge may recognize that the existing rules are ridiculous, but knows he would be in trouble if he didn't implement them. Half the time, businessmen use these rules as a weapon against their competitors. A car-accessory manufacturer will write to any number of powerful bureaucrats, detailing the rules that are being broken by another automotive-parts company's new factory. Oddly well-funded lawyers will demand of district courts that they, in the 'public interest', intervene to stop a company's rule-breaking.

Basically, implicit promises that rules won't be enforced always turn out to be worthless.

THE 'GREEN TAX'

Perhaps the most vivid examples of this come from the arbitrariness and confusion of environmental regulation in India. I mentioned earlier how Mumbai's second airport was held up because the Union environment ministry was worried that it might destroy a tiny fraction of Maharashtra's mangroves. A much smaller fraction than, for example, the fraction of people in casualty departments injured by falling off their beds. That's a classic example of how state and Union work at cross-purposes. It's worth noting, also, that of the huge number of stuck projects, only a fourth are being held up by New Delhi; the rest are waiting for various permissions from state capitals.

When looking at the environment regulators' pretty disastrous role in slowing down growth—all without noticeably benefiting the environment—we will notice the powerful mythos that can build up around anyone claiming to be an 'honest man just applying the rules'. We tend not to question someone making this claim. Odd—since this is a country in which anyone in power can always find a rule allowing him to do exactly what he wants. What appears to be rough justice is, almost always, arbitrary prejudice or political machination—if not something worse. Don't take my word for it.

Ask the environment ministers' colleagues. In the words of Montek Singh Ahluwalia, 'the method of clearances of environment and forestry is arbitrary, non-scientific and non-transparent'.

Are these rules really as complicated as all that? Well, let's look at just *some* of the hoops you need to jump through to have your project cleared by the Union ministry in charge of environment—not the local state's equivalent, or any other department. In general, according to Bibek Debroy in an *Economic Times* column, there's the Environment Protection Act of 1986, and the Environmental Impact Assessment Notification of 1994. There's also the Forest Conservation Act of 1988 and the Wildlife Protection Act of 2006. Usually, the crucial sections are those which require the data 'material to a decision on the application' to not be 'misleading'; or for all 'essential information' to be furnished.

You see what the bureaucrats writing the laws did there? They neatly put the onus on the person applying, rather than on the regulator. Something comes up after a project is cleared? Cancel the clearance! It was not the regulator's fault, for failing to make the slightest effort at the time. It was the applicant's, for not telling the government something it now claims it desperately needed to know.

And this is what happened, time and again. Businessmen, foreign or Indian, thought that they could go ahead with shortcuts— whether justified or not—only to be told, well after they'd sunk in a lot of money, that the shortcuts were being closed.

Whenever such discretion is being used, there's the possibility that it's being abused. So it was with successive environment ministers in recent years. Consider, for example, the much-feted Jairam Ramesh.[31] On the one hand, he insisted that as minister, he was just applying the rules. (I told you that assertion should cause your ears to prick up in suspicion.) On the other hand, both environmentalists and businessmen accuse him of playing complicated political games with permissions.[32] The bureaucrat-turned-environmentalist

E.A.S. Sarma, for example, said the Union environment ministry had different standards for projects depending on whether they were in states ruled by the Congress or not—a common complaint from businessmen, too.

Certainly, the latitude Ramesh was allowed by the law—and his leaders—to turn environmental positions into an opportunity for political advancement created several problems. For example, consider the question of dams. This has been an especially pointed debate for many decades; but India was forced to revisit the question in recent years because its Northeast—particularly the state of Arunachal Pradesh—was picked by Dr Singh as the location for a big push into hydroelectric power.

Now, hydroelectric power does indeed have several advantages—it's clean and it's renewable. And, as tiny, green Bhutan seems intent on showing India, hydroelectric generation doesn't have to come at the cost of ecosystems or forests. Some of the PM's plans—for giant 2000-megawatt dams in Arunachal, in particular—seemed, and seem, like pretty bad ideas. And that's probably why many people cheered when Jairam Ramesh basically subverted his boss—not for the first time, and not for the last—and tried to find reasons to postpone these dams. He held 'public hearings', something the ministry is permitted to do, in order to gauge local opinion on the dams. Such hearings are both necessary and useful.

If you look a little closer, things don't always stay simple. 'Public hearings' were held in the capital of neighbouring Assam, not in sparsely populated Arunachal Pradesh. Naturally, too few of those attending were, in fact, from Arunachal. As a method of getting *Assamese* views, it may have been acceptable, though it is possible to disagree even with that claim. As a method of getting views from Arunachal, it perhaps wasn't.

And this may have been very clever and cynical politics indeed—because Assam was going to have local elections soon.

Sons-of-the-soil parties, of which Assam has tragically more than its share, wanted to use dams in Arunachal as a way to mobilize votes—beware, O Sons of Assam, Arunachal is stealing your water!—something not unusual in Indian state politics. It looked, therefore, like Ramesh was very cleverly using the Union ministry's public hearings to show that the Congress, too, was concerned for Assam. If so, environmental regulations were being smartly deployed for political gain.

There's no point singling out Jairam Ramesh for criticism, though. If he was indeed using the tangle of regulations for his own ends, then he was far from being alone. In the Licence Raj, practically every recommendation or refusal from the Planning Commission or a ministry in New Delhi had some political subtext. Environmental regulation is being called the new Licence Raj for a reason.

The challenge is that we need to draw the right lessons from such errors—which is that we need to simplify the tangle of regulations to start off with. Better than a dozen people brazenly claiming to just implement the laws they've been given is a single person who improves the law. Neither Ramesh nor any other environment minister in the past has chosen to do that.

The cynicism with which government permissions were being handled led to some very high-profile problems. Few occurrences did more to dispirit Indian investors than what happened to a steel plant in Odisha planned and announced by a South Korean steelmaker named Posco. The factory the Koreans were planning would be worth, according to some estimates, $12 billion—by far the single largest bit of foreign investment in India. In 2007, they were granted permission by the environment ministry. In 2010, the ministry arbitrarily cancelled that permission, saying—as usual—that its decision three years earlier had been based on faulty information. In 2011, the company was allowed to continue building the factory again—after the delay had sharply increased costs for Posco—as long as various 'conditions' were met.

Well, at least things moved ahead, I hear you say? Unfortunately, even in clearing the Posco plant, the government sent out a terrible signal to investors. The act of giving the steel plant authorization to proceed happened to throw into sharp relief the government's double standards.

For, elsewhere in Odisha, an aluminium refinery was being set up by the large mining company Vedanta.

Now, like all mining companies, Vedanta is probably not among the best of corporate citizens. In fact, they cemented the impression that they were up to no good when they spent millions of rupees on a ubiquitous ad campaign that said they were 'Creating Happiness', without actually telling anyone what they did.

But whether Vedanta is a wonderful organization is not really the point here. The point is that the government, five months before it allowed Posco to go ahead with its plant-building on forest land, had denied Vedanta the same permission.

Amazingly, Jairam Ramesh denied permissions to the company even though the Supreme Court had, two years earlier, allowed Vedanta to go ahead. Were one uncharitable,[33] one could accuse Ramesh of trying to puzzle and worry those investors, like Vedanta, who had been willing to go to Odisha after an assurance from the local non-Congress chief minister.

The politics of Vedanta's refinery is worth spending a moment on. When the environment ministry cancelled its permissions to Vedanta, it explained itself by saying that some of the hills that had to be mined were sacred to the Dongria Kondh tribe that lived nearby. The tribe had already become something of a Cause. I mean, this was 2010—*Avatar* had just been nominated for every Oscar. Activists even took out a full-page ad in *Variety*, read by everyone in Hollywood, in February 2010, urging Avatar's director James

Cameron to speak out in defence of the Dongria Kondhs' rights; after all, they were just like that film's Na'vi, a traditional tribe seeing their sacred sites being ruthlessly mined. Except they weren't blue. And also they were, like, real people. The ad came out a few weeks before the Oscars, no doubt in the hope that Cameron would be moved, and mention the agitation before a billion-plus viewers in his acceptance speech. (He didn't win.)

Meanwhile, the Congress's heir apparent, Rahul Gandhi, turned up in Niyamgiri, where Vedanta planned to mine bauxite, to tell the Dongria Kondh he intended to protect their rights. It shouldn't surprise anyone that the Congress–led Union government looked very hard indeed for ways to ensure that Vedanta's project was disrupted.

Look, it seems easy to pick sides here. On the one hand are the unfortunate locals, their way of life, their pristine environment, being threatened by that most textbook of villains, the evil mining company. That the Indian state finally summoned up the vision and the heart to back the Dongria Kondh tribe instead of the giant mining conglomerate is something we should celebrate, right?

But it's not that simple. In fact, Vedanta is one of the best examples of why moral clarity is so very difficult to find in India. The way that the Union government and the Supreme Court eventually agreed to determine if Vedanta's mine should go ahead is, on several levels, disturbing. The Supreme Court told the state government to submit a report to the Union government that included 'the views' of local village councils. The Union ministry wasn't supposed to be bound by their views; by law, bauxite, the ore that becomes aluminium, is entirely the Union government's to dispose of. Unsurprisingly, the councils' views were unanimously anti-mining. Why is this unsurprising? Because the options presented to the councils were one-sided: the company wasn't allowed to send representatives with promises, while anti-mining activists were to be found under every rock.

What's worse is that the village councils did not own, or legally control, the land that was supposed to be mined. The mine was going to be a dozen kilometres away from their villages. Should local communities really be given so much of a veto? Can people prevent the mining of any part of an entire range of hills on the basis of their religious beliefs? Certainly, this went way beyond property rights, since the minerals underground were unquestionably owned by the state, and the land aboveground was not owned by any of the villagers—nor even held in common trust by the villages.

If your sympathy is with the villagers, you have to then ask yourself—do you really believe that religious belief trumps property rights, or the law? Then why, for example, should the land in Ayodhya that has poisoned relations between Hindus and Muslims in India for decades not be handed over to Hindu organizations on the basis of belief?

Yes, India has often been unfair to tribal communities. Governments and companies have not paid local residents a fair price for mining their land. But there's a big step from that to allowing anyone a religious veto over the use of large stretches of land. There's a balance here—one that needs to be thought about, and then built into transparent and fair processes and regulations.

In any case, the government's stepmotherly attitude towards Vedanta was noticed, and compared and contrasted to its attitude to Posco, another project in the same state. The fact that, to outsiders, the two projects looked so similar and yet the government had approached the two so very differently led most investors to conclude, correctly, that environmental regulation in India was just too arbitrary.

The sad fact is that at no point has anyone tried changing the laws that allow such arbitrariness. Turn back to Mumbai for a moment. Think about it: here's an island city, severely short of land. Shouldn't there be special, local rules for building in Mumbai that take the uniqueness of the city into account? Should it be regulated by a bunch of bureaucrats from Delhi? The answers seem obvious.

But if the answers to those questions are obvious, then you've got to ask a few more questions: Why have environment bureaucrats in Delhi then repeatedly made it tougher to build in Mumbai? Are they incapable of seeing the obvious until they've actually steered their ship on to the big block of ice? Or are they choosing to make things more difficult for their own reasons?

For they *have* kept things difficult, instead of properly simplifying them. For example, Mumbai is still part of a 'coastal regulation zone', which means that any building near the sea requires special permission. Given that most of Mumbai is near the sea, this is painfully ridiculous. After all, the purpose of coastal law was to protect the coastline from unchecked development. Surely it has occurred to the bureaucrats in Delhi that the coastline of Mumbai is *already* developed? But, instead, the bureaucrats have come up with ever more complicated rules as to what can and cannot be done and built hundreds of metres inland from the seashore. The Union government saw nothing odd about telling the state or city government how many floors gyms in Mumbai should have, in order to protect the coastline.[34]

If that doesn't sound crazy enough, try this: 50 new skyscrapers in Mumbai were held up by New Delhi because the bureaucrats insisted that you can't build more than seven floors unless the road you're on is more than 30 metres wide. Just to put that bit of raving insanity in context, New York's Broadway is around 25 metres wide for most of its length.

There are more such examples. But you get the point: environmental regulations have been used, and abused, by ministers and bureaucrats—for political ends, for personal ends, and sometimes just to show that they can. There hasn't been the slightest effort to change the laws; there hasn't been any effort to find regulators with a bit of independence and freedom. Instead, each new minister has entered office with the promise to be 'quicker' at implementing existing laws than his or her predecessor. But what happens if it's not the speed, but the nature of the law that's the problem?

When the Narendra Modi–led BJP government took office, one of the first promises it made was this familiar one, to 'speed up' environmental clearances. However, it did do some things that the previous government had not even tried.

Let's look at what they did.[35] They did away completely with public hearings where local residents could express their dissent over the expansion of coal mines. They did away with local consent for prospecting licences for miners; they abolished compensatory afforestation for prospectors, too, which required mining companies to plant trees elsewhere to make up for what they cut down while looking for minerals. The Supreme Court had banned heavily polluting factories from being set up within 10 kilometres of India's pitifully few wildlife sanctuaries; but through a bit of administrative jugglery of the sort it prides itself on, the government redefined the kind of factory that is classified as 'polluting', and rendered the court's decision pointless. The National Board for Wildlife, which is supposed to approve projects in and around sanctuaries, was reduced to a pale shadow; the board is supposed to have 10 non-governmental experts, but the government appointed only two. Two, that is, if you count the retired Gujarati forest official as 'non-governmental'. There are also supposed to be five non-governmental organizations on the board. In the past, such well-known NGOs such as WWF India and the Bombay Natural History Society have been among those nominated. The Modi government picked something called the Gujarat Ecological Education and Research Foundation. It is headed by Gujarat CM Anandiben Patel, which should guarantee its independence, eh?

Most telling, perhaps, is the case of Vapi, in Gujarat. This town in south Gujarat is supposed to be the most polluted place in India. The Indian Institute of Technology in Delhi measured pollution in several industrial parks across the country—and Vapi topped, easily. In response, the environment ministry announced a moratorium on any new factories there till the local administration came up with a clean-up plan. Sounds reasonable. A plan was announced, the moratorium was lifted—and then the plan was completely ignored. Two and a half years later, the environment ministry got tired of waiting and reimposed the moratorium.

But here's what's interesting: when the government changed, the moratorium was lifted. Vapi isn't, as far as anyone knows, any cleaner or less polluted. But, it seems, moratoriums can be lifted and reimposed purely at the will of politicians and bureaucrats in New Delhi. And nobody in New Delhi is interested in changing that state of affairs, naturally.

Yes, you need manufacturing. For that, you need less intrusive environmental regulation. But you don't get that through a regime that's arbitrary—whether or not the arbitrariness is supposed to help or hinder you. As the experience of the past ten years makes clear, the discretion that helps a business today might well harm it tomorrow. In fact, it will.

In the next section, we'll look at how high the stakes are when it comes to getting green laws right.

But what's worth remembering is that ending 'policy paralysis' isn't as simple as being more active. The problematic part of 'policy paralysis' isn't the paralysis—it's the policy. It's the policies that needed changing. The reason India came to a screeching stop in the years following 2010 was that the promises of the previous decade, of a more business-friendly environment that would help investment all round, couldn't be kept without a change in the laws, and without overhauling policy. And nobody then was interested in doing that.

Nobody is interested now, either.

PUT IT THERE, PRIVATE PARTNER

India's government failed to live up to its implicit promises to business—its promises that troublesome regulations would be, if not changed, then ignored. But here's a question: Why did business believe those promises?

The answer is simple. From 2003 or so onwards, Indian companies—and several foreign ones—gave in to a combination of stupidity, greed, and sneakiness.

a) Stupidity: because they thought good times would last forever, and bet everything on it.
b) Greed: because, if a desperate government was handing out concessions in return for promises, the companies decided they should take the concessions first and see if they could fulfil the promises later.
c) Sneakiness: because, in some cases, they took the concessions knowing full well that they would bully, bribe or blackmail their way out of the promises later.

Here's the basic business plan for India's fastest-growing companies this century:

They would sign up to build and operate, say, an airport; and they would agree to pay the government a certain amount for the privilege. But that agreement would be based on an unsupportable and unsustainable optimism. Perhaps the company would imagine that the number of passengers would grow 10 per cent a year, or something, and then they'd calculate the vast profits they'd make on that basis, and promise the government a share of it.

Now, perhaps the company's willingness to sign an agreement it couldn't keep was just stupidity, option (a). Or perhaps it was (b), greed—the government was handing out land with the airport, and the company knew exactly how valuable the land was, and wanted it, must have it, my precioussss. Or perhaps it was (c), sneakiness—they never intended to keep it. Once all the other contenders have gone away, and both they and the state have invested something in the project, they then tell their 'partner' in government: 'Sorry. Give us more money/ more land/ more time/ more rights. Without that, this project is no longer profitable, and we will walk out.'

It is impossible to list out how often this happened. It plagued almost every single public–private partnership that the central or the state governments entered into.

You see what happens, if every single auction the government holds, or contract it signs, with private companies can be renegotiated later? People start looking at the terms the government announces as fluid—as something they can change, under the right circumstances. If you're a company, you no longer think: 'Can I build this airport, or bridge, or road cheaper and better than my competitors?' No, you think: 'Can I influence the government into changing the rules and giving me more profit a few years from now, more than my competitors can?'

When you hear people say that the United Progressive Alliance had replaced the Licence Raj with a Contractor Raj, this is what they mean.

It happened over and over again. These are just three occasions:

Delhi Airport, run by the Andhra Pradesh–based construction firm GMR, levied a service fee on passengers that wasn't in the bid conditions. The amount they gained: Rs 3500 crore. The stated reason: the government changed stuff too, OK, and kept making us pay more, and our lawyers say we can charge you for it.

The Central Electricity Regulatory Commission allowed power plants owned by Adani and Tata Power to increase the price at which they sold electricity to the states over the amount they had promised in their bid. The amount they would gain: Tata, Rs 25,000 crore; Adani, Rs 18,500 crore. The claimed reason: the companies hadn't considered, when bidding for long-term contracts, the possibility that the price of fuel might increase, and should they be punished for that little error, was that really their fault, in a cosmic sense, and what is this notion of 'fault' anyway, huh?

Anil Ambani won a bid for a power plant that had a 'captive' coal mine, meant to provide that plant, and only that plant, with fuel. Mr Ambani's company then asked to use the free coal from that mine in another power plant they owned. They were given permission to do so by the Union cabinet—although they won the other plant without free coal attached. The amount they might gain: Rs 29,000 crore. The stated reason: They wanted the coal. They really wanted it.

Notice a pattern? Each time, the government gives in to a private company's demand. Each time, the private company that won a contract to partner the government wanted to change the terms on which it won the contract the moment there were no competitors around.

Why did the government give in each time? Perhaps, on some occasions, the company had a point, and it was the government that had failed to live up to its side of the bargain. Perhaps, on some occasions, the company was so 'well connected' in the government that it got what it wanted. Perhaps, on some occasions, the government had no option because the company could effectively blackmail it into agreeing. (In my opinion, each of the above three examples represents one of those three general cases.)

SOMEONE TO RELY ON

Perhaps the most effective example of government–corporate relations breaking down is in the case of natural gas and Mukesh Ambani's Reliance.

First, a word about Reliance. You may have noticed the name crop up here and there in this book, along with the name of this 'Mukesh Ambani' person. Trust me, neither name crops up in this book half as much as they do on a normal day discussing policy in New Delhi.

There is a tendency to imagine that Mukesh Ambani, India's richest man, essentially owns everyone in government. This is, frankly, a little ridiculous. But he does have an oversized hold on decision-making even so. The reason is very simple: Reliance gets things done.

Delhi's politicians talk about Reliance like Pakistani politicians talk about the Pakistani army. They don't like it; they are a little scared of it; but, dammit, they say, it is the only efficient organization in the country, and if you want something done you have to go through it.

That comes into play in this natural gas problem. You see, there's natural gas under the Bay of Bengal. This natural gas belongs to us, not to Mukesh Ambani. This point was argued and won by Mukesh Ambani, oddly enough. He was arguing this point to ensure that the government got to set the price at which Mukesh's Reliance sold natural gas from these fields. In one of those coincidences that make life in India so worth living, one of the primary customers for the gas being sold by Mukesh's Reliance was the Reliance owned by his estranged brother, Anil. And, some years earlier, Mukesh and Anil had promised their mother—again, I am not making this up, I wish I had this much imagination—that they would play nicely, acceding to a 'non-compete' agreement that included a particular price for gas. But now, Mukesh's lawyers basically argued that the agreement didn't apply—because the gas wasn't his, and so it was the government that got to price the gas and not Mukesh himself.[36]

Anyway, he won that case. And the government coincidentally raised the price of gas, which coincidentally made things tougher for Anil Ambani. Our recent history abounds with sweet little stories with a happy ending all round.

Everyone got really excited about this gas thing. Reliance claimed the gas fields were vast; entrepreneurs across south India set up factories—fertilizers, chemicals, power—that were predicated on cheap and easy natural gas.

And then the gas didn't come. Reliance said, a single tear trickling down its cheek, that the fields weren't actually as productive as expected. The government claimed the gas was right there, but Reliance was refusing to pump it out because they were, essentially, bullying everyone into raising the price further.

Meanwhile, all the people who had been led to expect cheap gas were losing money. Vast areas of south India that were lit by gas-powered electricity went dark for 14 hours a day. Eventually, the government gave in. Mukesh would get a higher price. Shortly thereafter, Reliance announced that, through sheer coincidence, parts of the gas field were, in fact, more productive than they had expected.

None of this need have happened—not the long dispute, not the errors of investment, not the power cuts in the south—if the government had written a sensible contract when it first handed out the natural gas concessions back in the early 2000s.

My point is this: it is foolish to go looking for out-and-out villains in this story. Mukesh Ambani was doing what was best for his company and his shareholders throughout. The government tried to get the gas out of the ground, and turned to the only company it could rely on to do that. Other entrepreneurs just made bets that the gas would get there. But put everything together, and it led to disaster.

The Indian state's desperation for private-sector money and expertise and efficiency led it to be incredibly weak. Any businessman could twist it around his finger. T.N. Ninan likes to say that India is a strong state when it comes to bullying the poor, but a weak state when it comes to controlling the rich.

BARGAIN BASEMENT

You know the amazing thing about the natural-gas problem? Here the government was trying to raise the price of a natural resource. The reason this is amazing is because, normally, India never does this. We have, historically, kept these things as cheap as possible.

That was the third problem that Manmohan Singh caused with his big private-sector bet in 2004. Remember his logic: we need the private sector to build our infrastructure. In order for it to be profitable enough for them to choose to build it, and then cheap enough for everyone to use, we have to keep their costs down. We don't have enough money; but what we do have in abundance is control over natural resources. We have rights to coal, and to radio spectrum, and to natural gas, and to so many other things; giving them, cheap, to the private sector will solve all our problems, right?

It's important to note that this had already been tried. Remember, in 2004, the telecom sector had begun to boom; and the great policy lesson from it was the difference between the 'National Telecom Policy' of 1994 and the 'New Telecom Policy' of 1999. What Vajpayee's government had done, in 1999, was to tweak one essential aspect of the 1994 policy: private companies trying to enter the telecom business would no longer have to pay up front for the radio spectrum they'd be using. No more auctions of valuable spectrum, either. A clever revenue-sharing method would be tried instead; this, essentially, made the natural resource cheaper for the company. This had clearly worked: cellphone call rates crashed, and the sector blossomed. Dr Singh's government, in 2004, presided over a massive expansion of Vajpayee's logic to a dozen other sectors.

There was, largely, silence at the time. After all, had it not worked with telecom? In fact, was this not the standard approach in India? Look at coal; India had always handed out its coalfields to those who desired them. And, yes, the consequence would be private profit.

Throughout its modern history, throughout its struggle to industrialize, India's government has used natural resources as its primary instrument.

I grew up in Jamshedpur, the home of Tata Steel, generally considered one of India's finest and most upright companies. We were brought up, there, on a diet of improving moral stories about the company's history—how Jamshedji, the Tata patriarch, had taken the decision, for patriotic reasons, to set up India's first steel plant; how he had gone to the United States rather than Britain for help, because the Horrible Imperialists didn't want to help India. This legend wasn't limited to the Tatas, or to Jamshedpur; even Doordarshan, our only TV channel in those dark days, used to show a little film about Tata's brave struggle that was meant to inspire us.

What nobody ever bothers to tell you is where they get their iron ore and their coal from. Yes, that's right: the government gave it to them. (Odd behaviour for such horrible imperialists, eh?)

Today, more than a century after the Jamshedpur plant opened, Tata Steel trumpets its cost advantage. Proudly, its website says it is one of the lowest-cost producers of steel in the world. But speak to any of its competitors, and they will point out why: Tata Steel has exclusive access to some of the finest iron ore and coking coal mines in the world—practically free.

This is probably why nobody even noticed when the government decided that it would triple or quadruple the rate at which it handed out coal mines to the private sector. If anything, most entrepreneurs looked upon it as only fair—as their right, in fact.

It is impossible to imagine that Dr Singh and his government weren't aware, when taking the decision, that some of the coal-mine allocations would be handed out to people with political and bureaucratic connections. Or, to be blunt about it, to people who'd bribe their way in. In fact, we know he was—he said, in 2004, that auctions might be the fairest way to distribute coal mines. When I get around to writing my epic 14-volume *Handbook of Irony in India from Earliest Times*, one entire volume will be devoted to 'Things Manmohan Singh said in 2004'.

An explanation that is offered by his defenders—which has the merit of fitting in with his government's general attitude in 2004—was that he was in such a hurry to build a power-surplus India that he didn't want to pause the mine-assignment programme while he installed one that was a little more tamper-proof.

Similar decisions were made in other sectors—most notoriously in telecom. There, it was decided to expand the number of companies in the business—a good idea—but without auctions. Again, the prime minister sort of objected; but the minister in charge, A. Raja, had solid reasons to claim policy precedent. He could just have looked at the not-too-savoury spectrum-assignment process under the previous government and thought, like so many entrepreneurs, 'Why not me?'

And Dr Singh didn't have the political backing to take him down; it might have cost him his government. This is where many people part company with him—they think this is one of the many occasions when Manmohan Singh should have handed in his resignation. In general, Dr Singh seems to have been expected to quit more often even than the average Microsoft programme.

So, to recap: India was stuck. In 2004, like now, it needed infrastructure and an industrial base. The big decision was: we will partner with the private sector to speed things up; we will give them easy money, and free land, and cheap minerals, and so on, and they will repay us with gratitude and honesty.

We didn't get the infrastructure we wanted. What we did get is corruption—because the government system just could not deal with this vast expansion of the state's ambitions. The government didn't have the capacity to build things itself, sure—but it also didn't have the capacity to make sure the private sector built it, on time, and without making illicit profits.

When it became clear the government didn't have the capacity to control its private-sector partners, something unforeseen happened: everyone else started trying to do the government's job.

THE ROT IN INDIA'S HEART

Talk to anyone you know in India, and you'd be told, likely, that corruption is a giant problem. Huge. Vast. Gigantic. Sufficient to bring down the country. To torpedo the economy. Were we not so corrupt, we would be like China—rich and totally completely absolutely corruption-free. Actually, even better, we would be like Singapore. No, Switzerland!

But we are unique in the scale of our corruption. We are more corrupt today than we have ever been. The middle class, honest and upright people that they are, have had enough; they know that corruption is holding us back. And corruption is because we don't have enough upright people at the top; we have all these damned politicians, with their 'democracy'.

Of all the many ridiculous things that we have told ourselves to explain our failures as a country, this is among the most ridiculous. It is also among the wrongest, and the most pernicious. Not to mention the most annoying.

As it happens, it isn't corruption itself that is holding us back. No. It is the fear of corruption. A debilitating, paralysing fear. It is, essentially, a shared national psychosis, a 'moral panic', to use a phrase that the sociologist Stanley Cohen came up with. A moral panic, said Cohen, was a high-pitched bout of anxiety that shared values were in danger—put in danger by 'a condition, episode, person or group of persons', who 'become defined as a threat to societal values and interests'. In effect, we don't talk clearly and openly about the true issue at the heart of the problem—discussing it becomes taboo because then *you* support immorality, and *you* are accused of being part of the problem. At a time of moral panic, anyone attempting to put corruption or the dangers of having venal politicians in perspective—even anyone warning of the consequences of overreaction —is not considered to be helping, but seen instead as being part of the problem. Apparently.

But here's the real difficulty: not everything that looks like corruption is corruption. And telling one from the other is part of what has slowed India down. But we can't sift out real corruption effectively if we're in the throes of a moral panic.

So do we plough ahead, ignoring corruption? Or do we shut growth down, while we remove every speck of corruption from the system? Are we even capable of imagining something between those two extremes?

Yes, India is rotting away, and it is nowhere more evident than when it talks of corruption. But it is not the corruption itself that's the rot. It is what's revealed by the moral panic surrounding corruption. The rot at the heart of India is the corrosion caused by a breakdown in trust; it is the acceptance of suspicion, of conspiracy theorizing; it is, even, the idea that injustice in the pursuit of the anti-corruption crusade is no vice. It is this collapse that bears considerable responsibility for India's growth slowdown—and, more, it has caused damage to India's political and governance institutions unmatched since the Emergency.

Think about it this way. Step one: We assign mines to companies, to help them grow and produce, in the fond hope that they will use it responsibly, and benefit industry and citizens alike. Step two:

We play politics and pass-the-file with environmental regulations, keeping minerals unmined even as the factories depending on them get built. Step three: We investigate the assignments of mines. Step four: We investigate even the non-assignments. Step five: We interrogate, and spread rumours about, the retired bureaucrats who signed off on the accusation, even when we think they're actually pretty honest. Seriously, this doesn't sound mad to you?

Partly, this has happened because nobody thinks hard enough about corruption in the first place. About what it is, and whether India has a uniquely virulent case of it. Things have changed since the Lalu era in Bihar. Back then, in the famed 'fodder scam' that set his reputation in stone, it was just a blatant abuse of power, a falsification of government records. That's just illegal, and still is. Like bribery, it's relatively easy to identify and isolate. But that's not the kind of 'corruption' that India's been enduring in the past decade or so.

Consider the landmark case of 'corruption', the euphoniously named Coalgate. This is born of that decision, taken by Dr Singh in 2004, to ignore the possibility he himself had raised of auctioning coal mines.

Coalgate was brought to everyone's notice by a report from India's national auditor, the Comptroller and Auditor General—then run by Vinod Rai, who represents India in Long-Distance Headline-Hunting at the Olympics. I don't want to be mean to the CAG. It has an important job to do, and it often does it well. But it too often seems to see its target audience as the news desk of national newspapers, and not the people it was supposed to report to in Parliament's committees. Its coal report could have been used to hold crony capitalists to account; but, instead, it focused on trying to put ridiculous and largely economically illiterate figures to 'losses'—an effort without precedent in performance audits anywhere.

Yes, yes, I'm getting to why this rant is relevant. The CAG chose to indict Manmohan Singh by starting its study of coal mine allocations from 2004, the year he took over. Why? Because that is when the government first mused that coal block auctions might be a good idea. So Dr Singh gets indicted—for having the right idea in the first place. Talk about perverse incentives. He should have just kept quiet—not something that's often said about Manmohan Singh.

Anyway, Dr Singh's decision on coal mine allocations basically continued the Indian state's comforting and historic habit of giving the mines to people who turned up and smiled nicely at a bureaucrat. (Just smiled, yes sirree. Nothing else.)

We now imagine that the idea itself, that coal mines be handed out so arbitrarily, is wrong. The Supreme Court cancelled telecom licences that were handed out like that, saying they were unfair. They have now cancelled the coal mines, too—if for somewhat different reasons that we'll explore later.

Well, perhaps mines shouldn't be handed out. Certainly, I'm more comfortable with people paying a market-determined price than in leaving these choices to a bureaucrat.

But consider also the consequences of cancelling those licences: people who bought them, in good faith—the Norwegian company Telenor, for example—also lost all their money. The sector was thrown into a crisis from which it took years to recover. If those licences are illegal, then why not also ask Tata Steel to return the mines they were given a hundred years ago? With a fine linked to how much profit they've made at the expense of the Indian exchequer?

The truth is that artificially cheap 'factors of production'—land, loans, spectrum, coal, iron ore, water, power—are a crucial ingredient of government policy in most countries. They may be a bad idea but they're accepted, too.

Look at the US. Do they have radio spectrum giveaways? Yup. Washington recently gifted radio spectrum worth tens of billions of dollars to various big companies—hidden in the fine print of a law Barack Obama introduced in 2012 that supposedly just extended tax cuts for the middle class. Are coal mines kept suspiciously cheap? Sure. The US Bureau of Land Management supposedly hands out mining leases to the huge coal-rich tracts it's responsible for, through auctions. Except that 85 per cent of the auctions in the past two decades have had only one bidder. And that one bidder is, let's say, rarely a stranger to the politicians in DC or the bureaucrats at the Bureau of Land Management. How cheap does the coal get? A 'winner' can bid just over 10 per cent of the price of coal locally—less than 1 per cent of the price of coal in China—and win. The US Treasury has given up $28 billion in revenue from coal leases in the past two decades.

Why does even the US do this? Because the idea is that, somehow, this coal feeds back into the industrial process—it sustains companies that provide jobs, or it makes the end product cheaper. Why isn't there a lot of noise in their politics when it happens? Well, that's a tougher question—one I'll get to answering in a bit.

Definitely, there's a lot of evidence that cheap radio spectrum is central to getting a vibrant telecom business going. Without really cheap 2G spectrum—which created the opportunity for the '2G scam'—you wouldn't have had really cheap calling rates. People made money off these policies, and they shouldn't have. But people making money off these policies wasn't the main reason they existed. We may choose to change them, but not out of an unreasonable fear that people are getting rich. That would paralyse us.

Raghuram Rajan pointed out, in his book *Fault Lines*, that an economy can be judged by who its billionaires are. If the billionaires are in information technology, for example, or retail, or consumer goods—sectors relatively free of government interference, and where state support is not what can make the difference between success and failure—then the economy is healthy and competitive. If the billionaires are in the resource-extraction industries—in mining or in petroleum, say—or in other such sectors where government permission and government regulation are central to making money, then the economy is in trouble. India is very firmly the latter. The United States, in spite of the examples I just provided of how it has embedded crony capitalism into its system without the slightest whine from its population, is the former—which explains, to an extent, the complaisance of its people. China, on the other hand, is doing as badly as India on the Rajan measure. Worse, in fact, since the top guys seem to be involved themselves—according to various news reports, President Xi Jinping's relatives have made vast sums of money in real estate, telecom and mining; and the family of Wen Jiabao, the reformist who left office recently, has made $2.1 billion through connections to powerful companies.

Unearned benefits grow in the dark. They are a product of poor regulation, a resource–based economy, and insufficient governance. They are a product of discretion, and of unaccountability. They are not a product of a unique moral failure. Nor are they a product of an inability to speak English, or sound plausible on TV.

India's laws and regulations allow for vast amounts of cronyism. Indeed, in some cases they actively demand cronyism. Change them. It's the only way out—either that, or fill your entire government and bureaucracy with stainless saints. And where, precisely, will you find them?

ALL THE LITTLE LEE KUAN YEWS

China and India—like several other Asian countries—are indeed consumed with anger about corruption. But not everything that we believe is corruption is indeed corruption.

Even so, the judgements of the past years have been clear and unyielding: that the Indian economy and its government operate without any morality, and need correction and control. People Like Us need to swoop in and save it.

This has led to the frankly terrifying increase in power in India of the strange many-headed beast that calls itself Civil Society. We may not know all its heads, all the NGOs and activists and so on that think they are the only check on the power of a constitutionally elected government. Yes, we can never know all the heads of this Hydra, for two more sprout whenever you look, but we can be reasonably certain all the heads speak English nicely.

That bit is important. It helps to understand that the Hydra is trusted where politicians aren't because the Hydra can explain things in nice, uncomplicated English.

Indeed, even bureaucrats and policemen are trusted more than politicians at this odd stage in our history, mainly because the police and the civil services are full of nice English-speaking men. Ah, we murmur to ourselves, if only these nice smart unelected men weren't forced to answer to those dreadful vote-bank-seeking vernacular-speaking elected men, they would fix things before you could say 'class bias'. Thus we rejoice every time an elected government is put on the backfoot by an unelected bureaucrat, some recently anonymous exam-passing form-filling procedure-fetishizing time-server. We rejoice—for We, the People, were granted a victory against those elected by, well, Other People.

Thus the saviour of our democracy—well, of the worthy salaried middle class of our democracy—is that democratic hero famed in song and story: the unelected state functionary. The bureaucrat, or the judge, or the copper, or the army chief—anyone, really, as long as you wouldn't mind your daughter marrying his son.

We believe that these bureaucrats will save us, if they are just given the power to do so. Perhaps they need to be 'empowered', as Narendra Modi told his seniormost secretaries; perhaps they need to be made 'independent', as the Supreme Court tells the Central Bureau of Investigation.

But wait—this is confusing. For the 'independent' CBI seems a whole lot like an 'unaccountable' CBI. Perhaps we should stop worrying about that, though. No way could the CBI be home to some corrupt megalomaniac. Not like J. Edgar Hoover and the FBI; Old J. Edgar would never have passed the UPSC exam. Or the interview—for in that, estimable moral character is unerringly sussed out, and it is ensured that only good, honest, humble boys get through.

Worst of all, perhaps, an 'independent' CBI isn't exactly working to 'empower' other bureaucrats. In fact, free of any restraints, the CBI is happily accusing retired bureaucrats of being corrupt, and producing as 'evidence' a bunch of perfectly straightforward and defensible decisions they've taken. And, unsurprisingly, those bureaucrats' currently serving successors are scared sign-less.

Literally—they're refusing to sign anything. 'What, pass this file? Me? And get hauled up twelve years later for corruption, grand larceny, treason, and bad handwriting? Not on your life.'

They aren't just confusing and contradictory concepts. 'Independence' and 'empowerment' for bureaucrats aren't any sort of cure-alls—though that's how we've been acting. Just one more independent and empowered post—one more vigilance commissioner, one more Lokpal, a more intrusive judiciary, a more aggressive CBI—just a little more power for these nice educated men, we think, and that will make all the difference. Surely we'd stop being run off the rails, then, by corruption and mismanagement! More 'independent' positions, positions put beyond being accountable to electoral politics, and democracy will be strengthened. The petty Musharrafs and miniature Lee Kuan Yews and tinpot Castros that populate the Indian middle class[37] all cheer anything that makes politicians less powerful, and bureaucrats more. Naturally—which English-speaking Indian would want to be a politician? Not one. But every single English-speaking Indian is a bureaucrat in his heart.

PART IV

THE CURSE OF 'JUGAAD'

So far, we've talked about all the various ingredients of an economy: land, labour, capital, natural resources. But there's one more thing you have to put into the production process: enterprise. Entrepreneurship.

Now, supposedly, India is a nation of entrepreneurs. This is one of those things that is a core assumption at Davos. Financial Times *op-eds have been written about this. Market-promoting economists have spoken piously about this. Tom Friedman has said so. It must be true.*

It is not true.

You can see how the impression got about: because we are, certainly, all looking to take shortcuts and make a lot of money. If you don't look closely enough, then you'd assume this was classic entrepreneurial behaviour. But it isn't. Entrepreneurs create value and take a slice of it for their own. They don't exploit existing processes to make a quick buck. You know who does that? Yup, your local water-tank inspector. Not entrepreneurs; rent-seekers.

This section is about how and why private companies, in a nation of bureaucrats, have failed to be innovative, and have failed to drive growth.

We will look at how the government has sought to protect and preserve the least innovative and most parasitical parts of the private sector, at the expense of those that could make real profits and employ struggling people.

We will look at hubris, and folly, and overconfidence, and bad judgement. We will look at how our largest private companies connived in the betrayal of the trust we put in them. And we will realize why that means reform and recovery will be twice as hard.

We will look at what it means to be a crony capitalist, and why it seems having absolutely terrible taste helps.

We will look at the gluttony and greed of the biggest names in Indian business, and we will realize that India needs a healthier path to growth.

WHAT'S WORSE THAN THE GOVERNMENT?

We are a deeply sarkari nation.

We are incredibly varied, right? Many people will insist that the only thing that really unites us is the cricket team. (Other people say 'Bollywood and the cricket team'; these people are not from south India.)

But perhaps that isn't true. Perhaps there is indeed a cultural oneness to India, something that instinctively unites all Indians, no matter their creed or ethnicity. I suspect it is this: we are all petty clerks at heart. Where other countries have a shared ethnicity or national language or a common fondness for apple schnapps, we have instead adopted and internalized the instincts and priorities and processes of our colonial-era bureaucracy. It's seeped into our souls, every one of us. Cut us, and we bleed in triplicate.

This doesn't mean that we respect processes, mind you: it means we seek them out in order to manipulate them. It doesn't mean we have a respect for queues, as another example; it means we seek the tiny extra status that comes from *cutting* queues. It doesn't mean that we seek to solve problems from a national perspective or whatever the Indian Administrative Service imagines its mission is; it means that we seek to create barriers between other people and their goals, and to sit atop these barriers while lesser people beg us to remove them.

This is fine if you are actually a bureaucrat. Well, it isn't fine, really, but at least it's expected. No country in the world prides itself on the efficiency and friendliness of its bureaucrats. It's like complaining your pit bull isn't excessively friendly to strangers—that wasn't what it was bred for, man, get a cocker spaniel.

What is extraordinary about India, however, is that we are bureaucrats no matter what profession we're in. Journalists, let me tell you, are bureaucrats. Which explains why most Indian newspapers could be renamed *What the Bureaucracy Leaked Today*. And also why our papers' prose style is usually indistinguishable from that of the average income-tax form.

Yes, journalists are bureaucrats. Shopkeepers are bureaucrats. Doctors are bureaucrats. Worst of all, businessmen are bureaucrats.

Dealing with the average Indian company is not really that different from dealing with the government. In fact, it might be easier to get a tax refund than to get your mobile phone service provider to return your deposit. For a country which claims to have 'service–led growth', we do provide exceptionally horrific service.

This means that the Indian consumer is a depressed, irritable and oppressed sort. But that's not all; the effects go deeper.

An inept private sector has been a willing co-conspirator with a controlling government; together, they have sent India careering into a low-cost, low-quality, low-innovation equilibrium that will be hard to escape.

DEMOTING PROMOTERS

Occasionally, I get invited to dinners. Recently, I was at a dinner organized by a 'Young Entrepreneurs Association', part of a major Indian chamber of commerce. The conversation puzzled me. You see, I had been to such dinners elsewhere in the world—and they hadn't been dinners so much as frantic networking opportunities. I remember going to one, at a business school in the US, with a friend. He paused before we entered, to make sure that his business card case was optimally placed in his pocket for a smooth draw—like Billy the Kid, except meaner and more competitive. Elsewhere in the world, people make deals, talk shop. But, at this dinner, nobody was doing any of that. Instead, they talked of vacations, and of home design. I spent the rest of the evening taking a poll of the guests; and it turned out every single one of them was from a 'business family'. They weren't entrepreneurs the way the world thinks of them; they were kids whose parents had given them some money to play with.[38]

Of course, there are exceptions to this generalization. There are Indian companies and Indian owners and Indian managers who are particularly smart, and public-spirited; who have developed new products and new processes that make people's lives easier. But neither our policies nor our society encourages such people and such organizations.

You know, we hear a lot about how India's companies are its strength, especially as compared to China's. We have a vibrant private sector; managerial expertise, open processes, corporate governance, and so on.

But pause for a moment and compare this with the facts. And not just our shared experience as consumers. Let's think of this as savers and investors. Is any of us likely to be excited at the prospect of investing in an Indian company? Not unless we know that it, like perhaps Reliance, has the inside track to great wealth. Or if it is a government-mandated monopoly, like Coal India. In fact, Indians have largely migrated away from owning shares in companies to holding their wealth in other ways. This isn't just because the returns are anaemic. This is because we don't trust the owners of Indian companies. With good reason: many of them exploit minority shareholders ruthlessly, deceive investors about their balance sheets, and squirrel money away for their own purposes. This is why we call most company owners 'promoters'. They can't be called owners, because frequently they, on paper, don't own their companies. The source of their control, on paper, is mystifying. On some occasions, they aren't even the largest shareholders. But they own their companies, and everyone knows they do. And so we are forced to call them 'promoters'.

Here's one of my favourite recent stories about how brazenly company owners will take away your money if you're foolish enough to give it to them. There's a company that rejoices in the noble name of 'JSW Steel'; it's part of the JSW group, owned by a man named Sajjan Jindal. The JSW stands for Jindal South West; the geographical qualification is necessary, presumably because Sajjan Jindal is one of a large number of brothers, all of whom inherited various resource-linked businesses from their father.[39]

(Remember that point I was making about how everyone asks: If Tata Steel can get nice mines, why can't I? Sajjan Jindal, shortly after being formally charged by the police in the payment of a bribe to Karnataka's chief minister for a mine, told his investors in an aggrieved tone: 'Even after a presence of more than two decades in Karnataka, investing more than Rs 35,000 crore and creating thousands of jobs, JSW Steel remains the only major Indian steel company with no captive mines.' This is how a resource economy works: competitive begging.)

The name 'JSW', you will note, is not particularly imaginative. Nor is it the kind of thing you would imagine is incredible intellectual property. Yet, in 2014, JSW Steel told shareholders that it would pay Rs 125 crore a year to a firm entirely owned by Sajjan Jindal's wife, Sangita. In return, Sangita Jindal would graciously permit her husband to use the 'JSW' acronym, which JSW Steel insists her company, JSW Investments, owns.

Here's the facepalm moment: JSW's sheep-like shareholders meekly agreed.

Perhaps I shouldn't blame them excessively. After all, at least Sajjan Jindal asked nicely. Half the time, shareholders don't even know what their companies are up to. Nor should I single out family-owned companies, really—it's a deeper problem. Consider Maruti, the bluest of blue-chip companies. Profitable, well run, a market leader, transparent, professionally owned and managed, right? An ideal place to invest your hard-earned mite, you'd imagine, comfortably telling yourself that its long-term leadership and those nice Japanese people from Suzuki that own it aren't going to steal off with your cash in the middle of the night.

Well, there are ways and ways of getting your hands on the small shareholder's cash. Consider Suzuki's way: it takes a large amount of money out of Maruti Suzuki and sends it to itself in Japan—but not as a dividend, which all the minority shareholders would have to examine and agree with, but as 'royalty' for using the Suzuki name. You think anyone still buys a Maruti car because of the Suzuki name? Maybe one or two people—enough to justify Rs 2454 crore going off to Japan in 2012–13? Thought not. Just to rub it in, do note that the amount that Suzuki 'earned' from the rights to its storied name in India was more than the conglomerate's entire profits for that year in Japan, Rs 2402 crore. For that matter, the royalty was also higher than Maruti's own profits, of Rs 2392 crore. One begins to suspect that the company is overpaying.

But, you say, how's this allowed in the first place? Well, shareholders don't really have a say in it, because it's a 'commercial arrangement', and the management can settle it with the guys from Suzuki. But, of course, Suzuki is also the major owner, and is likely putting the management in place. You think management is negotiating hard?

No, no, wait, you say. Somebody must be looking out for the other shareholders. Aren't there independent directors on the company's board who are supposed to do that?

Sure they are. And I'm sure they're extremely independent. But they're also extremely absent. More than half of Maruti's directors have an attendance record of less than 75 per cent—though you can attend a board meeting through a conference call, even.

Is it any wonder that Indians prefer to buy large amounts of gold and stuff it into Godrej Storwels? But, unless we start investing in companies, they won't have access to the sort of funds they need to kick-start innovation.

FLIES IN THE PILLS

So far, Indian companies have gotten away with being mean to Indian investors because other people have been willing to invest in them. They were coasting on years and years of good press—all those op-eds and speeches and analyst reports about how Indian companies were strong and Indians were enterprising and all that. It meant that, even if nobody in Patna was buying your stock, Peoria Inc. might.

But that might change, and soon. You see, even starry-eyed foreigners are waking up to the fact that, in India, owners can conceal anything they like about their companies from the people who have a right to know—whether the regulators, or their minority shareholders—or, for that matter, people they want to sell their company to.

Consider another story of villainy and skulduggery—and in this one the Japanese are the victims, not the perpetrators.

Once there was a company called Ranbaxy Labs. It had a wonderful reputation: it was profitable, it was pioneering. In fact, its reputation could even be called saintly: after all, did it not manufacture generic drugs, all manner of life-saving medicines? Was it not curing AIDS in Africa? Are not such companies deserving of admiration, capable of making a profit and yet selling affordable medicines? Ranbaxy was the backbone of a pharmaceutical sector of which we in India were told to be proud—and Indians don't need to be told twice to be proud of something.

Well, one sad and tragic day, the people who built Ranbaxy decided to sell it to a Japanese company called Daiichi Sankyo. The good people of Daiichi Sankyo had done their due diligence: they had inspected the books, talked to managers, toured the plants, and come to the conclusion that, yes, they were worthy of buying the gem that was Ranbaxy, the first foreign company to sell generic medicines in the US. When Ranbaxy was sold, there was much weeping and gnashing of teeth in India; a precious jewel had been given away for something as crass as money. India mourned.

Daiichi Sankyo paid $4.6 billion for two-thirds of Ranbaxy in 2008. They must have thought they'd got an exceptionally good deal—the very last act of selfless altruism performed by Ranbaxy's promoters. Six years later, the Japanese were glad to sell what remained of Ranbaxy to one of its competitors, for $3.2 billion. The company had lost half its value in six years.

It turned out they'd been sold a placebo.

Here's a little bit of what was actually going on in Ranbaxy, the pride of Indian pharma. Just a taste.

In one plant's supposedly sanitized room where medicines were made, there were flies 'too numerous to count'.[40] Elsewhere, the refrigerators that were supposed to keep samples at a predetermined low temperature were broken, with pools of water from melted ice inside. Some of the pills chosen at random and inspected had what seemed to be hair from an employee's arm; others had compressed and mysterious black spots that turned out to be the oil that lubricated the plant's machinery. And, to top off the ewww factor, one factory didn't have any running water in the toilets, so no employee had been able to wash their hands for a really long time. Remember, this is a medicine factory.

Meanwhile, it turned out that the medicines they were making weren't just full of nasty stuff, they didn't work to start off with. Ranbaxy had to plead guilty to felony charges in the United States, because some of the medicines they were making were 'adulterated'; they had to pay a $500-million fine.

One by one, Ranbaxy's plants were declared unsafe; eventually not one of the four could still export to the US—the major market for its generic version of Lipitor, taken by the millions of Americans who're watching their cholesterol levels. Millions of Ranbaxy's Lipitor tablets had to be recalled from chemists across the US when glass particles were discovered in them.

Craziest of all, it turned out Ranbaxy had been methodically falsifying its test records. Batch after batch of its generics was shown as genuine in the test documents—all of which were invented. Regulators in South Africa realized that AIDS drugs from the saintly people at Ranbaxy were little better than placebos when all the test data for various different batches turned out to be identical—and photocopied. They didn't even do a good job with the faking. Well, sometimes they tried harder with the faking. On one occasion, they forged some documentation about data they had to show regulators, which was supposed to be from years earlier—and, to take that new-paper feel away, they aged it in a steam room overnight.

In other words, in some parts of the world, it was just presenting completely false data. In Brazil, of the 163 medicines that it was selling, it had properly tested only eight.

Every step of the way, Ranbaxy behaved like a good Indian teenager taking a test: it cheated when it could, and gamed the test when it couldn't cheat. Sometimes, former employees claimed, it would just buy brand-name drugs, and submit them to the FDA as its own in order to pass the tests.

All this was known to managers in 2004. Two brave managers, both relatively fresh hires, launched an investigation; one eventually got to say his piece to the company's board. According to *Fortune* magazine, he told the board that 'more than 200 products in more than 40 countries' had 'elements of data that were fabricated to support business needs'. He wound up urging a recall of major drugs, and coming clean to regulators. *Fortune* says, 'Kumar completed the presentation to a silent boardroom. Only one director, a scientist, showed any surprise about the findings. The others appeared more astonished by Kumar's declaration that if he was not given full authority to fix the problems, he would resign.' Naturally, he quit in two days.

According to *Fortune*, elaborate falsification of data was discussed at length in email chains that included Ranbaxy's CEO and a member of the family that owned it. On one conference call, when the uselessness of its AIDS drugs in Africa was discussed, a senior executive apparently said: 'Who cares? It's just blacks dying.'

Remember, all this was, at the very least, known internally before Ranbaxy's owners sold it to the Japanese. As one US regulator said, the company's culture was 'corrupt to the core'. I suppose it's a small step from concealing the kind of drugs you're making before you sell them to concealing the kind of company you're running before you sell it. The former owners of Ranbaxy now run one of India's largest hospital chains.

In the end, you have to wonder what Ranbaxy thought it was doing. I mean, was it not possible for them to make enough money honestly? It isn't as if they had a business model that was built around brilliance, or around luck. They sold medicines that other people had developed. They sold them without having to spend money on developing them; they sold them without having to spend money on developing a brand around them. Just about the only expense they had to endure was that of actually making each pill—a negligible cost for non-generic medicine companies—and it seemed even that was too much as far as they were concerned. A truly terrible advertisement for Indian enterprise.

THE CHEAPEST OF REPUTATIONS

The tragedy, of course, is that Ranbaxy is far from alone in its business practices. Indeed, it's worth noting that the industry it represents has undergone a series of such humiliating recalls. In the middle of 2014, one of Ranbaxy's fellow-leaders, Dr Reddy's, withdrew 13,500 bottles of a blood pressure medicine from US drugstores; apparently, they weren't as soluble—and hence as effective—as they promised to be. And just a short while earlier, a third company, Wockhardt, had withdrawn 1,10,000 bottles of the same medicine, for the same reason.

While India mystifyingly celebrates its generics-pharmaceutical industry as world-beating, the rest of the world is busy coming to far more accurate conclusions about Indian enterprise and quality control. The European Commission estimates that 75 per cent of all fake or deceptive medicines in the entire world come from India. (Or, at least, appear to. On several occasions, Chinese companies have packaged fake drugs to be shipped to Africa—and labelled them 'Made in India'. Now that's true enterprise. Not that it works out perfectly. On at least one occasion I was told of, an African regulator uncovered the deception because he thought the Chinese-made fake drugs *looked too well packaged to actually be real, and therefore Indian.*)

Africa suffers a disproportionate share of this fakery—'Who cares? It's just blacks dying'—and the effect on India's reputation there can be imagined. Many clever start-ups in Africa let you SMS the details of a strip of Indian generics you've bought to figure out if they're counterfeit or not. A recent paper from the National Bureau of Economic Research in the United States found, after testing 1470 different medicine samples, that Indian drugs are of a noticeably lower quality if they're being sold in Africa than if they are being sold outside it.

One would think that the Indian government would take the lead in trying to stamp out counterfeiting. First of all, it's the kind of thing that should sort of dent national pride. Then, of course, there's the small matter of trying to save lives—including Indian ones. Instead, India's drug regulators have actually told us, in a peevish tone of voice, to stop asking for global standards to be applied, because frankly most Indian companies would fail and then where would we be, huh? The Indian medicine regulator—called the 'drug controller', which is a pretty cool title—has said that it will take at least ten years to get India's pharma companies to stop making quite as many useless medicines as they do now. After being shown up by the US FDA, which actually had to set up shop in India in order to conduct enough inspections, the Indian drug controller finally had to try and up its game. Except it didn't have enough people, and applied to hire at least 300 people a year for the next few years. Practically an admission of guilt.

Worst of all, India has—with that peevish, self-righteous whine that is characteristic of the country when participating in international negotiations—tried to use the World Trade Organization, which oversees trade disputes, to act against international anti-counterfeiting measures. Seriously. The government wants to ensure that not even a single shipment of its beloved generic companies' drugs to Africa gets inspected by dastardly Europeans on its way through Amsterdam to Nigeria. (Yes, shipments from Mumbai to Lagos might well pass through Amsterdam. Weird, but it tells you a lot about how global capitalism replicates the patterns of colonialism.)

India has even tried to hold up a free trade agreement with the European Union—its largest trade partner, and one with whom an agreement is desperately needed if we want to revive India's textile factories—in order to protect generic-medicine companies. The EU wants to subject any medicine-related disputes to international arbitration; this is unacceptable to the fat-cats of the Indian generics industry, and thus to the anti-intellectual property activists who think international arbitration is but one short step away from the president of the European Commission coming to their homes to personally stop them from downloading the latest season of *Game of Thrones*.

So, just to recap: Indian generics companies are saintly. They cure AIDS. They are national champions. They also do no research. They don't bother with quality control. They lie to regulators.

How do they make money and stay in business? The Indian government fights the world on their behalf. It protects them from anti-counterfeiting action. It protects them from trade challenges. It protects them from foreign regulatory action. And it gives them extremely lax intellectual property laws, so they can make fat profits off other people's hard work and research. Globally, pharma companies plough between 15 and 25 per cent of the money they make back into research and development. For India's top companies, that figure is below 5 per cent—and that's after some very creative accounting of R&D.[41] Indeed, even the local branches of multinational drug companies actually spend nearly as much if not more on R&D in India, as a percentage of their revenue here, than Indian companies do.

But, in order to protect an industry that has actually turned *not* innovating into a business model—I mean, how perfect for India,

205

right?—the government has kept intellectual property rights (IPL) weak. India's a global outlier in terms of protecting intellectual property, and always has been; instead of trying to fix that, we've practically started a very damaging trade war with the United States over IPR. Because we are a mature and respectable country, we have made our case in a level-headed and adult manner: we didn't give visas to the American officials who were going to visit India to examine and discuss our IPR laws. One extremely grown-up Indian official told the *Business Standard*: 'They are free to do whatever they can (but) sitting in their own country. They certainly cannot go around the government and expect us to open up our files to them. No country can impose their laws on others. Would they allow us to do so if we launched an investigation into their laws?'

Does this fondness for generics companies and lax IPR have any real costs for India? Many. For one, there's this little thing that the US has called the 'generalized system of preferences'—it gives special access to US markets for companies from developing countries. India used to be the biggest beneficiary of all the 110 countries that got this special treatment; in 2012, $4.5 billion of Indian exports entered the US duty-free, especially manufactured goods like car parts. But in the middle of 2013, India was taken off this system. And, because we have managed to effectively irritate everyone on Capitol Hill, it looks like getting back on the system is tough. In other words, our *real* national champions—the guys who, against all the odds, manage to innovate and produce real things from real, working factories—are going to have to suffer to ensure that the generics boys keep making their big money. (And also to ensure that a bunch of New Delhi activists can be smug about how a plucky little developing country is taking on the might of Big Pharma, how wonderful, the Revolution is imminent.)

Put these stories together—Ranbaxy, Sajjan Jindal, Maruti, the Young Entrepreneurs, and so on—and a disturbing picture emerges.

India is a country, it appears, where companies aren't interested in innovation. They aren't interested in quality. They aren't interested in corporate governance and being fair to their shareholders; they aren't interested in hiring the best manager, only the manager most likely to call the owner 'Papa'. They will make money out of playing games with regulators, playing games with the government, playing games with intellectual property, and keeping costs low, low, low.

Keeping costs low, low, low has, well, costs. Remember how Maruti's managers sent off about Rs 2500 crore to its Japanese owner, more than its profit for the year? Something else was happening that year: labour unrest at Maruti's plant in Manesar, near Delhi. It turned violent; one person was killed. An entire shift was fired. The company said that times were hard, and workers needed to share the company's pain. You know how much it would have cost the company to give in to all the workers' demands? Rs 24 crore. Yup, that's right. Less than 1 per cent of the *extra* amount it sent off to Suzuki that year. Some costs are more worth cutting than others, it appears.

And it is these companies that the government wants to go to bat for. Look, low-cost auto companies like Maruti are certainly needed; after all, we need jobs, even if the people aren't paid enough. But do we need jobs in which people aren't paid enough, and produce products that can't even compete in the open market? In fact, we need the opposite. We need global-quality goods—in this case, world-class cars—because there are too many Indians just to make cars for India. We need to make cars for other countries as well. In order to do that, we need to make cars that they'd buy. It turns out, our car companies know that we don't make cars that good. But they're willing to do whatever it takes to ensure that they can keep on making lower-quality cars while raking in assured profits. How so? Well, you can't import a foreign car without paying an additional 60 per cent over and above the price. This means that

Indian cars have a big price advantage built-in. Now, if India were to sign a free-trade agreement with the European Union, that 60 per cent tax on foreign cars would be halved. Suddenly, a Volkswagen would not be that much pricier than a Maruti. And Maruti and its competitors really don't want that to happen—so they're pushing the government into thwarting the signing of the Indo-EU agreement.

So, low-quality low-cost Indian carmakers don't want trade; neither do low-quality low-cost generics pharmaceutical companies. Seeing a pattern? OK, here's another: look at our famous information technology industry. The wonder of the world, the reason every American lives in fear of their job being Bangalored, etc. etc. It turns out they, too, are concerned about ensuring that they get protected in agreements with Europe and the US. Our companies—and therefore the commerce ministry, which operates as an even less efficient wing of India Inc.—have set, as a fundamental first step for an agreement, the requirement that Europe certifies that Indian companies are safe enough to give your private data to (they aren't. No Indian would) and that they can send whichever Indian engineer they want to work for clients in Europe. This has been their model forever, right—'body-shopping', in which energetic, smart, and cheap Indian engineers arrive in the West to do the job? That's their competitive advantage. But, frankly, it too is low-cost, low-quality—and low-innovation. Like generics companies, Indian IT does not really believe in investing in cutting-edge research. Many, many years ago, Arundhati Roy called Indian IT workers 'techno-coolies'. Typical—a phrase dripping with the upper-caste condescension for manual labour that is half our problem. Roy's anger came from the fact that Indian IT was working, cheap, for foreigners. But that isn't the real problem. The problem is the entire industry is broadly unwilling to go 'up the value chain', to become innovators and market leaders instead of low-level service providers. Yes, some have tried to, intermittently—including Infosys. But the overall devotion to Indian IT's business model remains.

To protect outdated and exploitative business models, the Indian government will turn down the trading opportunities that would allow new entrepreneurs to thrive. Without the discipline of trade, we won't be able to export; without exports, we won't be able to employ people.

But low-cost, low-quality, low-innovation India is so very, very precious to us. It needs protecting. And coddling.

ALL INNOVATION IS FRUGAL

'Jugaad' is a curse.

No, I am not being too harsh. Think for yourself: What else is that pernicious, disgusting word 'jugaad'? Once it was a mark of pride, demonstrating that in a tough socialist society with very little on offer we nevertheless managed, we made do. We held things together with Sellotape and paan stains and prayer, and we kept them working.

But what is jugaad, really? Today? It's contentment. It's self-satisfaction and self-praise when what you have produced is clearly substandard. Are you a car company? Make cars considered unsafe in any other country in the world, free-ride on government diesel subsidies, and try to make money through selling official spare parts at outrageous prices when your useless cars collapse after they meet their first monsoon pothole. Do not focus on quality; do not try to open up the markets abroad for the smaller cars, the ones with greater endurance, the ones cheaper to run, that you know you can make.

Having viciously attacked car companies all this while, let me now quote a guy who runs one. (This is to pretend I am being fair.) Here's Anand Mahindra, who runs one of the few car companies that have done well of late, on what ails his sector: 'Jugaad does imply a positive "can-do" attitude, but unfortunately, also involves a "make-do" approach. It can, hence, lead to compromises on quality and rarely involves cutting-edge or breakthrough technology.'

The problem with Indian companies, according to the Japanese academic Shoji Shiba, who has spent difficult decades trying to save this country's factories, is that they think manufacturing is just the act of production. Nobody is interested in quality, and few in innovation: 'Very few companies at the top of the pyramid have some R&D, and build their own products,' he told *Business Today* magazine. (Even 'on the operations side, efficiency and productivity are not enough. Happiness of the workers is also important.') But the problem is that innovation is not something that we believe is needed in order to improve a product; innovation is jugaad, merely a process that reduces the cost to produce it.

One understands the need for jugaad, if you are a small entrepreneur in a small village, with no capital and no institutional support and no electricity and no roads and a caste system that oppresses you. You come up with solutions that are shaped by your constraints. This is a valuable skill.

But it is ridiculous to suppose only Indians have it. It happens everywhere. Come on! Is there something that is, perhaps, 'expensive innovation'? Is it meaningful to talk of 'wasteful innovation'? Then what on earth are we talking about when we talk about frugal innovation? An innovation is only a usable innovation if it reduces costs. 'Frugal innovation' is like 'alternative medicine'; if it *works*, it's just 'medicine'. Or 'innovation'.

So what is our real uniqueness when it comes to jugaad? The same things that set us apart as a country: our hideous mess of regulations and prohibitions, our absence of infrastructure, and our sensitivity to cost. In other words, Indian jugaad is about cutting corners. We can even take this dysfunctional attitude with us, I fear, to countries where rules are more respected than they are here. People who grew up in communist East Germany, recent behavioural research into Berliners' values discovered, cheat more and with less compunction. Indian innovation, which grew up in a resource-poor, trust-deficient, regulation-heavy environment, is as unable to leave behind its past. Until it does, it will remain low-cost, corner-cutting, making do.

Jugaad is a terrible, terrible thing to be proud of. Let us hope that the rest of the world has a terrible memory and doesn't remember what it means. Because, after all, at some point, we have to start selling them things. We have to ensure that 'Made in India' isn't a joke; but it will be, if people look at the things we make and say: Ha, I wonder exactly how many corners they cut to make this.

Branding an emerging economy is never easy. 'Made in China', for example, is not considered to be a guarantor of quality. The Chinese, for a decade, have been selling us things that we grit our teeth and buy because they are cheap, not because we want to. Today, even when they are beginning to make mobile phones, for example, that can match anything made in Korea or in the West, they have a massive trust deficit to make up, even in a country that is silly enough to be proud of 'jugaad'.

Once a country's brand percolates into people's skulls, it stays there. In 2013, one pretty popular Hindi-film hit song was even titled *Pyaar China ka maal hai*—'Love is made in China'. That was not, as you can imagine, a compliment. The lyrics went on: 'In love, there's no guarantee; there's no warranty; there's not even a formal bill.' Ouch.

The rebranding exercise takes ages, but it eventually happens. In the 1950s and 1960s, 'Made in Japan' meant, in the West, 'cheap and tacky'. Perhaps 'Made in China' is going through the same ascension. But 'Made in India'? Don't hold your breath. Not while we're proud of putting quality last.

CRONY COMPETITION

The Indian Premier League is the worst thing in India, and perhaps the world. It does not just demean a noble sport; it is also widely and justifiably viewed as a civilizational nadir. A previously unimaginable blend of bad taste and bad faith, the IPL manages to simultaneously insult women, history, cricketing skill, and the intelligence of its viewers.

What is too little appreciated, however, is how much it reveals about the Indian economy. About its excesses prior to the slowdown; about the borderline-illegal self-centredness of the owners of Indian companies; about poor management being covered up by good public relations and a sycophantic press; about an apparent inability to do business openly and transparently.

I don't just mean the extraordinary obscurity that surrounds who actually owns some of the teams. The Indian public and its press have happily chosen to believe that many expensive cricket teams can be owned largely by movie stars and other assorted celebrities, and not shadowy financiers spending a few years unknown for tax purposes. This once again demonstrates India's unique ability to be dazzled and distracted by glittery things. Unsurprisingly, this country is also a major growth market for American pro wrestling.

I don't even mean the complicated question of how much tickets actually cost. If you watch a match in Delhi from box seats, for example, you get a ticket that has 'Rs 30,000' or something like that prominently printed on it but, naturally, you didn't pay that much, you got it at a sharp discount—or you were given it free by an oligarch who wants a favour. In effect, nobody pays full price for hideously expensive tickets, which allows the league to claim both that the games are exclusive and that their future revenue from ticket sales are incredibly high. If people start questioning the claims about ticket revenues, then too many other aspects of the teams' finances will start being analysed. This is not unlike India's real-estate market, where sale prices for houses are way too high, and yet many are empty—because no real-estate developer can afford to admit that they're too high. They might have to send them lower, which would affect the value of their companies' assets, and so on down the slippery slope to housing-market collapse.

No, the IPL reveals a great deal about the Indian economy because of the identity of the teams' owners—at least, in those cases in which we know who the real owners are. When one of the IPL's champions was removed from the roster in 2012 because the team's owners went bankrupt and couldn't pay league fees, people began to notice that being really, really bad at business seemed to be what most IPL owners had in common.

Let's see. The team that was removed in 2012 was the Deccan Chargers, owned by the Deccan Chronicle Group. The companies' value in 2007? Rs 5000 crore. Their value in 2012? Rs 200 crore. The group had lost 96 per cent of value, and was massively in debt. Who else? Well, shares in the Delhi team's owners, the Andhra Pradesh–based construction company GMR, were trading at around Rs 120 as 2007 ended; they're trading at around Rs 25 today.

Another team was removed in 2013; it belonged to the Sahara India Group, whose flamboyant owner was thrown into jail by the

Supreme Court for apparently running a Ponzi scheme. Subrata Roy, the owner of the Sahara Group—officially the Sahara Parivar, or Family—is one of a kind. He legally changed his name to Subrata Roy Sahara. He calls himself 'Saharashree', or 'Man of Sahara'; designated himself his group's Managing Worker; and had a special 'Sahara salute'. He had his wife record a music video as a paean to their marriage and his corporation—which coincidentally served to get pictures of his real-estate project and his airline free airtime on music TV. In it, he was pictured repeatedly walking down roads and in motorcades surrounded by people dressed as members of an American President's secret service. He himself also wore a dark suit and dark glasses, but was set apart by the fact that he was also wearing a cape with a red lining. He claims to employ a million Indians. A Noted Patriot, he occasionally brings a hundred thousand or so of them together to set a national-anthem-singing record. He also claims to have 30 million investors; though, oddly, when the regulators tried to return a lot of money to them in 2013, not one actual person showed up, which has got to be a far more unusual world record. But the most interesting thing about Subrata Roy Sahara is that *he was considered perfectly normal for an Indian tycoon.*

The league's overall sponsor was India's largest real-estate company, DLF: its shares cost around Rs 1200 each when the league opened, and around Rs 170 in late 2014, and thousands of crores of rupees of value has just vanished. DLF is one of the two companies to have lost most value since 2007. (Fortunately, the other was its main rival, Unitech.) Oh, and let us not forget that its dealings with the son-in-law of India's most powerful woman, Sonia Gandhi, mean DLF is the best-known crony capitalist in the land.

And, above all, there's the Chennai Super Kings.[42] I don't even know where to begin. OK, here's this: they're owned by N. Srinivasan, who also happens to run the board that controls Indian cricket. This is not a conflict of interest, because in India, we do not have conflicts of interest ever. Seriously—Manmohan Singh's telecommunications minister, Dayanidhi Maran, regulated the business of his brother, Kalanidhi Maran, Tamil Nadu's largest media mogul, and I am a hundred per cent sure he did it a hundred per cent objectively. Similarly, I am a hundred per cent sure that N. Srinivasan did not get people to keep picking lots of his Chennai players for the Indian team to maintain his cricketers' brand value, but because he cared about the Indian team.[43] When his son-in-law was jailed for fixing IPL matches, Srinivasan pointed out with perfect justice that it had nothing whatsoever to do with him. I confess to being a little puzzled as to why Srinivasan did not actually offer to investigate himself in case there was any wrongdoing. I am a hundred per cent sure he would have done it a hundred per cent objectively.

The amazing thing about N. Srinivasan is that he is not just a superb class-A above-reproach administrator for Indian cricket—and now world cricket, since the International Cricket Committee has been so impressed by his uprightness and dedication to duty that it has elected him chairman—but that he is an equally good businessman. Indeed his company, India Cements, holds an enviable record: it is *the* worst performing company, relative to its sector, among India's top 500. It lost 60 per cent of its value in the five years after the IPL started, while the rest of its sector held its own.

None of this is happenstance. The tawdry aesthetics of the IPL mirrors its owners' errors of judgement. Its disconnectedness from true cricketing skill, from the lives and histories of the cities that hosted its teams, is a direct consequence of the sort of companies that were funding it.

The IPL was built on crony capitalism and the easy money of the pre–crisis boom. Anyone, especially a crony capitalist, could get his hands on cash then, even for something as unproductive as a sports team; and the ambitious, self-obsessed crony capitalist took the money, why not? Back in those days, it was possible to binge on easy money, using it to fund what seemed like endless expansion, and some very dubious acquisitions. The more dubious the profitability of the enterprise you run, the more important it is you overspend on something flashy like the IPL: the more visible you are, as any successful Ponzi schemester can tell you, the less likely the regulators are to come after you, and the less you are seen by possible lenders as a risk. And, of course, it makes you more likely to find defenders, including politically powerful protectors.

THE KING OF GOOD CRIMES

If you are keen-eyed and enthusiastic, or alternatively, if you are an IPL fan,[44] you will have noticed one portly absentee in my recounting of the league's roll of honour. Fear not! The King of Good Times shall receive my full and undivided attention. Vijay Mallya deserves no less.

Here is the thing about the Goatee of Good Times: he, more than anyone else, personifies everything that has gone wrong with Indian business. It isn't just his, well, dubious taste. Though it is that, partly. You see, there was a time, prior to 2008, when the garishness and vulgarity of Mallya's personal style was actually seen as a good thing. It was the Age of Growth, the Age of Reforms, and the Age of Wealth; being shy about how much money you had was considered practically immoral. Such reticence, it was argued, might lead observers to think that being obscenely wealthy was somehow a bad thing. And where would such thoughts end? I'll tell you where. With Socialism, that's where. It was OK for Vijay Mallya's father, Vittal, a magnate of an earlier, Nehruvian, nature. Raghu Karnad writes in the *Caravan*: 'Vittal Mallya was "like a quiet chartered accountant", said one senior state bureaucrat, a numbers man with a receding hairline and a demure personality.'

Had Vijay behaved similarly, it would have been a dastardly betrayal of free-market economics. What was the point of reform if rich people couldn't talk about their yachts to absolutely everybody? Indians wanted to live well, not frugally; Vijay Mallya turned that from a personal mantra into a political maxim and finally into a business model.

Everyone seemed to have forgotten one crucial aspect of a market economy: you had better be good at your job. Inheriting an empire from your austere, careful father is not quite good enough. United Breweries, which the elder Mallya bought off Brits departing after 1947, owes its success not to the quality of its beverages—as anyone who has tasted Kingfisher can testify—but to its vice-like control of the liquor distribution system. Local Kingfisher distributors are often accused of playing dirty with the brand's competitors to maintain its monopoly—which is why, frequently, bars you go to will serve only Kingfisher variants or its associated brands, such as Heineken. Mallya's United Spirits has two-thirds of the market, especially dominating the whisky[45] market; it grew 20 per cent in 2008, the year of the financial crisis, when most sectors shrank. Mallya then declared his business 'recession-proof'. True. But not Mallya-proof.

Vijay Mallya is the biggest example of why, in the new post-reforms India, tycoons needed to advertise themselves. They needed to be flashy; the smoke and the mirrors would conceal the fact that their business plans were farcical. Instead of talking about the madness that was Mallya's decision to launch an airline and name it after his beer brand, Kingfisher, people talked instead of the nudge-nudge-wink-wink-saynomore onboard welcome video, in which Vijay assured us that he had personally 'hand-picked' the glammed-up cabin crew. Instead of talking of the overweening ambition that would cause Mallya to buy too many planes—and a rival airline—too soon, we talked of the overweening ambition that caused him to buy Tipu Sultan's sword at an auction in London. Instead of questioning the dubiousness of his balance sheets, we chose to question his decision to take his giant yacht, *Indian Empress*, to the Mediterranean, and to gossip about which political heir was vacationing with which actress on it.

It's conventional wisdom now that Mallya's erratic judgement led him to make bad business decisions, which have now brought down the group he inherited. For example, he couldn't wait five years to have his new airline fly abroad, as the rules specified—so he massively overpaid for the bankrupt Air Deccan in order to use its international licence, uncaring that Air Deccan's low-cost image would hurt the 'premium' brand he was building for Kingfisher. That premium image, problematically, came from adding costs wherever possible rather than from cutting them down, as the airline industry needs to do.

But there was another effect, too. Each time Mallya did something outrageous—used his liquor fortune to buy relics of liquor-hating M.K. Gandhi, for example—it served to underline his prominence. This man, it seemed to say, is madly flashy. He's never going away. He will disassemble his father's bungalow brick by brick and rebuild it on top of Bangalore's tallest building, the kind of thing that really deserves a paper in a psychology journal; he will have every new addition to Kingfisher's fleet, flying in from Toulouse, do an aerial parikrama of Tirupati before landing in Bangalore; he will insist his goatee is trimmed to look like Ganesha's trunk. Clearly this man, people thought, is a fixture of our public life.

And, in the end, that impression paid off—at least temporarily. He used that air of invulnerability and permanence, and his money, to get himself into Parliament. There he charmed and wheedled various powerful sorts, to ensure that when things came crashing down, they didn't come crashing down on him. In fact, he managed to ensure that the government's public-sector banks kept on lending to him even when it was amply clear that his airline was never going to make money. The banks—which are, remember, owned by the taxpayer—are not likely to get back more than 20 per cent of the thousands of crores that they lent Mallya. Nobody's completely sure how much Kingfisher owes, but it's probably in excess of Rs 12,000 crore. Just so you can compare and condemn conveniently, that's how much money the Chennai–Bangalore Industrial Corridor needs to be set up; it's how much the government of Telangana wants to give its farmers as a loan waiver; it's the total amount of foreign money given to charity in India in 2013.

Why did the banks keep on lending? The State Bank of India, the largest and most reliable in the country, wrote off Rs 1500 crore that it had lent to Kingfisher in 2011—and then gave it some more rope in 2012! Ah, the banks said patiently, but now we own the airline, so that makes a difference. Well done, SBI, you bought a too-costly-to-run company in a cut-throat sector with a terrible management team! Prudent banking, that. Since you're being so forthcoming, do you want to explain why you paid 70 per cent more for each Kingfisher share , over and above the price they were selling for on the open market?

Mallya had turned himself into an institution. He was well connected and visible. No bank wanted to foreclose on him. No government official wanted to put him in jail, even when the taxman claimed he had defrauded his employees by taking away their pension money—a criminal offence, and one for which the law makes it tough to get bail at that.

And the best part is: Mallya feels hurt. He feels singled out. He feels that jealousy has a great deal to do with his troubles today—and tweeted as much, when *Forbes* took him off the Indian billionaires list.

You know, perhaps Mallya's right in a way. Because he is far, far from being alone. Every single state-controlled bank has turned into a tap for India's crony capitalists. Remember when Indira Gandhi privatized the banks, claiming that they lent too much to rich people and not enough to the rural poor? Well, hello, ghost of Mrs Gandhi, you're looking well, sit down and have some Darjeeling while I point out what that clever and cunning plan led to.

Government banks accumulated Rs 5,00,000,00,00,000 in bad debts and write-offs between 2007 and 2013. Of those that were written off, the Reserve Bank of India revealed that '95 per cent' were 'large loans' to big companies. Did, on any occasion, banks force the management to change because they had run their company into the ground? Was some useless business-family scion deprived of his power and position and money for being irresponsible? Ha, the very thought. What kind of country do you think we're running?

SURVIVAL OF THE FATTEST

Back in January 2008, as India waited to know which celebrity and which oligarch got to own which team in the Indian Premier League, the Bombay Stock Exchange's blue-chip stock index, the Sensex, hit its highest point in history.

Today, it's close to record highs, once again. But hidden in there is a vital, vital story. Of karma, as it were. Some time ago I ran the numbers, looking at which companies had lost the most since that January 2008 record, and which ones had done well. Of the 50 biggest, our old friends at DLF had lost the most; and Anil Ambani's Reliance Infrastructure was close behind. A bunch of other oligarchs' big companies—Jaiprakash Associates, that built the Yamuna Expressway; Bharti Airtel; Tata Steel; and Mukesh Ambani's Reliance—had all lost big. Slightly smaller companies that had done badly included the various IPL owners' companies— Pune's, Hyderabad's, Bangalore's, Chennai's. There was a pattern, I argued then: 'A toxic mix of overweening ambition, of political connections and muddled balance sheets, of debt binges and careless acquisitions, of prestige projects and promoter egos.' The ones that did well? Careful companies, professionally run, that stuck to what they knew: Asian Paints and ITC, for example.

It is worth our while to briefly return to that time, to recapture that shining moment in 2008 before the first glimmerings of the financial crisis were to take the wind out of everyone's sails—literally, in Mallya's case, since the poor man had to sell his yacht. (If you have tears, people, prepare to shed them now: Mallya now has to rent *Indian Empress* for a month every summer, as if to pretend he still owns it.)

Return to that time, that glorious week that the Sensex set its record. One of Anil Ambani's companies, Reliance Power, was due to sell its first shares to a wider public. The wider public, being typically sagacious, bought all the shares he had to sell in less than a minute; 70 times as many people wanted shares as there were shares to be sold. Hmm. Everyone thought this was typical. Only to be expected. 'Investors seem to be confident in the future of the Indian economy,' said P. Chidambaram, without a hint of smugness. The company seemed to agree: its own slogan was 'Power On. India On'. Oh, hubris. Tell me something, hubris: Why are you so very funny in retrospect? Why?

Hubris and overconfidence were everywhere that February. I remember sitting glued to my television as India's most trusted business journalist, the CNBC-TV18 anchor Udayan Mukherjee, leaned forward in his chair that cold January day that Reliance Power was to start selling shares, in its 'initial public offer' or IPO. '2008 will be the year of mega-IPOs,' he told me and my fellow viewers, as we slurped our coffee in wild-eyed excitement. 'It will be the biggest primary market run in the past five-year bull run.' (No, it wasn't.) He added: 'There are no signs of any massive directional moves' to the stock market. Later that week, the Sensex fell more than it ever had before on a single day. And then it fell as much again, the next day. OK, perhaps I am being unfair to poor Mukherjee. After all, the day after the Sensex tanked, the exact opposite of what he had just breathlessly predicted, he did bravely tackle his error, writing a column, in which the first line was: 'The thing about life is that one makes mistakes.' The rest of the column was about how absolutely everybody *else* in India had made lots of mistakes that they really should have had the judgement to predict and avoid. He was absolutely right, too. There really had been a near-universal suspension of disbelief.

Reliance Power's shares could only be freely traded some weeks after the IPO. Within a day that trading formally opened in February, the company lost 32 per cent of its supposed value. All those investors who had bought shares at Rs 450 in January 2008 hold shares worth Rs 75 each in end 2014. The company is a fraction of how much everyone thought it was worth in 2008. Remember, this isn't just any company—it's one of the backbones of India's efforts to get power to its villages. And not just in 2008, or in some imagined, unbelievably bright future that only 2008-era Indians could see. Today, too. We are once again dependent on a company that lost three-fourth of its value in a few years. Indeed, Reliance Power just mystifyingly tried to buy the hydroelectricity generation plants of Jaiprakash Associates— remember them? They were also losing vast chunks of value—for Rs 10,000 crore. It's unclear where this money would have come from, or who would lend to a company with this record; all we know for certain is that the heroes of January 2008 were and are close to being India's largest private-sector power supplier. This is who we have to build India with.

What you expect from a good company, from a vibrant private sector, is the ability to predict and manage risk. Was that on offer here? Look at the 'prospectus' of Reliance Power, the little booklet that every company that's selling shares to the public has to put out. The regulators require the company to list the risks that it sees. Anything on the horizon likely to make investors lose their money? The company has to put it in. Read this prospectus: not only does it have schedules and timetables for completing power plants that are completely unrealistic in retrospect, but the question of where the coal comes from is never even addressed! Given that coal-fired power plants are shutting down across north India claiming they need more coal, it's amazing that it wasn't considered worth discussing at the time. If a private company can't figure out its biggest risk, should it be in business?

True, I might still invest in Reliance Power myself. You have to hand it to companies that fall on their feet, and find creative ways to get hold of other people's money. Consider this one: Reliance Power paid $10 billion to buy 36 Chinese-made coal-fired generation plants to put up across north India, equal to providing for a fifth of India's power needs. Much of the money to buy these came from, well, the Chinese themselves. True, Chinese turbines seem to care nothing for the fact that they are reinforcing stereotypes about goods from that country—since they have a habit of breaking down, and then having to be shipped back to Shanghai for repair while leaving entire states without power for a summer. But still. Pretty impressive.

India's companies and its governments—and its investors—have a simple rule: nothing must fail. The more outwardly successful you are, the more embarrassing it would be if you failed. It might suggest to the censorious hordes always waiting just out of sight that not everything in India is perfect. And we need them to be perfect, because otherwise people might not give us their money.

There is a problem with this thinking, and it isn't just that it is profoundly immoral. It is that it can't last forever. Keynes said the wisest thing about markets ever: 'They can stay irrational longer than you can stay solvent.' You can't bet against everyone else being stupid—nobody is rich enough, even if they are smart enough. But people cannot all stay stupid forever. Rational people, smart people, looked at GMR, the Delhi airport builder, for example, in the years till 2008 and wondered how it was getting so many investors given that it earned zilch. Rational people, smart people, saw GMR and so many similar private-sector 'partners' of the government defy their predictions, amid much talk of investing in India's future. Rational people, smart people, began to think they were wrong. They weren't. That became clear—eventually. Yes, it was in everyone's interest to let these companies thrive; but the logic of money eventually must outweigh the stupidity of a crowd.

You see, everyone had something to gain from the market going up. TV newsmen who should have been wondering what was driving it up instead got on screen wearing T-shirts saying '10,000!' when the Sensex hit that figure. When it hit 12,000, in 2006, business TV hired cheerleaders. Literal cheerleaders. There were girls in short skirts waving 'Go Sensex Go' placards.

Why? Because you have to convince investors on Wall Street— who are, if anything, even more shallow than investors here, but with far more money to burn and far less time—that India is profitable, is shockingly profitable, will always be profitable. You back companies that are little better than Ponzi schemes because your whole economy is being set up as a Ponzi scheme: the moment one foreign investor decides India's not actually providing the returns he expected, the whole damn pile of pretence comes tumbling down.

The true lesson from the high-growth years, the false and fake high-growth years, is one that has not yet been fully comprehended. Depend solely on keeping inputs cheap, and you will fail. Assume that coal is cheap forever, like the owners and investors of Reliance Power did, and you will run into trouble. Assume that foreign money will be cheap forever, and you'll run into similar trouble.

The reason I bring this up is because, perhaps, we are entering another few years in which international investors will look to India with hope. And we should certainly welcome them. But what happened in the past should also cast a shadow on our optimism.

They did not betray us by leaving. We betrayed them, by lying about the quality of our companies. And we betrayed ourselves, by trying to replace the departure of Western money after the financial crisis of 2008 with our own, no questions asked.

That was the government's response to the crisis: three 'stimulus' packages that essentially consisted of big cuts in taxes for companies. Altogether, the stimulus packages, a big giveaway to the fattest companies, consisted of almost 2 per cent of GDP—more than we spend on education and health. Oh, and in the process, we also got our banks to lend to people like Vijay Mallya, keeping them in business because they were Too Connected to Fail. Add another 3 per cent of GDP in loans to such companies that are being 'restructured'—in other words, just short of being lost forever. And there will be more such revelations of bad lending soon, I assure you.

And that got us some pretty supercharged growth for a year or two. But, again, quality will tell. Cheap financing, whether from gullible foreigners or from your friends in government, can't last forever.

India seemed to recover quickly from the global crisis. Yes, companies like DLF and Reliance Power had seen their value shredded—but other companies, good, honest, consumer-goods companies, seemed to be helping India survive the tough years. It seemed 'robust demand'—in other words, Indians' relentless optimism, and thus their willingness to keep spending—would not permit a downturn in India.

But, in the end, we've got to start making real stuff again. And building big stuff again. We are still stuck with the problem that Manmohan Singh had in 2004: How to build manufacturing? You need infrastructure. How to build infrastructure? Well, we don't know.

Dr Singh's answer, to partner with companies, foundered on government employees' inability to out-think and outsmart the private sector. (On the occasion, that is, when they were unbribed and thus tried to do their job.) But, today, we look at these giant companies, once embodiments of bright-eyed hope and anticipation, and see them for what they are: now slightly sleazy, paunchy, balding, and lascivious. Is it worth working through this marriage?

I mean, who among us would like to put our own money in companies that have lost so much since 2008? So why should we expect our government to? Perhaps that's India's central problem: we don't trust the people who actually got us to high growth earlier, because they burnt us once. How can we, in the absence of trust, get high growth again?

DEMOCRACY, THE UNLIKELY HERO

The devil's bargain the government made with the private sector is part of what sent growth up to eight per cent through much of the first decade of this century, making India temporarily the envy of the world. Other elements helped, too—but, oddly, all in the same way. That period of high growth—which Manmohan Singh, and his acolytes, and even his critics, seemed to think was normal—was, in fact, deeply abnormal.

Many people will insist they know what caused that abnormal high growth. It was the reforms of the past, some will say—Dr Singh would say the reforms of the early 1990s, his opponents in the BJP would say the reforms of the early 2000s. Yet others would mutter things about animal spirits and India Unleashed and Uncaged Tigers and various other phrases that sound like book titles.

But, actually, that period had one distinguishing feature, and one alone: Of really, really low input prices. Everything that you needed to make stuff was cheap, cheap, cheap. A lot of it, as I said, because it was government policy. And the rest because the years before the economic crisis were, well, just a very fortunate time.

It was a boom, remember? Finance hadn't discovered yet that there was a fundamental flaw in its business model, and therefore cheap Western money was sloshing around India like monsoon rain in a Mumbai street. Almost any Indian company could get financing—if not from Indians, then from Western financiers who seemed singularly unconcerned about the chances of being paid back. The world also helped us with cheap petroleum prices—crude oil cost between $30 and $70 a barrel. (To compare, prices stayed at $110 for years after the crisis and, many analysts think, are headed back up there again.)

And, of course, the government pitched in with cheap coal and cheap spectrum. Look at the startling growth numbers for Bihar, for example, and it's frankly depressing how much of it comes from the telecom industry—and thus is dependent on cheap spectrum. And everyone assumed that land would be given to them, too—if not free, then close to it. What else is a government for, if not to bully people off their land so that companies can get 10,000 acres on which they eventually might produce a useless car or two?

Companies and states alike could look like real rock stars thanks to this policy. Look, even I would feel really rich if I didn't have to pay for food and rent and coffee.

You think these good times are coming back soon? They aren't.[46] If there's a lot of Western money sloshing around in India, surely we're wise enough now to know that it doesn't mean it will still be here next week.

And too many people have finally been moved to anger by the years and decades of free inputs, this horrific subsidy we've been giving our companies. No government can, with impunity, give things away for free again.

At some point in economic policymaking in India, politics intervenes. This is something democratic countries have to deal with. The choice of instruments open to their policymakers is far, far fewer than in authoritarian countries. The Chinese can keep iron ore near free for their steelmakers, as they did, and eventually conquer the entire global steel industry, and there won't be a peep out of their people. I mean, if you're a Chinese citizen, you're massively oppressed yada yada yada—is skewed resource policy really going to be your first point of complaint? But India doesn't have that dubious luxury; the people have a voice.

Remember, China's solution to the whole infrastructure-financing problem is one that India simply wouldn't be able to implement in a hundred years. The Chinese practise something that economists call 'financial repression'. (Being economists, they often think this is worse than any *real* repression in China.) That upstanding and altruistic institution, the Chinese Communist Party, has an iron lock on savings rates. It keeps—represses—interest rates artificially low; this means that you, if you were a Chinese citizen, would not get a fair rate of return on your life savings. You'd have to work much harder and longer to save the same amount for your retirement. How much does the Chinese government take off your savings? Well, over 4 per cent of GDP, as it happens—not what I'd call a small sum. This is why authoritarian governments are the best conmen; you don't even know when they're taking your money. And what does the People's Republic do with all this money? Well, a quarter goes to banks; a little under that to the big companies; and the remainder to the government. That gets spent on buying dollars, so as to ensure that the Chinese currency is kept artificially low and Chinese goods are kept artificially cheap—so the factory I work in can stay open. And it gets spent on building infrastructure. That is, always remember, how the Chinese have solved the problem we're plagued with.

Indian voters wouldn't stand for this kind of nonsense. We have the opposite problem—savings rates in several places, such as provident funds, are kept excessively high. Call it a freedom bonus.

However, this has major consequences for growth. India's spell of off-the-charts growth was primarily caused by a big spike in investment. But voters don't care about investment, do they? The electorate, and the policymakers who answer to them in democracies, care more about how much they have to spend than they do about the investment-to-GDP ratio. And that's supposed to be the object of economic policy as well: private consumption expenditure, the amount in people's wallets.

Here's the strange thing. In that period of high GDP growth, growth in private consumption expenditure was steady—but not outstanding. Indeed, in parts of the country, a slightly weird thing happened: zippy GDP growth happened right alongside staggeringly low consumption growth. In Uttar Pradesh, for example, even in the years when things seemed to be going well, consumption growth averaged only 1 per cent annually. You think voters won't notice?

Voters will notice, and they won't allow it to last over a long period of time. They will expect consumption and their own wealth to increase steadily along with growth. Behind all the talk of 'aspirations' and 'jobs' and so on and so forth lies a simple point: growth needs to put secure income growth first. We're simply too democratic a country for anything else to be OK.

Nostalgia for the growth of the past is, like much nostalgia, deceptive and dangerous. It was driven by things that simply aren't available today.

Yes, there are noisy claims made that, if we just restore the conditions of the past, then the high growth of the past will return, too. Return to an 'investment-friendly' climate, we're told. In this argument, 'investment-friendliness' apparently means blinkered regulators. And the government bullying consumers and landowners on your behalf, and giving you stuff for free. And policymakers using brute force to divert resources that voters want to spend on themselves. None of these things is coming back, and so the growth that they induced isn't, either.

The people who urge this on us have either failed to understand what went wrong, and why growth slowed, or they have other, more obvious reasons. ('Give us your stuff for free, or we'll shoot the economy! Honest! Don't try anything, you hear?')

The truth is—and this is the most important, and the least told, lesson of the past decade—that India needs another way to grow. We can't rely on resource giveaways, and we can't rely on *jugaadu* companies, and we can't rely on cheap oil or cheaper foreign money.

Democracy is this country's immune system. It told us that our growth was unhealthy and unsustainable. If we return to unhealthy habits, we'll get sick.

India needs a healthier path to growth.

PART V

THE ONLY WAY TO GROW

India is, to put it mildly, in a bit of a mess. So many problems need to be addressed so quickly and so close together that it seems that there is no way out. The entire growth model looks broken.

Even if it is, it can be repaired. The way forward is easy to understand, if not to implement.

But we have a chance, today, to make tough and radical changes. And that is because enough people are convinced that some painful decisions will have to be endured. The sense of drift and purposelessness, whether justified or not, has grown too strong.

Indians, it seems, have tired of waiting for their leaders to praise and propose radical reform to them; they are now making the case for change to their leaders. If we learn the right lessons from the mistakes we have already made, then we do indeed have a chance to find a better way to grow.

In this section, we will isolate the five bad choices we have made that must be corrected. And we will sketch out the five big steps forward that we can take.

We will look at how government can change itself, and how it can help us change for the better, too.

By the end, I will hopefully have convinced you that deep and transformative reform is not just necessary but possible—and that nothing short of that will work.

Growth is not our birthright, but we shall have it.

LESSONS FROM *MOTHER INDIA*

In 1927, everyone was furious. A woman named Katherine Mayo had written a book about India. It was racist, propagandist, and generally mean-spirited. This was bad enough. It had become something of a bestseller. This was worse.

The book, *Mother India*, was supposedly about how India was an enfeebled country, poisoned by vices of every nature, and quite unfit to govern itself. Most of it was an attack on everything Indian, carefully planned to produce the most ewww per word. Most infuriatingly, large chunks of it were true.

Mayo's plan was to show, above all through questions of public health, exactly how British rule was the only thing keeping India alive. Hence, there were long sections—among the most cringe-inducing—devoted to how generally unsanitary conditions in India were in 1927. People defecated outside; government-built toilets weren't used; cities like Benares were literal cesspools, where clogged sixteenth-century sewers 'await the downpours of the rainy season, when their suddenly swollen contents will push into the city's subsoil with daily increasing force'.

And the consequence? Mayo quoted a fellow-American: 'From long consumption of diluted sewage they have actually acquired a degree of immunity. Yet all of them are walking menageries of intestinal parasites, which make a heavy drain upon their systems and which inevitably tell when some infection, such as pneumonia or influenza, comes along. Then the people die like flies. They have no resistance.' She added, in her own voice: 'These conditions, added to infant marriage, sexual recklessness and venereal infections, further let down the bars to physical and mental miseries; and here again one is driven to speculate as to how peoples so living and so bred can have continued to exist.' Like all writers of her ilk, Mayo was obsessed with racial continuity and survival, and with what she was convinced were entire continents full of sexual deviants.

This epic trolling of 400 million people—that many in the first edition, that is; for subsequent editions Mayo carefully replaced all instances of the word 'Indian' with 'Hindu', for maximum irritation—managed to incense even Mohandas Gandhi. *Mother India* was, said Gandhi, 'the report of a drain inspector sent out with the one purpose of opening and examining the drains of the country to be reported upon'.

This does seem to be an odd metaphor for Gandhi to use, though. After all, the village-obsessed Gandhi was one of the few prominent Indians to actually care about drains. At one point, he wrote that the primary task of the workers he had sent out to India's villages was to improve sanitation. It wasn't just a question of increasing wealth, he insisted: 'Our poverty plays a very small part in our insanitary condition.' Elsewhere: 'The cause of many of our diseases is the condition of our lavatories and our bad habit of disposing of excreta anywhere and everywhere.'

Why, you ask, have I chosen to open with this set of rather dismaying reminders? Because, as it turns out, India's experience with sanitation is a marker of how difficult it is for true change to take root in India. Ninety years after *Mother India*, almost seventy years after Independence, and India is even more of an international disgrace than ever it was. Two-thirds of rural India still has no toilets. Of course, this is subject to vast variation; Kerala, parts of Bengal, Punjab, and the Northeast don't have the problem to the same degree. But that means, too, that across India's heartland—Uttar Pradesh, Bihar, northern Madhya Pradesh—there are entire stretches where 90 per cent of people see no difference between their larger neighbourhood and a lavatory. As a UN report on the subject says, with an air of exasperation not normally heard from that sedentary organization: a billion people 'continue to defecate in gutters, behind bushes or in open water bodies, with no dignity or privacy'. Look at a map of the world in terms of how many people are defecating outside, and India jumps out at you. We're Number One! Though once again, just like cricket, not in a *cool* thing.

Naturally, our disdain for indoor toilets has had dreadful consequences. It may be a little harsh to declare that we are, as that unnamed American told Katherine Mayo, 'walking menageries of intestinal parasites', but, certainly, we haven't been able to keep our water and food pure. This is more than just disgusting and embarrassing: it's a major health problem. The Princeton economist Dean Spears, who has done more than anyone recently to study this problem and its consequences, has pointed out a series of worrying facts. The one that worries me the most is that, in villages with more toilets, 6-year-old children are much more likely to 'recognize letters and simple numbers'. Turns out, shit makes you stupid.

OK, so this is a problem. But we've so many! Why is this of particular interest?

Because it reveals a great deal about exactly who we are as a country. Not the problem of open defecation itself, but its persistence and growth to these unique and staggering proportions.

First: the diagnosis. It comes from people such as Mayo, but also from men such as Gandhi, and from other voices who must be considered more disinterested than either. India, we are told, has a problem.

Then the denial, the one form of intellectual argument we have mastered. India has no problem; if it has a problem, it is nobody else's business; everybody else also has this problem; everybody else has other problems, why don't you talk about those instead; why are you saying this is a problem, it is a part of our 5000-year-old culture; we knew the answers to all problems in the Vedic era; even if we have this problem, it is not our fault; even if we have this problem, we cannot accept any of the solutions that have been shown to work elsewhere; even if we have this problem, it is much better than it was; perhaps we have this problem, but it is none of your business.

Then, the disregard. China can work at the problem, and ensure that only 1 per cent of the country doesn't have access to a latrine; even Bangladesh can get it down to 3 per cent. We, on the other hand, have left it at 50 per cent.

You see, not until there is a crisis do we even acknowledge the beginnings of any problem. So it is with this one. Today, it is becoming clear that the public-health consequences of not using toilets are, frankly, unmanageable. Not only is it making us stupid, but it is making us short. This fact may have led to one of the other characteristic consequences of talking policy in India: misdiagnosis. Our kids were shorter than, say, sub-Saharan Africans; therefore we were stunted; therefore the kids weren't getting enough to eat. Malnourishment, therefore, was a national crisis—Manmohan Singh said so himself. Nobody considered that we may have showed the symptoms of being malnourished—'stunting'—partly because kids under the age of 1 were expending all their energy on fighting off all the hideous things they were picking up from the disease-ridden water. And because we didn't consider it, we decided instead to fight the symptom, setting up a giant effort to fight malnutrition—which may not have been a problem of the same degree. As Spears has argued, reducing open defecation, and thus preventing the diseases it causes, is by far the cheapest way to reduce infant deaths.

But, eventually, this runs into a bedrock of opposition that goes far deeper than you'd expect. The reason that sanitation is one of Gandhi's preferences that Independent India happily abandoned is because it requires deep and painful change. We are not set up, institutionally or culturally, to manage such change. We run away from it.

We don't even want to talk about why, sometimes, problems can be painful to resolve. Consider this: on average, Hindus are far more likely to avoid toilets than are Muslims. Why? Well, it can't be wealth; Muslims are generally poorer. It can't be just that more Hindus live in towns, where you are more likely to have a toilet; even in rural areas, almost 80 per cent of Hindus go out to the fields, while among Muslims, just over half do. One survey of rural India discovered: 'Many of our respondents do not want to own or use the kind of simple, affordable latrines that would save lives and reduce stunting . . . Why are such latrines socially unacceptable? Firstly, many people think that having such a latrine near the house would be ritually polluting . . . Muslims are generally less averse to owning and using affordable latrines, which need to have their pits emptied every few years, than Hindus, who tend to view such latrines as ritually impure and are extremely concerned about emptying pits, or having them emptied.' Are you hearing what I'm hearing? India is unique in the extent of this problem; its persistence is born of concerns over impurity. Aha, you say: 'caste'. Gandhi could have told you that, and he did. But do you think Indian policymakers will accept it? Not on your life. We will insist it is purely about getting more toilets to people—even though the toilets the government has built for many families are going unused: 'Forty per cent of

Hindus with a working government latrine regularly defecate in the open. In contrast, only about 7 per cent of Muslims with a working government latrine regularly defecate in the open.' There is something deep at work here, something that goes beyond easy technocratic solutions. Perhaps just building the toilets isn't enough. The big takeaway: even the best policy suggestions can founder on our innate stubbornness.

For the first time since Independence, there is perhaps a spot of hope that India will clean itself up. After all, there's a crisis, which means we might actually be forced to do something. Till now, we have used typical half-measures to approach a reform which should have been attacked with ferocity. And also because the new prime minister, Narendra Modi, is smart enough to actually figure out that this is as much a social change as anything else—and has campaigned for it in those terms, speaking of 'toilets over temples', and of open defecation as something that impinges on women's safety.

So, what does this disaster teach us?

First: don't be in denial. We have a problem with sanitation, which we should have openly acknowledged decades ago. Thanks to that, we have ducked doing anything actually painful.

Second: don't persist with problem policy. Clearly, all these years, whatever we thought we were doing to improve sanitation did not work. But we kept on doing it anyway.

Third: don't go in for half-measures. We have paid for a few government toilets to be built—and then not bothered to figure out why they were not being used.

Fourth: own your reform. If there is any hope of changing India, politicians have to make it the centrepiece of their politics. 'Reform by stealth' cannot continue—and it does not work all that well, either. Just because Indians are unconvinced about its benefits doesn't mean that it should be hidden from them; politics should work to convince them.

If anything, ninety years on, we have to acknowledge this: Mayo was partly right. We do have a problem. Mayo was a racist, and it would have been futile to expect respect from her. But, even then, we expected respect. And were furious when we didn't get it.

Respect is our birthright, apparently. We are very fond of demanding our birthrights. We are slightly less capable of figuring out what they, in fact, are.

THE MEMORY OF FACTORIES

Just as respect is not our birthright, neither is growth. An overconfidence about our destiny has been the hallmark of policymaking since 1991. It's almost as if we genuinely believe all the lies about ourselves we tell foreign investors. Never trust people who read their own PR.

If anything has emerged from our story so far, it is this: that we stop short of real reform. We think tinkering around a bit is the Indian Way. Gradualism. Are we not a 5000-year-old civilization? (We aren't, actually, but that would require another book to explain.) We cannot be hustled along by all you economists with all your theories. We are wiser than that. We have our Ways.

Here's why I think, in spite of all the disappointments that India has served up to optimists over and over and over again, that the rickety old bus that is the Indian economy could still discover hitherto unsuspected horsepower.

First, because I think that a genuine appreciation of the scale of the challenge, and of the need for real and painful change, has been built up. Remember the challenge: that 13 million young people enter the workforce every damned year. This is not something that any civilization, no matter how old it imagines itself, can endure unchanged. And the pressures that it creates within itself are explosive. Which is why, this time, there is a very palpable willingness to accept even painful change. We sense that, where we must go, there are no maps.

And growth itself has its pressures. Even rigid political systems in homogeneous societies struggle with the transformations imposed on them by sustained high growth—the People's Republic of China, for example. But when it is accompanied by a major demographic shift, then there are neither guides nor precedents. Yes, there are no maps; all we know is Here Be Dragons.

Throughout this book, the ghost of Indian manufacturing has sat at the table with us. We have turned our back on it for years, for our conscience is not easy to prick; it is only now, when we realize that there is no place for our young people to go, that we realize how important it is.

But here's the crucial, hopeful titbit: the need for manufacturing isn't something that only Delhi policy wonks or Wall Street analysts are talking about.

Let me tell you a story. This is a story from eastern Uttar Pradesh, one of the most difficult parts of India—fiendishly complex, byzantine in its politics of kinship and patronage, riven with division, and struggling under the burden of some of the worst human development indicators in the world. This is the region where the men of Padrauna sat outside their shuttered factory, desperate to protect its machinery from looters—that may include the factory's titular owner. This is the region where young men in Ayodhya, smartly dressed, signal their desperation to be your guide to the famed—and disputed—centre of the old temple town by rubbing their bellies in simulated hunger.

In the far southeast of this region lies the district of Mirzapur. It is poor even for eastern UP; not all of it is covered by the rich brown loam of the plains, for this is where the plateau begins, with its red earth and rock. Here, four of India's poorest states—Uttar Pradesh, Madhya Pradesh, Bihar and Chhattisgarh—meet. It is the home, among millions of others, of Ram Charan, a man who—like his father before him and his grandfather before that—plays the drum. He has never left Mirzapur; in fact, he hardly ever goes down to the district town, in the plains. But, he told me, his younger relatives are a problem. They want to leave. And they will have to, he added, dropping his voice; because if they stay, there will be trouble. They do not know how to behave. When he said this, there was no note of disapproval in his voice. For, when young Dalit men 'do not know how to behave' something else is being said: they do not know their place.

They will have to leave, he concluded, because there are no jobs here. This was a familiar refrain, so I nodded with an air of patience. He looked at me sharply and said, 'Once there could have been.' And then, with the help of a friend standing nearby, he ticked off the factories that had been within walking distance—cement, carpets, and glass. But they could not reopen, I told him; they might never make money in Mirzapur. He did not disagree; but patiently explained that I had missed his point. His point was that he knew, as did everyone around him, where jobs came from. They were not fools, he said, 'demanding jobs from nowhere'. They knew jobs came from factories. And if there was none here, the young men would be sent to where they were.

Jobs do not come from nowhere. They come from factories. And young people will move to where they are.

For decades, since Rao, our leaders have feared to tell us these truths. They have run from the needs and the consequences of reform. They have hidden what we need behind a bushel of evasions and promises and outright lies. Today, Indians already know. And their smarter politicians may have started agreeing with them, too.

The anticipation of real change has built up to a point where it is impossible for any politician to ignore, even given their history of pretending that the Indian people cannot endure anything but painfully gradual change. And people appreciate, also, the displacement real change might cause to their lives, and the social and personal costs—because, finally, the costs of not changing are so immediate and so overpowering that they fear not changing more than they fear change.

Stopping short of genuine reform has been our besetting sin. This time, it is no longer an option; and this time, it is no longer necessary. Our politics' job has been made so much easier—because circumstances have done the convincing for it.

Whatever else may have been behind Narendra Modi's clean sweep of India's left-behind north, it did reveal how widespread the expectation, and the demand, for the deepest change was. Modi was not a candidate who was expected to do anything by half-measures; he was not a candidate whom people looked at as anything but a radical break from the old order. He was not a candidate who they thought would shy away from inflicting pain, if he thought it was necessary. We can disagree about what Modi is, or what he has done; but what he is hoped to be is not something there can be disagreement about.

If he tinkers at the margins, if he stops short, it will be the Indian state's final betrayal of those who have so patiently expected so much from it. This time, I fear they will not be as quick to forgive.

FIVE BAD CHOICES

There are five bad choices in our past which have got us into trouble. And we show no signs of abandoning these horrible choices. Some are half-measures. Others are a product of the government's desire to, lapdog-like, please everyone who matters. We need to own up to how they've got us into trouble, and how we need to fix them.

Here are the five:

Private–public partnerships; our tendency to make 'special' exceptions to rules; being convinced that we can solve our energy problem safely and cheaply; our tendency to distrust market prices; and how we manage the environment.

DISSOLVING A PARTNERSHIP

The biggest and most urgent question, surely, is how government 'partners' with the private sector. Without that, we can't solve the under-capacity problem, the not-enough-bridges problem, that underlies everything else we're struggling with.

If the story of the last ten years has told us one thing, it is that the private sector cannot be forced by government to do what it is told, and it cannot be trusted by government to do what it says—it can only be expected to do what it wants. And it should be allowed to. But, if it is to be a 'partner', it cannot be expected to build vast bridges and not try to skim vast sums of money, too.

Worst of all, there is no reason to suppose that it does a great job. I have walked along more than one new flyover in Delhi in the deep of night, just a few weeks before it would open, and have been shocked by how casually work on which hundreds of lives depended was being carried out. We have been fortunate so far— but the danger signs are already visible. India's first landmark PPP in urban infrastructure was supposed to be the line of the Delhi Metro that connected its new airport with the centre of town. A high-speed luxury line. Wonderful. It got built, too—though over cost and over schedule. A few months later, it had to shut down.

Apparently, the ball bearings on which the rails were set simply couldn't take the speeds at which the train was supposed to go. Eventually, it reopened—though at the normal speeds of the Delhi Metro. Reliance Infrastructure, the private company in this case, left the project; nobody knows for certain whether it or the public company that runs the Delhi Metro should be held responsible for building an incredibly expensive high-speed rail line that cannot run at high speed.

You would think that a system which has had exactly zero major successes to boast of would be examined somewhat more critically. After all, every single PPP project has ended in one of two ways: either as an expensive and eye-catching failure or as a scandal of gargantuan proportions.

We need a smarter way to build infrastructure. We need another solution to that problem that has plagued every country since the Roman republic got rich men to build aqueducts if they wanted to be consul: How to pay for infrastructure.

There are a few ways to make PPPs work better. One is to recognize that the 'building' part of infrastructure—big, lumpy investment, insecure returns, lots of crazy risk to manage—requires completely different companies from the 'operating' part of infrastructure—with steady, long-term revenues, and largely predictable maintenance costs, and easily insurable risks. We need two different sets of infrastructure companies to do these two tasks.

If it were the case that the private sector could make money on infrastructure without cutting corners, we'd have honest money in it, not fly-by-night operators or big crony capitalists. What do I mean by honest money? Ordinary people's savings—as shown by their investments in the stock market, or by what banks do with their deposits. But, together, those account for only 35 per cent of the costs of public–private partnerships. And that share declined over time. But which investor would want to change that? It is unlikely that you will be able to find one person out of our 1.2 billion who will look at the bunch of infrastructure companies we have now, and say, 'I trust those guys with my savings. I think they have a proven track record. Also, they look honest.' Somehow, we need to change that.

And we need longer-term finance from the rest of the world, too. The Japanese and the Chinese, sure, they're willing to lend us a bunch, because they have all these savings and nowhere to put them. But our need is so great that we can't ignore the pools of money in the West, pools that are freer than those from East Asia. We need long-term money from the West to come to India; we need the California state pensions authority, say, to come and put their accumulated savings into building a railway line or port in India that will only pay off over a twenty-year horizon. You know when the headlines keep on saying 'pension and insurance reform' is needed, and you turn the page to read about the cricket team? That's exactly what they're talking about: letting pension funds and the other big reserves of patient, sensible capital from the rest of the world into the Indian economy so that we don't have to rely on our own robber barons.

One other way—and this will take longer, perhaps—is to work on smarter people in government, people who might do a better job of regulating private-sector 'partners'. That requires, of course, a wholesale restructuring of the government. But, in the end, regulation of these projects might be more trouble than it's worth. If it's the government that must evaluate risk, impose safety standards, control costs—then why not build it yourself?

That is the least popular, but best answer, I'd say. Pay for it ourselves; bid out sections of the job to private contractors, if necessary, but without any clever non-monetary sweeteners, which is where the lies and the deception and the corruption creep in. Nor can cost be the only criterion, ever. The wisest thing ever said about

PPPs came from an American astronaut: 'It's a very sobering feeling to be up in space and realize that one's safety factor was determined by the lowest bidder on a government contract.'

Ah, you say, but don't you remember? We can't pay for it, right? We can't afford to build stuff without the private sector paying up.

Well, it's tough. But it turns out that we pay even when the private sector is supposed to be paying. Remember, it was supposed to pay half of the $1 trillion we needed. And the reason we needed PPPs was that the government just didn't have the money to do it all. But this is how much of a failure the PPP era was: what happened was the opposite of what had been planned. Instead of the private sector upping its contribution, the amount the private partner put into the average PPP project *decreased* dramatically.

Look, because we've kept out foreign long-term capital, and we've turned off small Indian investors, we have a set of incumbents in the infrastructure sector with very special qualities: they can 'manage' political risk. In one of those very few iron laws that economics has, this means that they want supersized returns—at least 16 per cent, according to one survey, excluding the money they expected to legally make on the side. Is that what you get on your fixed deposit? *After* inflation? Thought not.

But does revenue from infrastructure give you big money, normally? Come on. You need a hell of a lot of crumpled ten-rupee notes handed in at toll gates to make the sort of money these guys expect. Naturally, they want more; and that's how they bully the government into giving them an extra share afterwards. Or they want something else—land, or coal. That has its own dangers.

Now, we're busy trying to ensure that the projects these guys started to build really get finished. We'll bend environmental rules to make that happen. We'll change the terms of the contracts. We'll give them cheaper raw materials and promise them higher prices. We will ensure they get access to more money even though they haven't paid back what they have taken in the past. We will put our entire banking and financial sector at risk, and then give shaky banks lakhs of crores of taxpayer cash to shore them up, all in order to ensure these companies and their wealthy-as-sin owners stay engaged. That is completely wrong. Even if you want the projects to eventually go through—a decision that the market, and neither politicians nor bureaucrats should make—you don't need these companies and these owners. They made bad decisions. Take away their assets and give them to someone else. Restart the infrastructure sector, sure. But that involves shutting it down first.

As I said: building and running infrastructure require two completely different sorts of companies. One makes money, one spends it—but that doesn't mean that you can try to put an 'equals to' sign between the two and hope it all works out.

The private sector has had a great run. But, if we really want to solve India's chronic problem of under-capacity, we clearly can't expect the government to sit back, watch TV, and hope the companies will do everything we need them to without causing any trouble. Indulgent-Parent Government must go. Stern-Parent-Who-Supervises-Homework-Closely Government must take its place.

Either the government vastly increases the number and training and pay of its regulators, so it can keep a closer eye on its partners. Or it vastly increases the number and training and pay of its own builders. One of those two has to happen. And it won't be cheap.

TRUST PRICES

The second thing that needs to change: how we price our natural resources. The era of cheap coal, assigned spectrum, free land, abundant groundwater has to end. I don't believe that the reason we just handed these things over to the private sector was simply because we were building opportunities for bribery; that's been the narrative for the past few years, and it's crashingly foolish as well as short-sighted. As the story of the Tata mines—and the prosperity they continue to deliver to 'India's best company'—reveals, there's nothing new about handing out natural resources to companies. Nor is it unusual—China's world-beating steel industry was built, in ten years, on input subsidies. But it can't last.

One big reason is because it is counterproductive. It changes and warps the reasons why people want to get into industries. Power plants actually become about mining coal; telecom becomes about reselling spectrum; highway construction becomes about building up a land bank; steel becomes about iron-ore exports. Instead of involving the private sector in building India, this policy puts them in charge of exploiting India. Which, naturally, they will do with both hands, as also toes, and teeth, if allowed.

There is a very simple rule about natural-resource extraction.

Wherever or whenever companies have been unleashed uncontrolled on natural resources, powerful cabals have formed. Oligarchies. They have brought governments to their knees—which some think may have happened here recently, when Reliance Industries was bargaining hard for a higher gas price and south India suffered under debilitating power cuts. Terrible tension has built up between governments and powerful oligarchs—look at the beginning of Putin's rule in Russia. Or the tension is between foreign and domestic commercial interests—the history of twentieth-century Iran provides an example of why that's a problem.

The best way to control private companies is the price mechanism. It keeps them honest, to whatever degree they can be. In most cases, prices work—like in coal, which should be auctioned rather than promised. In some cases, they work less well—such as in natural gas, where there is no such thing as a 'market price' for natural gas, because the damn thing can't travel anywhere without a pipeline or being artificially liquefied. For some reason, the government wants to allow natural gas—where there is no market and the private-sector companies in charge of getting it out of the ground can thus overcharge customers—to follow a price mechanism. But for coal, where there could be a market, the public-sector company in charge of getting it out of the ground has been told to hand it over to its private-sector customers heavily discounted. I couldn't even begin to speculate why that's the case.

India has to start trusting prices more. The government can't fiddle around with them forever, and think they're very clever—because the private sector is way better paid, and way smarter, than any collection of overworked bureaucrats. The best way to control a private company is through another private company, and that's exactly what prices do.

All companies play hard once natural resources are involved, because the pay-offs are just so huge. Consider, for example, the case of the two big power plants built by Tata and Adani at Mundra in Gujarat. The two of them won bids to supply electricity to western states; they promised to price the power they sold cheaper than their competitors did. Unfortunately for Tata, Adani, power consumers in western India, and good sense in general, it turns out that the two companies had not bothered to calculate—or had deliberately ignored—the chance that the price of the imported coal they burned to turn into electricity might increase. When it did, sharply, a couple of years ago, they found they weren't making as much money as they'd like—and so demanded that the western states pay more for their electricity. Eventually, the electricity regulator gave in and raised the price that the states would pay Tata and Adani. And are you ready for the best bit? When, in August 2014, the Supreme Court looked like it might force Tata and Adani to stick to their contracts, they simply shut down large parts of their plants and caused rolling blackouts across the north and the west of India. Told you: they play hard.

The government's reaction to all this has been to minimize the amount of coal that is actually sold on the open market. That's right; it wants more coal to be sent at heavily subsidized prices to various companies, and less sold on the open market so that the right price is found. Essentially, we're doubling down on a flawed strategy. You shouldn't give the private sector free stuff—it's amazing how quickly they get addicted to it.

And free stuff makes you stupid. It makes you lazy. It makes you corrupt and it makes you dirty. The Centre for Science and Environment releases rankings every now and then of companies in various sectors. Which are doing well in terms of minimizing their environmental impact? Which kill the fewest fuzzy animals? Etc., etc. You know what they discovered? Here's their head, Sunita Narain, writing for the *Business Standard*: 'It is interesting to note that the top three companies work against economic odds. They import fuel and do not have captive mines for iron ore. In gas–based Essar Steel at Hazira and Ispat Industries in Raigad energy costs are as high as 23–30 per cent of the turnover. In Rashtriya Ispat Nigam in Visakhapatnam iron ore constitutes 17 per cent of its turnover and coking coal another 31 per cent. But in Tata Steel in Jamshedpur, Jindal Steel and Power in Raigarh or SAIL in Rourkela, the cost of iron ore is only 3–10 per cent of the turnover.'

Yes, that's right. The companies that have to deal with the market, with properly priced inputs, are the ones that don't depopulate and despoil their surroundings.

All coal, all natural resources of any kind for which an open and free market can be constructed, should be sold on an open market—a continuing open market, not just through auctions which can be rigged.

Yes, all natural resources. Land, too. Iron ore. Even groundwater, if we can work out how. Will this be painful? Yes. It will mean a ton of contracts will have to be reworked, and the private sector will scream. But it's essential.

THE REAL PRICE OF COAL

The next two things that must change are related to why natural resources should be priced truthfully, and even more closely related to each other. The first is our magical thinking about energy, in which we pretend we become 'energy independent' of the rest of the world easily and cheaply. And the other is how we manage our environment.

And both start with our coal obsession. India has the fourth- or possibly fifth-largest reserves of coal in the world. We are tired of paying for imported petroleum or natural gas, and policymakers worry that in the future it will be the most import-dependent large economy in the world unless ways to power itself from its own resources are found. In other words, we need lots more coal out of the ground. Lots.

But here's the problem. We need to price it properly. It can't go cheap to power plants or factories. But that's exactly what has been assumed will happen. Because of that, India has built a vast coal-powered electricity infrastructure. And it has accelerated its dependence on coal. The economist Subir Gokarn has calculated that, for five years before 2007, coal-fired power plants constituted one-third of all new electricity-generation capacity; over the next few years, they were half of new capacity; and recently, all additional plants have been coal-fired. But coal mining hasn't grown at the same rate.

The question is: Should it? Everyone assumes it should; and the answer is to open up more areas for exploration. Coal India, the state-owned mining monopoly, has 55,000 acres, at least, of forest land that people want it to start mining in. Private companies assigned coal mines have also sometimes been given forest land. If we just start digging in these places, our problems will be solved.

But I think they won't. The real reason that we are convinced we must get all the coal out of the ground even at the price of destroying whatever forest cover we have left is because we have massively over-invested in coal-fired power plants. And we are unwilling, as a country, to take the hit for that bad decision. We don't want to import coal either, because that will mean being dependent on the rest of the world, and we don't like that—never mind that the likelihood of every coal producer in the world ganging up on India and refusing to sell it coal is vanishingly small, so what are we scared of?

Today, coal provides 65 per cent of our energy, but even then coal-fired power plants are always hungry for more. We need to reverse course. Coal-fired electricity is cheap as compared to the alternatives, we are told. But, truthfully, that's only if we say coal is cheap, cheap, cheap, and we don't price many of the other inputs they use, such as the copious fresh water they consume. Once we start doing that, then suddenly electricity generated from coal doesn't seem so cheap at all. It's looked cheap so far—but that's purely artificial.

So what do we do? First of all, on the environment: remember, the price system is your friend. If you price water for coal plants properly, then coal-fired electricity gets cheaper. If you price forest reserves properly, reflecting the fact that they're increasingly scarce and valuable, instead of being abundant and therefore free, then coal itself gets cheaper. And so does iron ore, and bauxite, and any number of minerals.

This will lead to howls of outrage. Minerals, after all, led to a great deal of prosperity. Iron ore exports to China are what kept us in dollars for years; and without minerals much cheaper than they are in the rest of the world, why would anyone set up a plant in India, we're asked. The answer is simple: you can't fight true prices forever. If you claim that bauxite, say, is available free, and an entrepreneur comes in and builds a factory to produce aluminium from that bauxite, a time comes when you get caught out in that lie. For that bauxite has a price. It has a price in forests destroyed, and that price will eventually have to be paid; it has a price because someone has rights to that land, and that price will eventually have to be paid. If you reflect that eventual price in the claims you make up front, only then will you avoid trouble down the road. In other words, we have no free minerals. We have minerals that cost as much as they do elsewhere in the world—because they're under the ground, and we're using the ground for other things. As people everywhere do.

So far, our approach to environmental regulation has been simple: we build up a complex system and then ignore it when it suits us. Remember all the examples of double standards over the past few years? But the answer to that is clarity of the highest order, not more exceptions and shortcuts.

Since 1991 and Narasimha Rao's original sin of concealing reform under a patina of lies and misdirection and denials, successive Indian governments have adopted a common approach. They have tried to avoid changing laws or regulations, but promised to apply them less restrictively. They have changed the rules of administration, not the laws in the books. And this is precisely why growth has slowed; this is precisely why corruption seems to have exploded. Environmental regulation is the best example, in some ways, though not the only one. The government's claim that 'self-certification' and labour-inspector websites are the same as changing the labour law that actually oppresses entrepreneurs is another example.

But look at environmental regulation. We have so many laws, and not one effort to make them effective, and clear and easy to follow. Or look at the regulations governing mining. In late 2014, the Supreme Court cancelled all coal-mining licences that had been allotted since 1993. Why? Not because the assignments had been accompanied by corruption. Not because they violated various environmental laws. But because they violated the letter and spirit of an Indira-era law that said only the Government of India could mine coal. Not one government had bothered to change that law—an error that threw sectors comprising 5 per cent of India's GDP into a maelstrom of chaos and confusion overnight. Many in industry trust the prime minister; some trust their local chief ministers or a bureaucrat they are dealing with. But reform and investment of the scale that India needs should not depend on having a leader you trust. It must depend on having laws and regulations that survive leaders you don't. The old reform paradigm—in which a powerful man says 'these laws are bad, we will not enforce them'—has outlived its effectiveness.

So, change the law to make it transparent and fair. Then apply it, transparently and fairly. Have measurable, justifiable norms. Make sure people pay for despoiling the environment, and don't imagine it is their right to do so. And more problems than we can imagine will go away.

The reason we crave energy independence is that we feel insecure being dependent on the rest of the world for our fuel. But, just as we price things wrong if they lie in our forests instead of at our ports, we magnify those dangers, while minimizing those that can come from exploiting our own mineral reserves to the fullest. This is a book about economic threats to Indian prosperity, and not about political threats to the Indian government. But the baseline is this: nothing damages growth more than political instability or violence. Nothing makes you less appealing as an investment destination. Whether it be Naxalism, Maoism, left-wing extremism, 'Gandhians with guns', or some movement with an unknown name and ideology that's being incubated right now, you want to deprive them of their oxygen—exploitation. People, for reasons coldly rational, must be given a degree of control over their local environments and their livelihoods. They must be given property rights and personal autonomy—or they will revolt, inevitably. Price *that* into your minerals and see how cheap they are.

Trust prices. Trust prices, and you then trust people.

TRAINS AND PANELS

It's because we don't trust prices, or people, that we're thinking about energy all wrong. India has been starved of energy for so long that we think it's only fair that we hand it out at as low a cost as possible. When you do that, however, you get Kanpur. You get a place where everyone is aggrieved about not getting electricity, where everyone wants to steal it, where nobody makes money from supplying it, and so, where none is supplied. People are willing to pay for electricity that comes in 24 hours a day, seven days a week. They are willing to pay to have the choice to turn on a switch. If the electricity costs more, then they will not turn on the switch as often. But they want that switch to work.

This applies, of course, to all our public infrastructure. Many commuters in Mumbai would be willing to pay more for trains in which there's a higher chance of them getting one of those much-desired seats. Or, if one is to speak of the holy grail, for commuter trains which are air-conditioned, so one arrives at Churchgate looking more like a stockbroker of high repute who manages vast amounts of money and less like the old rag his wife uses to clean the kitchen counter. The central government, which was voted in on the promise of change and firmness, did not exactly live up to expectations when it wimped out and withdrew an increase in commuter rail fares in Mumbai.

Mumbai's commuter trains are, in many ways, emblematic of what has to change. They are a source of endless fascination, and not just to the 7.5 million people they carry daily. We love them. But they have been completely unchanged since when? The 1960s? The 1930s? Even Western Railways is uncertain about exactly when the interiors were last redesigned. Nor is this a random point about aesthetics. You see, the carriages were designed to take 200 people at a time. But, at rush hour, one can take more than 500 people. There is even an official term for this (as I said, I love bureaucratese): 'Super-Dense Crushload'. A train has reached SDC levels, the *Sunday Times* reported in 2009, when it has 550 people in every carriage—or 16 people per square metre. Typically for Mumbai, tolerance has been increasing over time: in 1998, SDC levels were 10 people per square metre. (I know this couldn't be because people are getting thinner.)

They're so crowded that the windows have to be kept open, for ventilation. People vie for window seats, in contestation so fierce that it can cause old friends to never again speak to each other. Of the competition's lucky winners, 16 or so will be hit and maimed by stones, which kids throw at the trains' open windows for fun. They're so crowded that people can hang out of the holes where other less adventurous countries would have doors. Every year, hundreds of those people fall on to the tracks and die.

Also, Mumbai is very humid, and not all of the 15 other people sharing your square metre smell great.

We get what we pay for. Mumbai's suburban rail is the cheapest form of transport in the world. It costs us less than 10 paise per kilometre to travel. The government wimped out of raising it to 20 paise per kilometre or something. Not only do fares this cheap mean that the railways lose money on what should be a profitable service, but it also means that they never have the money to replace or refurbish or upgrade the carriages.

I think it's ridiculous not to raise fares. At the very least, make the trains pay for themselves. Subsidies to the trains don't reach the city's poor—a World Bank study revealed that the poorest 27 per cent of Mumbai's population receives only 15 per cent of local rail subsidies. In fact, allow the railways to invest in better services, and let people pay a bit more. Once people see that services are improving, they'd be willing to. In 2015, a couple of air-conditioned carriages might be introduced as an experiment, costing between 28 and 35 paise per kilometre. I'm betting enough people will pay the extra bit.

(Air-conditioning, after all, is the greatest triumph of human ingenuity. We in the tropics were not meant to leave our houses in the noonday sun, but if we are to be forced to by this capitalism idea that the temperate West has inflicted on us, then air-conditioning is the one thing that makes our lives bearable. It is a talisman of modernity, an imposition of human will on an unforgiving and unfriendly environment, and the most wholesome of addictions. One blast of freezing, dry air restores decency and humanity to people who were in danger of melting into stinking puddles of anger. In fact, I would support any party that suggested a Right to AC Act: everyone south of whichever latitude Jammu is on deserves access to air-conditioning. And I am willing to pay, to sacrifice. Turn off my TV, my fridge, my laptop, and my lights, if you must, but leave me my air-conditioning and my thoughts. It is the one thing that raises life in the tropics above mere survival, and on this point at least, if nothing else, I am in agreement with Lee Kuan Yew. And with anyone who has ever been inside a Delhi mall in May. Want to supersize growth and productivity? Invest in air-conditioning. One study of typists in 1950s America discovered that they typed

25 per cent faster when air-conditioning was introduced. In other words, AC is better than the Internet even.)

As with electricity, people will be willing to pay for train services if they think they're being treated as consumers and not as cattle. We have to start accepting that people will pay fees for the services that the government provides them, as long as they see the prices as fair—and the services as improved, and available. We may not be the most perspicacious of countries, but even we have figured out by now that 'free' means 'rationed'.

With electricity, for example, that's priced close to what it actually costs to produce in terms of coal and water and forests destroyed, people will use it more carefully—as long as it's always there. And once ordinary people pay properly for electricity, then we will be able to pay power plants a reasonable return—while charging them the real prices of all the raw material they consume. At every step of the way, we need prices to be allowed to work; right now, every step of the way, we are trying to *stop* them from working. Want to know how we are performing the miracle of simultaneously destroying our forests, infuriating the people who live there, importing vast amounts of coal, charging high prices for electricity, *and* delivering rolling power cuts? That's what happens when you pretend you can micro-manage a complex production chain like electricity's—and, somehow, keep prices down every step of the way. What are we, Superman? I bet even on Krypton they charged full price for electricity.

OK, it's clear that I don't like coal. And I think that if we priced it properly, as well as the things we produce from it, then we would paradoxically be less dependent on it. But, you say, isn't it the case that we need it? After all, what other ways can we create energy?

Look, I don't pretend we can give up on coal. I do know that we shouldn't overestimate how much we need it. And, yes, there are other ways to power India.

Consider renewables. At some point in the next few years, solar power is going to really take off. But we have to be careful to get it right. Solar power should not just be about massive farms of solar cells out in the desert somewhere. Those, it turns out, struggle to make money—and so, naturally, will attract subsidies and the crazy rent-seeking that follows. Instead, solar power should also be about a closer control on your energy supply—micro-grids, rooftop panels, and such like. Walk down some streets in power-deficient Patna, and you see entire shops devoted to solar-powered tube lights and fans; a single panel, connected to a single light or a single fan. This can change people's lives, and that's why they're buying them in huge numbers. Decentralize how power is generated and consumed, and suddenly fewer people start stealing it. The key to making power profitable and always-on is in that: eliminating the 25 per cent 'leakage', or theft. And that can come through encouraging them to control their own power. Generate it locally.

In India, we don't like innovations. Solar power, in spite of government subsidies and favourable policies, has struggled with one big *faux* flaw: it doesn't fit into the rigid 'grid' system we have developed for coal- or gas–based power plants. Solar energy's output fluctuates, because we can't control the sun. It isn't as easy to predict how much it will be putting into the 'grid' that connects all power producers. And so, regardless of the best intentions of forward-thinking people in Delhi, the actual people who operate the national power grid discriminate against solar power.

Solar power has to go off the grid. Let rows of households wire themselves up and together get a solar power set-up that takes care of at least some of their needs. Do this in enough places, and you'll see the pressure on 'regular' power plants ease.

This is an idea that makes perfect sense. Naturally, it grossly displeases the government, though it won't tell us why. Thus, in many places, you need to fill out reams of paperwork just to link a few panels together and set up a local micro-grid. In effect, you'd have to register as a power producer, and get all the permissions, as if you're setting up a big thermal power plant in your backyard. And one wing of the government doesn't like solar being connected to the big national grid—but other wings, in some places, make such connections mandatory. Yes, they are exactly that schizophrenic.

Oh, and there's nuclear power.

What's that you say? It's dangerous? Right. How many people have been killed by nuclear power? Not a lot you can recall, right? In fact, there have been fewer than 20 in India over the past half century. A few hundred altogether everywhere, many of them in occupational accidents. The only time a nuclear accident has killed people who weren't employees was at Chernobyl; the UN said 43 people died, of whom 15 were neither employees nor emergency staff.

You know, if you are going to go nuts and claim power plants are killing people, can you not pick the form of energy with the *most* spectacular record of safety, and the one *least* likely to kill innocent bystanders?

One of the leading scientific voices in the climate debate is Columbia's James Hansen. He wrote a nice peer-reviewed paper a few years ago trying to work out the real human costs of coal, as opposed to nuclear power. Nuclear power, he calculated, just in the nine years between 2000 and 2009, 'prevented an average of 76,000 deaths'. You see, we *know* coal kills people far more often than the same amount of nuclear power. You know the number of people killed by, say, the Tarapur nuclear plant in densely populated Thane district near Mumbai? Zero. This does somewhat undermine the claim that we are unable to manage nuclear power well, that we'd cut corners, that none of us would sleep safe in our beds if there was a nuclear power plant next door. In fact, there's a nuclear reactor right in the middle of Mumbai, in Trombay, and everyone even forgets it's there. Zero, zero, zero.

But researchers at Harvard's Kennedy School calculated, in a 2013 paper, that the average number of premature deaths of locals caused by each coal-fired power plant in India is 650. That's 650 *per year*. Six hundred and fifty. 650.

This is one of those points where one just runs out of things to say other than, over and over again: '650–zero.' '650–zero.' '650–zero.' '650–zero.'

All I can really add is this final point, meant for those anti-nuclear types who I must assume skipped maths class: 650 is more than zero. It is an infinite number of times more. We cannot calculate how many times more than zero 650 is. All of mathematics fails to provide us with a number for how much safer than coal plants nuclear power has been in India.

Long-term energy independence is realistically unachievable through coal. Because we will never get enough out of the ground to make us truly independent of the rest of the world's resources; and because long before we get as much out of the ground as we want, we will have sparked off a forest fire of insurgency; and because if we're paying the right price for coal, it might cost as much to import it, anyway. So, if we want to pay less for foreign oil, we need to look to the future: to nuclear power, and to renewable energy.

Sadly, we have over-invested so much in coal and natural gas, so much money might be lost, and so much karma for bad decisions is to be avoided that even very smart people in government and the private sector might find themselves mysteriously unable to understand these very simple points.

WHO'S YOUR DADDY?

You may have noticed a certain nagging similarity between all the errors that we've talked about so far, between all these things that need to change but haven't yet. And yes, there is indeed something that they have in common.

India's government remains convinced it knows best. Most policy that it claims helps business also increases government power. It increases bureaucrats' discretion, and their ability to choose who becomes rich. Post-1991 India has become far better at hiding its controlling, socialistic instincts. It camouflages them behind words like 'incentives' and 'subsidies' and 'input concessions'; but it's still all about government control. Cheap natural resources? The government determines who gets them and why. Environmental regulations? Let's just make everyone criminals and then a kangaroo court of apparatchiks will decide who gets into trouble. Paternalism is the founding philosophy of the Indian state.

And that leads us to the final thing that India needs to change, but doesn't seem to be getting around to doing: its tendency to 'pick winners'.

The question of industrial policy, as it's technically called, is much debated. In places like South Korea, it seems to have worked—the government went out and picked sectors that could flourish in the global economy, it partnered with private-sector companies like Samsung and Daewoo and made them industrial giants. But for every country where it worked, like Korea or Taiwan, there are places where it didn't, like Ghana or Brazil. The difference, people say, is that Brazil may have focused on internal demand instead of world trade, or that it had too much debt, or that it was a natural-resource exporter, or any of a number of reasons. (I am always suspicious when I am given more than one reason for something.) But, even if any of that's true, even within the countries that made a go of their 'picking winners' strategies, you rarely hear about the bets that failed—the sectors that didn't take off, the companies that were duds. Here's one: the automobile sector in Taiwan. The government's been pushing it since 1953. Failed miserably. There are dozens of others.

Frankly, in India, which do you think is more likely—that the government will pick the right sectors and the right companies, or the wrong ones?

One of the very few departments in New Delhi that actually got shut down in the early 1990s—when reform carefully skirted around the idea that bureaucrats should lose their jobs or even do another job—was something called the Directorate-General of Technical Development. The DGTD, back in the bad old days, was in charge of telling companies which bit of technology to use. Thanks to it, and to the whole industrial policy of which it was a crown jewel, India had developed a supremely uncompetitive manufacturing sector—one that collapsed into dust at the first breeze of global competition. The lesson from experiences like the DGTD is that industrial policy should stay far away, in particular, from things that involve the government picking appropriate technology, something that can change swifter than a civil servant changes ties.

But, instead, the government is focusing on a Rs 10,000-crore venture capital fund for high-tech sectors. It's set aside Rs 20,000 crore for the next few years to fund 'electronics manufacturing clusters'.

Look, I get it. The guys in Delhi are justly irritated that Indians want lots of nice mobile phones and tablets, but we keep on importing the damned things from China or Taiwan or wherever. Can't we build our own?

We already have some preferences for domestic electronics manufacturing—making imports slightly more expensive than making stuff at home. That's how Micromax, for example, can capture a reasonable share of the market. But look more closely at your Micromax phone. The screen will be made in China, the battery in Taiwan, the circuits in South Korea. At best, it will be assembled in Gurgaon. Micromax is what, in the 1980s, used to be called a 'screwdriver company', where everything that mattered was imported—but the screwdriver that turned to assemble it was in India, in order to claim tax advantages. That's what happens when you set up domestic-preference systems; and it will get worse, the stronger the preference is.

I'm not claiming that government can't help things along at all—after all, it could serve as a buyer, if nothing else. In particular, for high-tech military stuff, which you could legitimately say needs to be made here for security reasons. The United States Department of Defence was a big consumer of high technology back in the World War II era and shortly after, and helped get the transistor going among many other innovations.

Equally odd, if not odder, is the idea of government running a venture capital fund for local innovation. Think about it: private capital will always figure out where high-tech is going quicker than government will. It backs the right horses, not government. You know what would work instead? That the government doesn't insist that everyone investing in a start-up list on their forms everyone unto the seventh generation who ever gave them money. If you want to help a little plant grow, figure out why it isn't getting sunlight. Don't move it to under a tube light and then buy a diesel generator to keep the tube light running.

Yup, the domestic market for electronics is huge. There's enough demand here for companies to invest—if they think they'd profit off it. If they don't think they can make profits off it, work out why. Don't give them money so everyone can pretend they're making a profit, when they aren't.

This is, at worst, state control and inward-looking protectionism. At best, it is benign industrial policy. Both require you to assume that bureaucrats know best. When it succeeds, it is on those occasions when bureaucrats actually *do* know best. Look within yourself and ask if it could happen here.

These strategies are not very different from what we tried in the 1950s and the 1980s. And, again, I want to emphasize that, under some circumstances, they can work. We had a decent growth rate under Nehru and again under Rajiv. But there are times and places where industrial policy works—in particular, when a country is plagued with failures and gaps in its markets. It very emphatically does not work when the country is plagued with failures of the state.

Like everything else that's patchwork, this was also on the United Progressive Alliance's agenda in 2004. In 2005, the UPA passed the Special Economic Zone Act, which is the gold standard for piecemeal thinking, for picking winners—and similarly deserves a Golden Globe for failing, and an Oscar for doing so repeatedly and yet somehow surviving. (*Really* long death scene.)

Here's how things started. Before 1991, someone decided to set up little 'export promotion zones' or EPZs in relatively underdeveloped areas, where Indian companies would set up shop and produce cheap clothing, say, for the Western market. These zones would be exempt from some of the more onerous regulations the rest of India was subject to, all the ones that people generally complained about. Naturally, not just anyone could set up shop there. You had to prove your worth, your honour, your good intentions—several times over, in triplicate, and ideally in a small envelope as well.

For some reason, these failed to take off. Death #1.

Then, in 2000, a man named Murasoli Maran—India's commerce minister, and named for the newspaper he used to edit, which is confusing, but also the kind of thing that happens with hardcore intellectual-politicians, of which he definitely was one—took a trip to China. There he saw the wonders of Shenzhen, the Special Economic Zone at the mouth of the Pearl river, just upriver from Hong Kong and downriver from a vast hinterland. Shenzhen was not quite what it is today, with 15 million people, a super-busy container port, and an appropriately tasteless amusement park which has one-third scale replicas of the Eiffel Tower, the Taj Mahal and the Pyramids all next to each other. But it certainly wasn't the sleepy fishing village it was in 1979, when Deng, seemingly offhandedly, suggested that the local government—if it was so determined to reform and export and all that jazz—'set aside an area and call it a special zone'. (After all, Deng pointed out—precedent being all-important in those days, and an idea was only truly sanctified if Mao had done it—there had been a special zone back in 1940, on the border with the Japanese and the Nationalist Chinese. The Party had earned money for its weapons by growing and selling opium in that Special Economic Zone, one of those fun bits of Chinese history the People's Republic generally forgets to mention.) Deng's suggestion had taken root and blossomed; Shenzhen had links to the outside world via Hong Kong, and to the people and resources of interior China via the Pearl river, and its vast scale—400 square kilometres—had allowed an entire ecosystem to develop free of the restraints of the rest of China.

Anyway, Maran was duly impressed, though presumably not as impressed as he would have been today by the one-third scale

Eiffel Tower, and when he returned to India, he decided that EPZs would henceforth be our own Special Economic Zones, or SEZs. Changes would be made to the regulations, those exact changes that had been holding the EPZs back from success. SEZs would be three times as large as EPZs! And private developers would be allowed! No other major changes were, of course, necessary. Lots of tinkering with the regulations was enough.

For some reason, these also failed to take off. Death #2.

Then, in 2004, the UPA came into office, all bright-eyed and bushy-tailed and energetic and determined to make a difference. (How sweet it is to be young, how bitter the draught of age.) It examined the SEZ problem and at once saw the flaw. There was no Law. The UPA firmly believed the Law was the Thing, and the Thing was the Law, and they were one and the same. Legislate employment, and people would have it; legislate food, and they would have it; legislate small tins of sardines falling from the sky, and people would not leave home without an umbrella and a can-opener. How, then, could you have SEZs without an SEZ Act? And all the problems would be fixed this time. The new SEZs would be twice as large as the old SEZs! And private developers would take the lead! No other major changes were, of course, necessary. Lots of tinkering, etc., etc.

For some reason, these too failed to take off. Death #3.

Wait, you say, that isn't what the numbers say. The numbers say that, within eighteen months, 237 new SEZs were set up, when the UPA had inherited only seven. By 2012, there were almost 600, with a total area of over 700 square kilometres—bigger than Mumbai.

Well, yes. A lot of people did sign up. But it wasn't exactly the kind of crowd that we were hoping for. You see, the government was offering to help you acquire the SEZ land, right? So, thought India's clever and public-spirited businessmen, why not sign up for an SEZ, and get our hands on large amounts of increasingly valuable land? Of those 600-odd SEZs, less than a third actually operate. The rest are simply land banks for private developers. Oh, and the main tenant of most of those that operate? The information technology sector—not textiles or manufacturing, as planned. The IT companies simply wanted to ensure that the tax breaks that they had been promised under a previous legislation wouldn't be taken away, and so they relocated to low-tax SEZs. A large part of SEZs' not-very-impressive export earnings are thus from IT companies which would have been bringing home that money anyway.

Remember, the point of SEZs was that they would be so large that they would create little self-contained economies, where the regular rules of doing business in India would no longer apply. Shenzhen was a little Hong Kong in the People's Republic; India's SEZs were to be little Chinas. As my colleague Kanika Datta has pointed out, that doesn't quite work when your SEZs are, some of them, as small as a single square kilometre. (Some IT-related SEZs are—a building. One building. Well done, whoever signed off on those. I hope your retirement is comfortable.) The largest Indian SEZ would have been 140 square kilometres, less than half Shenzhen's size—and even that didn't take off. Too much land had to be acquired and there were the usual protests.

In general, if companies come to you and complain that they want to leave SEZs because the tax breaks aren't high enough to keep them there, the SEZ is failing in its purpose. It isn't supposed to be a low-tax enclave; it's supposed to be a high-connectivity enclave that just happens to use temporarily low taxes to keep a lid on companies' set-up costs.

And so, I repeat: Death #3.

The problem is that this is not the final death. Once again, plans to revive SEZs of various shapes and forms are being suggested— and most of them involve restoring tax concessions, which private companies insist is all they really need.

When the Shenzhen SEZ was created in 1980, it was in a country struggling with the after-effects of titanic ideological disputes, in which millions died. SEZs were a way of allowing a little space for rational economics in a political set-up which simply couldn't bend that easily. It was an artefact of its time and place. It succeeded because it was as if another Hong Kong had been set up, not because of some magic inherent in the very idea of a special zone. Indian politicians are, generally, lesser men than Deng—perhaps because they have had to confront fewer obstacles. Deng, in their place, would see no need for an SEZ, but our leaders do, because SEZs mean they don't have to repeal any bad laws—they just have to pass another bad law. And then they can tell foreign investors that we, too, have areas that are just like China.

The simple truth is that SEZs are a declaration of failure, not of hope. They say: we cannot hope to reform and repair our country. We might be able to fence off these few square kilometres, quarantine them from the awfulness of the rest of our beloved homeland, and hope that somehow a world-beating export sector is created in them. Within these few square kilometres, we have gleaming infrastructure! A well-trained workforce! And weather like Southern California! Cross that bridge, though, and you're back in India, and there's nothing we can do about that.

Think about it for a moment. If we think certain policies will work inside an SEZ to enhance production, why on earth should they be restricted to an SEZ? The only reason that they are is that we do not wish to make the political case for why these policies are, indeed, good and valuable.

Because we don't want to own the reforms process, because we always stop short of the hard work and pain that real reform entails, we stop short of what we need: to turn the whole of India into a Special Economic Zone.

THAT PATCHWORK FEELING

Throughout this book, traffic has kept on cropping up as a metaphor. We've talked about how the smooth ride from the Delhi airport is interrupted by the irruption of a terribly planned flyover; about how only one bridge has been built of an entire island-hopping chain of bridges that was supposed to decongest Mumbai, and so you fly off that bridge into traffic-jams-as-usual.

That, right there, is what SEZs are about. That patchwork, piecemeal feeling is the primary characteristic of Indian economic policy. We work on 'de-bottlenecking'—trying to work out what is holding up an economic process, and removing or bypassing that specific obstruction. Of course, that means we immediately land up at another dashed obstruction.

We should, instead, be working to remove all those obstructions at one go. Or, in fact, ensuring that they simply melt away. Try to tackle one obstruction at a time, and you are stuck in traffic for what seems like forever. Hit a green corridor, create an expressway, and you sail through to your destination. (OK, now I'm going to stop with this metaphor, while I'm ahead.)

We focus on these patchwork solutions, on tinkering, not only because we are lazy, or half-hearted, or unwilling to stand up and say: Yes, reform is good. It is also because we have not been able to get rid of the idea that our government will be able to identify each individual bottleneck and apply a bit of legal or extra-legal lubricant to it. On the one hand: an overarching change to our legal structure; on the other: an ever-so-slightly more efficient government looking at each problem and solving it. Yes, the former is hard. But does anyone really believe the latter will work?

All the five mistakes I've laid out are so interconnected that it's difficult to figure out which obstruction can be removed first. SEZs need cheap inputs, i.e. land; better environmental regulation needs less focus on coal and energy independence; that will need fewer concessions to the private sector; and so on. How, precisely, can you tackle them independently?

All five also share this peculiar combination of overconfidence and bashfulness. We're too shy to really reform; but we're still confident that we can figure out every problem in time, discover every big thing before it happens.

Which is delusional. Basically we are saying this: that the government knows better than everyone else how the economy will grow. Which sectors will grow, which areas will export, which companies will contribute. And, don't get me wrong, sometimes this works. There are times and there are places where it could make a giant difference.

But in India? With our government? With our history and experience? No.

We, instead, need to trust other people more. We need to trust that they can make the decisions that will lead to an export or a manufacturing revolution. We need to accept that all the obstacles that the government would struggle to identify and remove one by one could be removed all at one go by India's citizens and companies—if they were allowed to try.

Trust prices, and trust people.

FIVE STRIDES FORWARD

Those are the five wrong turns we've taken, born of one error of judgement: the Indian state's overconfidence. How something so inept can yet be so convinced that it will get it right next time can be mystifying—till you remember that every one of us knows a real human being like that, too.

But, naturally, retracing our steps isn't enough. We also need to take five big strides forward. There are five things that we have shied away from, five things we have feared to do—partly because they seem like a betrayal of our past, partly because we have claimed that we have a special 'gradualist' approach to reform, and partly because we have, till now, just not cared enough.

Here they are, in the order that we'll be talking about them:

First, we must make sure that every single market is more flexible, less constrained than it is today. In particular, the markets for all the things that go into manufacturing—land, labour, capital, and entrepreneurship.

Second, we have to get more money to government. This means—and I hate to say it, because this is one of those phrases that just get thrown about a lot, like just invoking it will make a difference, as if it's some sort of mantra—'black money' needs to come down.

Third, we have to make sure the money that's coming in gets spent on the right things, and doesn't go leaking away in grandiose government programmes that don't work the way they're supposed to.

Fourth, we have to fix agriculture—the one sector of the economy that remains completely untouched by the reforms of 1991. The time has come for its special exemption to end.

And fifth, we have to completely change our attitude to towns— from grudging their very existence and wishing they would just go away and stop bothering us, to actively encouraging more of them to spring up.

Let's look at these one by one.

WHEN BIGGER IS BETTER

The first thing we have to do, and perhaps the most important, is to complete the agenda of 1991. The reforms that began that year were about relaxing controls on product markets. We stopped telling companies what they could produce, and how much of it; we stopped forcing consumers to buy certain goods and not others. But the markets for products are only half the story. Equally important are the markets for what goes into making them—labour, land, capital, and entrepreneurship, the factors of production.

The wrinkle is that each of these is not just a commodity—each is a livelihood, a way of life, as well. Reforming these requires changing how millions of people live, and what their plans are for their lives. This isn't easy, and it is particularly hard if you're trying to reform an economy while claiming that you aren't—which is India's preferred way of going about it.

But we cannot put it off any longer, either. The lack of reform in these markets has meant that we simply aren't productive enough. And also, we simply aren't competitive enough—nobody in the world wants to buy things made in India. Changing that needs more than pretty slogans; it needs more than carving out a piece of land and calling it a Special Economic Zone. Changing that is about ensuring that the right ingredients for vibrant companies and factories come together—and the government can't force that, it has to create the conditions in which ordinary people can make it happen.

So, first: labour. 'Labour law reform' is what we keep hearing about; labour law reform is the biggest way in which the state intrudes upon factories, keeps them small and relatively unproductive. It has to go. If you run a factory, you should be able to take on extra workers when you get a big order, while telling them it's just temporary.

Actually, that can happen today, too; contract workers are everywhere in certain industries. But it's both illegal and unfair. It's illegal because the Supreme Court has said that you can't have contract workers in your 'core business' under the current law. Everyone has the option to do so nevertheless—but at the cost of being harassed by the cops and the inspectors. In other words, we have effortlessly found the worst of both worlds. And it's unfair because you then have 'permanent' workers and workers on contract working the same assembly line, doing the same job, but with one of them being five times the other.

It takes a lot of energy to ignore unfairness. Unless unfairness is somehow sanctified by irrational belief, whether religious or ideological, it is dangerous. People can't come face-to-face with it every day and be unchanged. The kind of unfairness produced by India's labour law is particularly pernicious. There is no reason that a contract worker can give to himself to rationalize why he is struggling and his colleague is not. There is no explanation that his foreman can give him that is satisfactory. The foreman usually knows this. And, perhaps consequently, the foreman is as often as not brutal and arbitrary when dealing with the contract worker—almost as if to make up for the fact that the permanent worker is un-fireable. It is pretty obvious how the tension inherent in these relations can escalate into confrontation, or explode into violence.

So, first: a restrictive labour law creates unfairness, and it induces violence.

But that isn't the only consequence. Manish Sabharwal, who runs the giant training-and-temp agency TeamLease, keeps on banging away at the point that every single additional job since 1991 has been in the informal sector. And, he adds, these laws confiscate half of a worker's salary, diverting it into supposed benefits that are poor value for money and that employers usually lie about providing, anyway.

What happens when all you can really get is an informal job, one which doesn't pay enough? Well, it drastically reduces the payoff to becoming 'employable', to use one of Sabharwal's favourite words. If I think there's decent work at the end of the time and money I invest in my own skills, I might do it. If I know there isn't, I won't. I would rather, like my friend Prakash from Bareilly whom we met in Part I, hang around and do odd jobs and wait for the occasional big bonanza. Sometimes, a single phrase explains things best, and this life of impermanence is still summed up for me by a phrase I remember reading long ago in a book about Gujarati labourers, by the Dutch sociologist Jan Breman: 'wage hunter-gatherers'. There is, as many, including Aman Sethi, have noted, a certain freedom to this life; but the possibility of investing in yourself, of voluntarily giving up some freedom for a promised future, doesn't ever arise.

And the most incredible product of our restrictions, surely, is exactly how much they stifle innovation and growth. The World Bank looked at firms in the US and India, decades apart. In the US, they found that 35-year-old companies had, on average, grown 10 times on two crucial indicators—they sold 10 times as much and employed 10 times as many. But 'in India, the productivity of a

35-year-old firm merely doubles, while its headcount actually falls by a fourth'.

Larger firms are better, most of the time. They provide more benefits and higher wages for their employees; they are capable of more innovation, according to that study from the World Bank, and compete better in global markets. That's for firms with over 100 people; but remember, in India, between 80 and 90 per cent of manufacturing companies employ less than 50 people. Most employ less than 10.

We need larger firms and bigger factories, or we won't compete in the world's markets. And until we embed ourselves in global markets, we have no way of employing everyone we need to. There are simply too many people joining the Indian workforce for them to only make stuff for other Indians. They have to get to work on creating and exporting goods to the rest of the world, too.

I haven't talked a lot about trade in this book; but this is one of the most basic points that is possible to make. Everyone understands, it seems to me sometimes, that manufacturing is good.[47] Everyone understands that exports are good. But I don't think they understand exactly how important it is that we insert ourselves into global supply chains. Getting people in India jobs is not about easy import substitution. You can't con people into making stuff in India through SEZs, or tax holidays, or whatever. It would be a mistake to obsess about the fact that we, for example, are importing mobile phones, and try and force people to manufacture them here. Instead, look at how mobile phones are made: the screen in one place, the battery in another, the core chip in a third. You need to be one of the places that make a part; you cannot start by trying to force yourself to be the place that makes it all. This is not the 1970s; you can't try the same strategies that people tried then. Especially because they failed in the 1970s.

You see, here's the central problem with not being open to

imports: competition with the best in the world is the only thing that keeps producers trying hard. Exports won't grow if imports aren't a threat. We only started exporting cars to the rest of the world when we started importing them too—because only once we started importing them did our carmakers have to start making cars that people actually wanted to buy.

Oh, and we keep banging on about the size of the Indian market—but let's get over it. We have more hungry producers than we have potential consumers. This means we, humbly instead of arrogantly, try to look at what people would want to buy from us that we could make. Instead of arrogantly proclaiming the strength and depth of the Indian market, humbly ask what our weak industry can make for you. What can we do for you, not what can you do for us. In our arrogance and self-delusion, in this national machismo that compensates for decades of being ignored, we think our job is to sell 'the India story'. No. It is not. It is to sell Indian goods. And for that to happen, we can't be arrogant, and we can't think small.

The fear is that we will settle for just the tinkering. India's government, I believe, also has a righteous anger about India's horrific red tape. Prime Minister Modi has talked about the 'Inspector raj'; he's said that he would be happy if we repealed one bad law a day. But action is harder. Consider this: of all those labour laws that hold back manufacturing, the government has repealed practically none. What it has said is that it will ensure the nice, kindly man, the labour-law inspector, will harass you less. Because there's a website on which he'll have to submit his report. I think we can agree this is classic tinkering.

Small-picture solutions are not big enough. To sell Indian goods to the world, we need to understand our labour markets are simply not dynamic enough. To create the jobs that 13 million new workers a year demand, you have to ensure those jobs are not millstones around an entrepreneur's neck. Make generous severance compulsory, sure; and expand social services, too. But don't have employment laws that make employers think twice about opening a new wing to their factory.

HOLDING UP LAND

Next, land. If anything, this has been the most fraught of disputes in India. We are an incredibly crowded country, and that has been getting worse as few people leave agriculture, and farms just keep on getting divided into smaller and smaller portions. Frequently, land is the only financial asset that people have, the only thing they know keeps them from destitution. They have no skills, no safe-deposit box, no bank account; but they do have a patch of land. More, many people understand exactly how land translates into security, but if you give them a fixed deposit in a bank instead, they just don't feel as secure.

On the other hand, you have the unquestionable need to build more factories—and the somewhat more questionable need to open up more land to mining. Some of those who worry about land acquisition ask: Why can't industries just be built on barren land? On far-away land? On less fertile land? Less irrigated land? Simple problem: barren, less fertile, less productive land is frequently further away from population centres and road networks. If you think about it, you will realize this is not a coincidence. If you're going to build more factories, you can't restrict them to barren land.

And the final problem is that this is an area where individuals alone can't write contracts with each other and get things done easily. Building a factory frequently means getting together several parcels of land. Let's say you get 90 per cent of the landowners in the vicinity on board by paying a reasonable amount to them, one they're happy with; suppose the remaining 10 per cent, out of irrationality or maybe out of greed, refuse to part with their land until the price is 10 times higher? Or 100 times higher? Clearly, there's an impasse here—economists call it the 'hold-up problem'— and it's one that states throughout history have solved by stepping in with overwhelming force.

India's solution was to just allow the state to take over everything it wanted, on behalf of anyone it wanted, for any purpose at all, as long as it could vaguely be defined as 'public'. So many things can be, you know—in a chronically housing-starved country, even housing projects with 17 swimming pools can be claimed to serve a public purpose if the bureaucrat in question is daring enough.

You can get away with this sort of thing if you are a colonizing, imperial power, which is when the original land-acquisition law was drafted; but give us sixty or so years of freedom, and we will push back. People were furious; many because they didn't want to give up their only asset for what was not enough money; others because they didn't want to give up their only asset for any money at all; others because they wanted a job at the factory, or equity in the factory, or to be resettled in the neighbourhood; and an infinitesimal minority because they really wanted to stay farmers, and to stay farming that specific patch of land. Naturally, most of the sympathetic coverage focused on that last bunch. This is how the media operates, it's useless to complain—that bunch gave us the best story, human interest and all, never mind that they're not representative, what are we, social scientists?

And so now we have a different law. This one, according to Sanjoy Chakravorty of Temple University, will ensure that nowhere in India will land be cheaper than Rs 25 lakh an acre—or, in other words, between 50 and 100 times more expensive than it was ten years ago. One begins to suspect that we have overcompensated. And it isn't just the price—there is an entire phalanx of bureaucrats you will have to go through to sell or buy land, all evaluating and inspecting and certifying and identifying. At the very least, this will delay you. At worst, it will also further escalate your cost.

Look, you need to have something in the middle. Naturally, higher price than before; equally naturally, not a fiftyfold increase.

And, again, we need to keep the state's actual participation to a minimum. It may be essential to solve the hold-up problem to get the government to come in at the last minute and be persuasive in the way only people with armies can. But it is also true that this should happen as little and as late as possible. In other words, get more people willing to sell.

People will only be willing to sell when there is a real market for agricultural land. People have to get used to the idea of land as something you can buy and sell, not something you inherit and hold on to. The time when we could have redistributed land properly has passed. We failed to reform landholdings when we should and could have. The states that did redistribute land then are now much less abjectly poor. But if the others restart that process now, we will just end up making landholdings smaller and less viable. The only thing to do is to move towards a genuine land market.

Sadly, we don't have a market in land for two reasons. The first is that we are never sure who owns what. Seriously. Local Indian papers sometimes have advertisements in which people are asserting their rights over one little piece of land or another by claiming to have documents in Persian going back centuries. Sometimes they need to do that in order to mortgage or sell land that's been with their families for generations. They have no actual land deed; there is no national register of land. One is being made, but it is proceeding at the speed universally associated with 90-year-old ladies on the pavement. It needs to speed up; and, once finished, it needs to be completely paperless—ideally online and accessible to anyone.

The second, and possibly more pressing, reason we don't have a market in land is that it is illegal. This is considered a good idea. See, otherwise farmers might be exploited. City slickers would turn up and offer them some cash for their land, and then farmers—being, in this telling, incurably naïve and unable to see the real value of their only asset—would give them the land and then the city slickers would resell it to other city slickers for a vast sum of money. This would be exploitation, and the only way to stop it is to ban any sale of farmland to anyone other than someone else wanting to farm. Oh, and he better not already have too much land.

Excellent. Small problem: what happens now is that the city slicker just buys the land at an agricultural price, gets a cousin in the capital to declare that patch of land is now industrial or residential, and sells it on to the developer—at a vast mark-up. You see, in an effort to protect the farmer, we have effectively ensured that he gets very little of the value of the land he sells. As you should have figured out by now, this is pretty typical for Indian law.

Change these two things, develop a market in land, and much will be improved. People are willing to sell. Earlier this year I stood by a well-laid rural road in what would have been, a few years earlier, a pretty inaccessible part of eastern Uttar Pradesh. I was prodding the men by the side of the road as to whether they sent their daughters to school. They were offended that I even needed to ask; what did I think they were, people from western UP? They were even OK, they pointed out, with their girls getting jobs after they graduated. But where were the jobs, they added morosely, the usual complaint. It would be nice, said one, if there were a few factories here. I snorted at this; surely they would be the first people to complain if their land was taken away for a factory. They laughed—and then got up, and walked me up and down the verge of the road, pointing out the fields that they felt were unprofitable, and could be sold and a factory built. People are ready to sell.

But companies are not ready to buy that easily. They've been spoiled—by governments falling over backwards to give them land that's been expropriated from their owners. And have you noticed how much they ask for? Thousands of acres, vast tracts of land, to put up one factory. For these guys, the land crisis doesn't exist. They want to build a park-like industrial township to produce five cars a day. Go to Stuttgart or to Yokohama and see how much space they use up to build 500 cars a day. And, once again, you realize that the Indian private sector needs a smidgen of sense to be beaten into them. Look at the famous Infosys campus in Bangalore. Can someone explain to me why a software company, which really could operate out of everyone's networked living rooms, needs a tract of land that one normally associates with airports or small European duchies? Big enough for a bowling alley and heaven knows what else?

Don't give them vast campuses. Let them buy on the open market—and force them to pay well, but not exorbitantly. The answer is simple. It's just admitting it that's hard.

ACCOUNTING FOR OWNERSHIP

Then there's capital. That, too, like land and labour must be much more mobile than it has been so far.

We know that Indian companies rarely change hands. Remember the story of Kingfisher? It was run disastrously into the ground by a feckless owner. And yet his creditors simply refused to force him out. Ownership and management are considered sacred in India. We allow 'promoters' to get away with anything, with defrauding their minority investors, exploiting their workers, and breaking the law. Because it is 'their' company, even if they only technically own a fraction of it.

This needs to change for two reasons. First, you can't expect labour laws to change without having similar rules for capital. Why should workers agree to have their livelihoods depend on business decisions taken by management and ownership—when those guys have absolutely nothing on the line?

And it has major effects on workers' skills, too. As Shubhashis Gangopadhyay has argued in *Business Standard*: 'If workers are not sure that their managers have the right incentives to take good decisions, they will be wary of being retrenched or suffering pay cuts to remain employed. This will not encourage them to make the necessary investment to improve their skill unless they want to leave this job for a better company. If the system is such that all managers are protected in their jobs, then there is no company worth moving to and labour has no incentive to invest in human capital.'

Second, it needs to change because we need more efficient and better-run companies. The way that happens, theoretically, is this: If a company fails, the owner is responsible. He loses control; he is forced to sell, or his creditors take possession. They find someone else to run it, who does a better job. The company's value is preserved—but the owner who screwed up doesn't benefit from the process at all.

This is not what happens in India. We behave as if a company's value is only preserved if the original owner stays at the helm. (Partly, that is because the original owner can make a credible threat: Keep me in charge or else I will somehow strip this company of all assets when you try to make me leave, and you won't know how I've done it because Indian law is so archaic.)

So, the first thing we need is investors who are more active. Large parts of many Indian companies are owned by 'institutional investors', such as the giant government-controlled Life Insurance Corporation. They appoint their nominees to the boards of the companies—but, typically, these nominees just rubber-stamp the decisions that promoters take. If, instead, they started asking a few sharp questions, then capital would be held accountable in a way it has not so far. It really is a pretty simple solution, and one that the government can implement comparatively easily: make LIC and the other big holders of Indian stocks much more active supervisors of the companies that they partly own.

The second thing is to improve the productivity of capital—lots of money that's stuck in projects that are going nowhere, in factories that are badly run. But the investors and owners can't cut and run. Creditors can't get a small fraction of what they invested, write off the rest, and get out of there. This is what would happen in most well-run economies—but, in India, the British forgot to write a real bankruptcy law, and so independent India never got around to one either. Draft and pass a bankruptcy law, so we can shut down enterprises and projects that would otherwise tie up capital and investment.

Above all, we have to hold capital accountable. The mess that's been made of India has not been made just by truculent workers and an interfering government. An entitled capitalist class, which believes that it is due profits without innovation and without sweat, is a large part of the problem.

And so, finally, to that most intangible of constituents of the manufacturing cocktail: entrepreneurship. That ineffable quality of risk-taking, of innovation, of idea-making—amazing how the English language falters at describing something so basic to modern economic growth, isn't it? It just shows you how recent, compared to language, the idea of industrial development is.

What we want from entrepreneurs is simple. We want new ideas. We want new techniques. We want them to set up small companies, and to—on the strength of their ideas, not their connections to the government—make them big.

But do we, in fact, reward such behaviour? (Hint: We do not.) Instead, our most beloved companies manufacture generic medicines, or tariff-protected cars, or do basic outsourcing work. Our least beloved, but most powerful, companies work in those sectors where their ability to get licences and permissions and concessions out of government can be turned into vast wads of cash.

So how do we change? First, we have to start valuing intellectual property more. We are a nation of plagiarists. We don't even reverse-engineer that well, it's far too much work. Value and protect intellectual property, turn it into money, and millions of smart young people will want to start creating it.

And we need to ensure that small companies, once they start, have the opportunity and incentive to turn big. But, once again, we have laws about this: laws to protect small companies that force them to stay small. The Indian state is such an overprotective parent; it hates to see its beloved, coddled micro- and small-scale enterprises grow up.

Here's a partial list of products that can only be made by small companies: pickles, bread, mustard oil, groundnut oil, wooden furniture, laundry soap, steel chairs, locks. And we wonder why, after opening trade with Southeast Asia, we suddenly started importing a lot of cooking oil from there. Besides the outright reservations for smaller companies, there are a tonne of other incentives—preferential taxation, lending, God knows what else— that means that, if you have a small company, you are incentivized to keep it small. Naturally, therefore, if someone has a great innovation, we never get to hear of it.

People who visit from abroad are frequently struck by the brilliance of some of India's smallest entrepreneurs. This gives rise to the myth that India is a country of a billion entrepreneurs—surely, if so many small companies are run by people so good at their job, then there must be something in the Indian character that is open to entrepreneurship. Sadly, that's a misreading of the facts. The reason that so many small entrepreneurs in India are so impressive is because, in other countries, the impressive small entrepreneurs tend to get bigger. Not in India.

TOWN AND COUNTRY

The next two steps have to take us beyond the unfinished agenda of 1991, to an agenda abandoned long before that. Our obsession with agrarian purity and our disdain for villages have got to end. As is typical for India, it has picked up and preserved all the most terrible things about Gandhi—puritanism, a belief in the irrational, a conservative infatuation with the village—and very little of the good—non-violence, kindness, hygiene.

It needs to end. Let us tell the truth about the village and about rural India: It is a sink of depravity. It forces people into boxes. They fail to ever transcend their caste background, their kinship ties, their landowning status.

We need to get people off the land and into cities. Cities are cauldrons of innovation. More, they are the crucibles of solidarity. The mill village of Mumbai, back in the early twentieth century, was one brief shining moment when it seemed many of the divisions of the villages were not melting away, but becoming less relevant. Cities are like that—especially cities where people have to work together. To the extent that our cities still preserve caste and other hierarchies, it's because they are no longer imagined as machines for working together, but merely as places to live.

First, therefore, agriculture. Allow people off the land. First, by letting them sell—which returns us to that question of markets. Actually, getting a market off the ground might need more than reducing regulations. Banks will have to start lending out money to people to buy land, so those who are better or are more enthusiastic about farming can expand their farms, while those who want to get out can. At the moment, in many parts of India, banks don't lend you money to buy farmland. They have lots of cash available to fund your irrigation project when you do buy your land, but you can't buy it when you don't have the money, can you?

And let people mortgage their land easily, too. As Aruna Urs, who farms in the south, tells me, that has three benefits: It lets farmers who are struggling exit easily; medium-scale farmers like him can scale up, easily; and people can move to more productive areas of the economy.

In the end, that's the crucial thing. Our agriculture simply does not earn enough; and it has too many people. This is an iron equation we're dealing with here. Make it more productive and also move people off it; the two things go together.

Here is what, I believe, we have not yet understood: we are no longer a starving country. We no longer need to ensure that enough food is grown; for decades, we *have* been growing enough food. The country that invented granaries cannot build enough to store its vast stockpiles of grain; and yet we plant and harvest more. It is time to slow down, to pause, and to recognize that this is one thing we no longer need to worry about. There is enough wheat. There is enough rice. It is time to end incentives for production, and to create incentives for productivity.

Currently, we try to ensure that production is kept up through the government's vast 'procurement' programme, in which rice and wheat are bought up by state agencies at a vast premium to what they cost to grow. The idea was, originally, to ensure that enough was grown. But, over time, the aim of the programme has changed, as is inevitable with such interventions; and now it is used, above all, as a method to get money to farmers. Keep the 'minimum support prices' high, and you do not need to worry about income support for farmers. I have no objection to making sure rural incomes are high. But this isn't quite the best way to go about it. It distorts the choices that farmers make—those who should be finding ways to grow vegetables, which grow more expensive every year, are instead growing wheat we no longer need. And as for rice—well, it strikes me as nothing short of insane that a crop meant for the floodplains of wide rivers engorged by monsoon rains is instead being grown in the arid semi-desert that is the Punjab, the inhospitable land rendered welcoming by a lavish, unsustainable, and irresponsible use of tubewells, which deplete that state's water table in order to pump artificial floods up to the surface so it can pretend to be rice-rich Bengal.

The same economic madness that has marred India's approach to industrial growth has warped agriculture, too. We want to help poor people. Excellent. But, we will not give poor people money. Instead, we will help them by trying to keep products' prices low. And, to keep a product's price low, our preferred method is to keep its producers' costs low—but by giving the producers stuff for free. (How far we will go to avoid giving poor people money!) In industry, we give away coal and iron ore and so on; in agriculture, we give away power and water. That's how Punjab grows rice. And that's how 60 per cent of Maharashtra's water is used on 3 per cent of its land, growing water-guzzling sugar cane even in districts where drought is less an exception and more the norm.

Here, too, we have failed to trust prices.

Agriculture can be made more productive through, again, infrastructure. Build canals and small local dams; dig tanks and wells. Make sure it's less dependent on the monsoon. All of east and much of south India simply don't have irrigation facilities; without that, they can't do as much as they want. Get new crops—genetically modified, if necessary—to farmers. Get new techniques to them. Once we ran something called an 'extension service', in which government agronomists fanned out across India taking new processes to farmers. This has essentially shut down in the past two decades; nobody seems to know why. Seriously. It's a mystery. Puzzles everyone. One of the few things that worked; now it's gone.

And agriculture can be made more productive through another kind of infrastructure as well. Build not just the paraphernalia required to get water to your crops, but also the arrangements to get your crops to the cities. So far, many farmers grow rice and wheat because it's the state agency's responsibility to buy and store them. But that is a practice that must end if India's increasingly wealthy and demanding people are to start getting the vegetables they now expect to have with their lunchtime rice. But another thing that stops them from growing vegetables is that tomatoes go bad way faster than grain does. They need better roads, cold storage facilities, refrigerated trucks or railway compartments. They need middlemen who are corporatized and efficient, not corrupt and bumbling bullies. Many Indian states have rules that say farmers can only sell their produce at government-nominated wholesale marketplaces. The supposed idea is, once again, to 'protect' farmers from exploitation. In actual fact, the system winds up working against smaller farmers, who are bullied into lowering their prices by the cartels of local middlemen who control the wholesale marketplace. And then the cartels bully shopkeepers at the other end of the chain. In Gorakhpur, in north-east UP, I once listened to what a man with a cart of vegetables told me about what he went through when he tried to cut out the middleman, and come to an independent deal with a trucker. The cartel found out where he lived, and turned up in the middle of the night—and beat up not just him, but also his 12-year-old son. These are just some of the abuses that foreign direct investment in retail is supposed to end.

The power of the cartels is extraordinary. Vegetable vendors in Delhi claim that there are five men who control the trade in tomatoes across the northern states. Tens of thousands of farmers, millions of tonnes of tomatoes, 300 million consumers—all dependent on half a dozen men. The best way to fix this is not just for each state to change its rules, but for the country to change its rules, too. One simple national registration, ideally online, and you should be a legitimate trader. And once you are, you should be exempt from any state or local fees. This is a legal possibility. Indeed, a draft law exists. Why is nobody pushing forward with it? Well, the cartels—like cartels everywhere—are rich and powerful and politically connected. Oh, and they have 'pro-poor' arguments to deploy.

A more reasonable supply chain benefits consumers as well as farmers. We have suffered, for ages, from high food inflation. In other words, the price of food keeps increasing. I believe that is, in part, deliberate policy—or at least the foreseeable by-product of deliberate policy. Successive governments have kept buying agricultural produce from farmers at high prices, in order to keep rural prosperity going; and the entirely predictable effect of that has been that price increases across the board. We have dealt with this throughout our history, because farmers have always been the focus of government transfers. Thanks to their political power, and thanks to the worry that they're always one step away from disaster, we have endured food prices going up by an average of 6.7 per cent a year every year since Independence. Today, our monetary policymakers wonder why consumers believe that food prices will continue to increase, in spite of so many promises being made to control inflation. The answer is right there: we have always had high food inflation. Not even Raghuram Rajan at his most plausible can wipe out that collective memory. Inflation is the absolute least of our worries. Grow fast and hard enough, and inflation is forgotten. And if the growth is in agricultural supply, then inflation might slow down for the first time in our history.

THERE IS POWER IN A FARM

We try and protect farmers, not farming. Which is a terrible idea, as we've already discussed. Especially since it means that the lives of those who choose to go into agriculture are needlessly hard. Those without land who work on other people's farms, for example, are out of any sort of welfare net, other than perhaps the rural employment guarantee scheme. (Which pays them, remember, about Rs 100–150 a day. This is barely above the poverty line, and yet you'd think, from the squeals let out by well-heeled people, that we're putting them up in air-conditioned comfort and feeding them caviar. I know I keep on circling back to this: but there is no real and persuasive evidence that the guarantee scheme has destroyed rural labour markets or government finances. Nothing reveals how cynical our policy conversation has become more than its obsession with finding flaws in the employment guarantee scheme, the only welfare programme in our history that has targeted and gotten through to landless labourers, and whose fiscal impact has never been greater than that of, for example, the tax cuts handed out in 2008 to those earning more than Rs 1.5 lakh a year. The scheme cost, last year, only 55 per cent of the amount we paid to subsidize the Indian middle class's gas cylinders. If some of those nice middle-class people who are so worried about fiscal prudence had attacked the far more expensive subsidies for their own cooking gas even one-hundredth as often and as shrilly as they did the rural employment guarantee, they would have more credibility.)

We try and protect farmers, and not labourers; if we cared about labourers, we would try to ensure they had some access to formal savings—why are they not, for example, offered access to the provident funds that other employees are? The government has finally decided to work towards getting large numbers of rural, landless Indians into the formal financial system, and getting them accident and life insurance. But that's only a start. They need access to savings accounts, low-cost, low-hassle accounts into which they and their employers can deposit a few rupees at a time.

You might well ask: Why is it that we support agriculture in this odd and inefficient manner? Why keep fertilizer subsidies going, instead of support for income? Why exempt all agricultural income from taxes, instead of handing out transfers to poor farmers or landless labourers? Why promise free power and water when there's ample evidence of what that does to the environment, to government finances, and to farmers' own choices? Why subsidize the production of more rice than can be eaten in India, when every kilogram of basmati that leaves our shores means we are exporting 5000 kilograms of water?

Think of it this way. Small and marginal farmers have only a quarter or thereabouts of India's farmland—and it is usually the bits that are least responsive to fertilizer. Thus if I keep fertilizer cheap, I'm helping the wealthier farmers, the ones who are at the top of the social hierarchy in rural areas. Tubewell ownership is even more concentrated among the largest farmers; and so power subsidies for tubewells amount to all taxpayers, even the poor, subsidizing the richest farmers.

So the current ways in which the state supports farming are

tough to change because you'd have to go up against the wealthiest farmers. And these guys don't just control local politics—frequently, they *are* local politics.

See, here's the vital thing you need to know about agriculture—the economic structure of farming is, everywhere and in every country, the template for social power, and for the national imagination. America is about the West and the pioneer and the homesteader. France is about the organic farmer and the small baker who cultures his own yeast. Japan is about its own rice and its own shrimp. More, those who exercise power over the land are the powers of the land. (Even if they do not have direct power, they still have moral authority, as in France.)

Thus, in India, the landowning caste or ethnicity in any area is almost always politically dominant. Touching the source of their power—traditional agriculture—is very difficult indeed for a politician. This is why farmers in Punjab, the richest in India, get so much free power and water it bankrupts the state government and dries out the water table. This is why there is no such thing as a tax on agricultural income.

What is needed is for us to take on these interests. They deserve very little sympathy in any case; but, even if they did, we can give them other stuff, instead. Repeal the land-ceiling laws that constrain the size of their holdings. Let them write their own contracts with big purchasers, like supermarket chains—that is not permitted at the moment in many states. Give them all these other things they want, but ensure that agriculture becomes a regular sector, a productive sector, rather than something that is seen as a moral touchstone for Indian society. The only people who benefit from coddling agriculture are the people who have, for generations, bullied other people in their village. Destroy their economic protections, and you do not just save agriculture—you renew rural India.

INDIA-CLASS CITIES

And now for the seas the rivers of people must flow into: India's cities. You know, we dislike cities so much that we haven't even bothered to build sewage lines for most of them. Trivandrum, for example, has sewage connections for less than 40 per cent of its houses—and this is in oh-so-advanced god's-own-country Kerala.

The general plan has been the following: Look, if we don't plan for people to arrive in our cities, then they won't arrive. Plan B: Oh look, they're arriving. Well, let's not make it comfortable here. If it is they might stay, or more people might arrive. Plan C: Damn, they're still coming in droves, although the city is now crowded, dirty, and unlivable. Let's try and push them into staying in the villages, instead. Plan D: They're still turning up, in trainfuls! This is ridiculous! Some of them are even settling in the centre of town, where real people live! Evict them, the thieves. Send them so far away from the city centre that they will have to walk four hours to get to their workplaces. At least we can pretend, then, that they aren't coming.

Indian policymakers have always been very comfortable with the idea that *they* live in the cities, while most of the people they rule live in villages. This is the natural order of things, and has been since

Gandhi. Our job is to make inspection tours, and then go back to our air-conditioned metropolitan cubbyholes and write little laws that make things better. Our job is not to find space in our own lives for the people we rule. This is why, for years, the only political party in this country that was serious about city administration was the Dalit party, the Bahujan Samaj Party. When it ruled in UP, its first priority was to improve city administration, to build sewer lines and privatize electricity. Only the Dalit party understood exactly how important it was to have liveable cities to move to.

Today, the understanding that urbanization is unstoppable has at last percolated into the mainstream. But it is still dangerously confused. The current government, for example, is obsessed with 'smart cities', though nobody knows exactly what that means—the Government of Singapore even sent a request to the Government of India asking for a definition. The last lot promised 100 new cities along the Delhi Mumbai Industrial Corridor; this lot has promised a similar number of 'smart' ones. Whatever; it's wonderful we're now at least acknowledging the need to plan for urbanization.

But until something more basic about how we imagine cities changes, we will fail to create ones that are real magnets for people.

You see, we cannot afford cities that are 'world-class' in the sense in which entitled Indians who travel the world use the phrase.

They see Central Park, and they think that's all that New York City is about. But cities have never been about gardens; they have been about factories. They are not about gracious living; they are about spurring production and trade. So it has always been through most of human history; the very rules of civilization, of civic life, have been written to help people come together to craft things and trade them. We entitled travellers want our cities to be 'world-class' replicas of what those in the West have just become; but Mumbai cannot become the New York of the past few years, a sanitized preserve for the world's super-rich, because that is not how cities are made. New York became New York not because of bankers, but was built on the sinews of real industry. It was a city of textiles, of meat and of sugar. Yes, today the Garment District hosts fashion designers and the Meatpacking District is where the cool late-night bistros are, but their names should remind us of how and why they came to be.

We can't have cities that please the eye with rolling parkland and with no poor people in sight. If we try, we get the opposite.

Many, for example, worry that increasing the floor-space index or FSI, which regulates how high buildings can go, will make cities denser. This is nonsense. Cities only get denser when more people move there, and the amount of land available for them to move on to stays the same. How high you can build on that land makes no difference to this equation, and thus to a city's density. Increasing FSI, which allows you to build more floors on a given parcel of land, just ensures that the people who move there have more space—they don't have to crowd into tiny closet-sized apartments or live in slums. In 1971, Mumbai's slums were 22 per cent of the population; in 2001, they were 55 per cent. That's a consequence of the fact that, in the same period, Mumbai actually *decreased* its maximum allowable FSI. This means that buildings that were built in the old, more liberal floor-space regime, can't even be demolished today, because they'd have to be replaced by buildings with less space, in a city several times larger.

I hate China comparisons. I really do. But every now and then, they're essential fodder for our anger. In Shanghai, as Alain Bertaud points out, the average resident had 3.6 square metres for herself in 1984; and 34 square metres, almost a tenfold increase, in 2010. In Mumbai, she would have had 4.5 square metres in 2010. As Bertaud adds: 'The main goal of the regulatory policy has been to control the size of Mumbai by penalizing any new development, fearing that economic success would attract more people.' Yes, we have deliberately planned for our cities to fail. That has been our intent. If they succeed, then more people would move there, 'who would have to share an already deficient and immutable infrastructure'. Bertaud concludes: 'This is a very pessimistic view of urban development.' Ah, understatement, so very French.

But the image of a 'world-class' city has colonized our minds. Actually, maybe I'm being unfair. It is imperial-class cities that we want—so the word 'colonized' is even more accurate. You see, we think that we all deserve to live like imperial bureaucrats of the sort who designed New Delhi, the worst city in the world, to demonstrate to the country exactly how little empire cares for convenience. The Raj's civil servants built a city with huge bungalows for themselves in the middle, the most powerful men in the country squatting proudly on acres and acres of land in the centre of a city. And this, this imperial excrescence, this supercilious display of naked power, is what we imagine all cities should be like. Flat. Flat and vast, with nothing piercing tree cover—trees that, I would like to point out, are not even native to the semi-desert that Delhi's in, but were still dragged there by British planners at the cost of water that the city's inhabitants could ill afford at the time. Climb, sometime, to the top of the Taj hotel in downtown Delhi. (There is a reason why the phrase 'downtown Delhi' jars us.) Look down at the estates of our rulers. See how some of them have set up little farms. Yes, that's right; slap-bang in the middle of one of the most crowded cities in the world, rich people are *farming*. This happens nowhere else in the world. It is a magnificent expression of contempt for urban planning, for equality, and for natural justice. It spits in the face of common sense, and is thus entirely fitting for India's capital.

That beautiful, leafy, green, sprawling centre is designed to make the lives of those on the margins ever more difficult, forcing them to commute over vast distances to work. The city's heart is kept a suburban Arcadian paradise, while its margins become dense, congested replacements for inner-city development—just without the accessibility.

Jawaharlal Nehru called New Delhi 'a visible symbol of British power, with all its ostentation and wasteful extravagance'. Typically clear insight. But, again typically, the accuracy with which he described this exploitative geography did not cause him to work to change it. Instead, he allowed our nominally egalitarian government to slide slyly into the palaces the twice-born of the Raj built for themselves. That was an original act of sin, and it has poisoned the generations that came after: the patterns of domination developed by the Raj were replicated by the new Indian state in everything else it did, too. Sunil Khilnani describes New Delhi in *The Idea of India* as being about 'the creating and ranking of social structures . . . its hexagonal grids were demarcated into segments for "gazetted officers", European "clerks" and Indian "clerks". . . distance from the central acropolis was gauged by rank.' The racist, imperial fantasy that is Lutyens' Delhi has captured India's imagination; just as the Nehru–Gandhi dynasty is being replicated all over India, so is New Delhi's exclusionary aesthetic.

We need to free India's cities from the tyranny of New Delhi, not just as a ruler, but as an example. Instead of world-class cities, we need India-class cities.

We cannot have cities that have centres with practically no people, but lots of wide open spaces.

We cannot have cities with spacious boulevards set aside for motor cars, but no place for three-wheelers and bicycles and special bus lanes.

And, above all, we cannot have cities from which every form of industry has been forbidden, which is what environmentalists and the Supreme Court seem to want.

This is what we have got wrong: Cities are not a place to live. They are a place to work. Cities are for factories, too.

Until we start planning cities which have factories, not just high-income office blocks; until we raise floor-space permissions so that people can live comfortably close to their workplaces even if they are not the richest people in India; and until we over-invest in public transport, and make car drivers sit sullenly while buses whizz past them in dedicated lanes, we will still fail at urbanization.

Smart cities aren't about how they are administered. Smart cities should be about how they are designed. And who they are designed for. They should be designed to provide livelihoods and living room and lives for all those who want to move there—not just for those who already have.

That's when we will really start to grow as an economy, and as a people.

TAX AND SPEND

The final two strides forward are also a matched pair: where the government gets its money; and how it spends it.

I am not really making a case here for higher taxes. Perhaps they should be higher, but that's not my immediate concern. I am, however, making a case for higher tax revenue. India's government currently collects around 14 per cent of gross domestic product. In some parts of the West, that's around 40 per cent; but I'm not even suggesting that. I'm just saying it needs to get higher.

One way to get that going is already in progress: the goods and services tax, or GST. This is completely revolutionary, the sort of economic backroom plumbing that can change your life without you even noticing. It means that every commercial establishment will find it slightly easier to pay taxes—and also, they will discover, it's become slightly more difficult to avoid doing so. It means that there will be, hopefully, more in common between the taxes you have to pay in Maharashtra and Madhya Pradesh than there has been so far. You see, another thing that's been keeping companies small is that expanding into another state is a tremendous expense. Do so, and you need to follow not only an entirely different set of regulations—but also a completely different set of taxes. Not to mention the fact that your truck has to wait for a week at the border to pay taxes to cross. Properly implemented, the GST can change all that, and replace all this confusion with a simple common tax rate that's easy to pay. Hopefully, that will increase tax revenue sharply.

But the GST won't be enough. We have to look at income taxes. Again, I'm not talking about raising them. But we have to at least close the hundreds of loopholes that allow our richest people to get by without paying any taxes at all.

For that's precisely what's happening. This is something we all know, really. Those of us who earn a salary get our money taken away 'at source'; but, for our doctor, our lawyer, our builder and his supplier, our shopkeeper and his wholesaler, taxation is an afterthought. In every Budget since 1997, we have avoided not just raising income taxes, but broadening their net, too. In China, 0.1 per cent of people paid income tax in 1986; twenty years later, it was 20 per cent. Over here, it has been a steady 2 to 3 per cent of the population. We have not even tried to bring the rest of the country into the tax net.

All this while the rich have grown, well, very rich. Back in the dim past, I once earned some spending money digging up old income-tax records for high-wealth individuals. (Typically, the moment we asked for them, and the tax guys realized they had to give them to us, they panicked and stopped producing the data from the next year. We had clearly violated some implicit contract between the ruler and the ruled.) The economists I was digging up the records for, Thomas Piketty and Abhijit Banerjee, later discovered that in 1998–99 the share of income that India's top 1 per cent took was 9 per cent. A decade on, that was 30 per cent. For the top 0.1 per cent, things are even better—that is the only part of the entire population of India to have had income grow faster than the economy as a whole.

Clearly, we should be getting our rich to pay more income tax. But, while in China income tax will soon be 5 per cent of GDP, in India it's just 0.5 per cent.

And, of course, we should tax their property, too. It's property taxes—collected and spent by local authorities—that should pay for local improvements and infrastructure.

Yes, we can fix this, and bring more people into the tax net. But it won't happen through midnight raids and intrusive inspections and reporting on your neighbours—all the beloved instruments of the little tyrants in our tax offices. No, it comes from changing how we do business, and how income is recorded and earned.

Look, the less cash we use, the more we can track evasion. This is one of those basic things we all know—cheques are taxable, cash is not. We need to get more people and transactions into the formal financial net. Start with real estate. As with salaries, deduct tax 'at source' in any land-related transaction. Shut down real estate as an avenue for black money, tax land value properly, and tax collections shoot up.

And, finally, make sure everyone has a bank account. The more efficient and convenient it is to use the banking system, to transfer money electronically, the more likely that we will be willing to pay taxes in order to use formal finance.

Black money is a terrible moral failing, certainly. But, as with corruption, as long as we think of it as a moral failing to be punished, it will only grow in scope. Think of it as a disease, and we might start curing it.

Right, let's suppose that we eventually raise all this money. That the government is floating in cash. How should it spend it?

There are a dozen claims on the government's purse. I'm not going to decide between whether a health system or an aircraft carrier or a new airport is more important. That, in the end, is really a democratic decision. I have my opinion, but in this at least

I will recognize that it is my opinion and not a truth sent from on high for your edification and solemn observance.

I will say just this: some of it should be spent on infrastructure, because the private sector is useless at building it. And we should charge citizens fair prices, not give it to them free.

OK, I will say one more thing: prize efficiency. Prize it. Search it out, praise it, duplicate it, replicate it. Places where we feed people cheaply, like Chhattisgarh? Figure out what they're doing and replicate it. This is, fortunately, something that our politics seems to be working on. Programmes that work in one state are being picked up by others.

Abhijit Banerjee and Esther Duflo have a simple three-part description of the many Indian welfarist interventions that fail. They call it the 'three Is': ideology, ignorance, and inertia.

If an intervention is spurred by ideology, they say, it may very well fail, for India's ground-level circumstances have a way of defying ideological certitudes. Look, I'm not knocking ideology: it helps define a vision. In a country as confused as ours, with so many differing power centres, a broad ideological direction is perhaps the only way in which we can ensure they're pulling together. That is why, in fact, our politicians' failure to articulate a reformist, market-friendly vision for India's future has hurt us so badly.

But, when it comes to the practical application of a broad ideological vision, they have to be just that: practical. The rural employment guarantee scheme is practical: only those actually desperate are likely to do the back-breaking work for the poor pay that it offers.

Then there's ignorance: ignorance of how the people that state actors are supposed to affect actually behave. Recent research by Rema Hanna and Iqbal Dhaliwal, for example, discovered that when government 'primary health centres' were given biometric methods of assessing employees' attendance, then attendance did go up. And so did several health indicators. But, it turns out, those very centres also saw more people diverted to the private health clinics at which the staff often moonlighted. It seems that, if you forced people to do their jobs, they find some other way to screw the system—for example, by diverting more potential patients.

And, finally, there's inertia. When a bad programme gets written into policy, it stays there. I think we can agree this is so common in India as to not even need examples. Inertia means that, if a programme fails to improve people's lives, we assume that's because not enough is spent on it. More is pushed through pipelines that don't just leak, but also frequently head to the wrong destination in the first place. According to a study conducted by a think tank for the finance ministry at the beginning of the UPA's term and quoted by the economist Bibek Debroy, subsidies were altogether 14 per cent of India's GDP; taxes only 17 per cent. This leaves only 3 per cent for other vital functions of government, and for public investment. And, worst of all, 9 per cent of GDP—the lion's share—went into 'non-merit' subsidies, heading to people who weren't the direct targets of the intervention. Like that Rs 50,000 crore a year I mentioned earlier that we spend on subsidizing gas cylinders. Only a quarter of India's households use gas cylinders. And you know what? I'm betting they're not the poorest quarter. Not even close.

Unless we wish away democracy, and unless we wish away inequality and poverty, this country will always prioritize welfare spending. That it did not, for decades, was a product of how imperfect a democracy we were in the 1950s, and how complete was the grip of the pre–independence Indian elite on the post-independence Republic. Those years were an aberration. The basic drive behind Indira Gandhi's socialist populism, then the middle-caste upsurges of the 1980s and 1990s, and the entrenched welfarism of the Sonia Gandhi years, is the same: the understanding that people vote, that they are sovereign, and that they will not endure a state that does not help them.

The only thing that may have changed is that they are tired of *ineffectual* ways to help them. This is wonderful. But unless we imagine that everyone in India has suddenly gone out and bought Ayn Rand, little else has changed. They still care about their own prospects and expect state action to support them. Perhaps they will plead less for state support—and expect it more.

So we need to start thinking more intelligently about how we design welfare interventions. Over the past few decades, high state-mandated prices for agriculture have helped transfer income to rural households. Indeed, that's stepped up over the past decade, and is perhaps the crucial element behind widespread rural prosperity. What appears like hurtful food inflation to those of us sitting in cities might actually help those who get the money from higher food prices. But, although effective, this is not an efficient method of transferring money: it targets rich farmers disproportionately, for one.

I don't think we can expect to give up our strange attempt to build a welfare state simultaneously with basic state capacity. True, this isn't the way it has happened anywhere else; mostly, states have delivered on public goods like law and order and roads first, and then on welfare schemes. Alongside roads, they have built legitimacy—and then used that legitimacy to create broadly supported welfare systems. But we have to be realistic: that will not happen here. There will, for the foreseeable future, be more than enough voters who do not see the state's responsibility as ending at public goods.

We cannot wish away welfarism. (I believe we should not wish it away, either. We can call social democracy a luxury, unaffordable for a poor country. But it seems we do afford a lot of bloody luxuries. And did I not start this book by saying that we had better stop thinking like a poor country? It seems ethically confusing to righteously demand the infrastructure of a rich country while also saying sorry, no welfare, we are not that rich a country. But, as I just said, that's merely an opinion.)

We cannot wish away welfarism; but let us at least be smarter about it. While the rural agricultural worker, for example, may have seen income more than outpace costs, the urban working class hasn't been doing as well. Orley Ashenfelter and Stepan Jurajda, two Princeton economists, produced something in 2012 called a 'McWage Index': the number of minutes that you need to work at a McDonalds, in various countries across the world, to buy the fast-food chain's tasty and nutritious Big Mac—which, as *The Economist* first pointed out, is standardized across the world, and so is a reasonable guide-rail for various comparisons. (Yes, yes, we don't have Big Macs, we have Maharaja Macs, but it's largely applicable still.) By showing how long people have to work to earn a delicious burger, you show how wages for low-skilled urban employees differ across countries and time. Clever. Here's what's interesting: between 2000 and 2007, the McWage Index grew 8 per cent a year in India. From 2007 till 2011, Indian workers actually lost ground; it took 168 minutes of work to earn a Maharaja Mac in 2007, and 195 in 2011.

In other words, we have another black hole for our welfare state: just as rural landless labourers were never targeted by anything before the employment guarantee scheme came along, young urban low-skilled people, hurting the most in the post-2008 slowdown, are also not part of India's welfare state. Unsurprisingly, they're the angriest Indians. And they're not easily reached by the kind of welfarism we've seen earlier: they move about, they are less tied to pre–existing identities and patronage networks.

Three hundred million people have moved away from their homes in ten years. They should not be forced to move away from government welfare when they do. Subsidies should follow these people; subsidies should not be given to the things they produce, like wheat, or to the things they use, like kerosene or electricity or fertilizer. Move from subsidizing products to subsidizing people.

They have to be treated as individuals. That is, in any case, the true gift that a town gives to an Indian: personhood. You need no longer be a footnote to tradition, a mere appendage to your family and caste.

So start thinking about individuals, not households. Think about transfers in cash, not transfers in kind. Think about income support, not price support.

I am not just saying this because it will save money, though it might.

I am not just saying this because it will help target the urban underclass, though it will.

I am saying this because I want people to change the way they interact with their government. I don't want them needing to be close to a particular ration shop, because that's the only place their food entitlement is accessible; I want cash to arrive in their bank account so that they can travel elsewhere for work, and still have the money. I want a poor rural household's income to be protected, and not the price of the crop they grow—so that, if necessary, and if they think it wise, they can switch over to growing something else, or to not growing anything. I want individuals to benefit rather than families, so that heads of households have less power over their dependents, and so families that want to split apart—for work, or because they simply can't stand each other—are able to do so.

Make the citizen–state relationship about cash, about rights, about services, and about entitlements—and not about concessions and promises and favours and queues. Do this because then it means that citizens become owners of the state, instead of the other way around. Your government is no longer a faraway enemy, or a deity that turns up to grant a boon if you stand on one leg long enough.

The *mai–baap* state must die. We can no longer stand in front of it, hands folded, to beg its notice and its discretion; we must be given our entitlements, without actually talking to anyone at all if possible.

And the best part is, perhaps, that if we can start targeting individuals rather than families or areas or castes or classes, then we erode the layers through which government benefits trickle down. Those are the layers which reproduced in a different guise all the structures of oppression that our founders wished to destroy. Cut out the middleman; talk directly to your government. Indians who have benefited from speaking as individuals will be Indians with less of a debt to power structures of the past. They will become, perhaps, the bricks that build a progressive India; leave them to the mercy of immutable identities and group loyalties, and they will be the keystones of something much darker.

Individuals can matter. That, for me, is the real promise of transfers, and of the Unique ID project.

TOO MUCH TO ASK?

I admit it. I am asking a great deal of the Indian state. The ten things I have demanded of it are not easy, or they would have already happened. They require it to let go of things it loves doing. They require it to accept that it does not do some things well, which is insulting at the best of times.

And they require it to reform its own self, too.

This may be the toughest thing I ask of it. The Indian state is resolutely unwilling to change, more so than almost any other. We have inherited the colonial structures that a few thousand Britons used to rule millions of Indians, and we have transformed them into a way for a few thousand of us to rule millions of our fellow-countrymen. This is an extractive state, to use the terminology that Daron Acemoglu and James Robinson have made famous, and not a supportive one. The transformation from one kind of state to the other is painful. It has accompanied revolutions in other countries—in 1688 in Britain, for example. It has taken generations.

We have to do it in a few years, and without any bloodshed. Surely that's not too much to ask?

The Indian state needs to be better at one thing, above all. It needs to manage our differences better.

That is what the judicial system is for, after all. If we have been wronged, we should not fear to take it to the police, but we do. And so many of us are wronged without redress every day. If we are embroiled in a dispute, we should expect at least a better than even chance of justice; and we should expect it before the house we are quarrelling about falls down due to old age. This is not too much to ask.

Judicial reform might happen—if we expand our courts and change the way the government litigates (they challenge everything, because otherwise the cops might turn up at the bureaucrat's door and ask if he was bribed to let charges drop). Oh, and suppose judges stop insisting on the lengthy if enjoyable cut-and-thrust of oral arguments and allow written submissions? Even something so apparently small will help. We have all sat through interminable meetings discussing issues threadbare that we know would be settled in minutes over email.

Police reform? Harder. The states have to do that, since they control the police forces. And the states are the location of so many of our troubles—of politicians that want to look at cities and see bags of money, for example. But all it takes is one state to take the plunge; to make sure its police is more accountable to the people it serves and protects. One state, so that everyone can start copying it, the way states do. One of 29. Is that really so much to ask?

And then there's reform of the administration itself. Here are Devesh Kapur and Arvind Subramanian, putting it better than I could: 'The Indian state has been variously characterized as a "soft" state; a licence-raj state; a *jugaad* state; a "flailing state". In recent years it has also become a "bypass" state. Everyone in India—from firms to citizens and even the state itself—seeks to bypass its multiple failings and weaknesses. Each new poverty program seeks to bypass the wreckage of previous programs with seemingly smarter design. But in each case the results are similar—the state may not be enabling, but it can be severely disabling. India's three decades of rapid growth based on IT services may well be a consequence of that sector never having been regulated because it was not known to exist. But that model has run out of steam and India is reaching the limits of the bypass state model. A weak state has effectively gifted labour-intensive manufacturing to India's biggest strategic competitor—China.'

Look, this is the problem with our government: it is overworked; it is corrupt; it is inefficient; it is dumb.

The people are not dumb. (Not usually.) But, as an institution, our government is dumb. It just cannot respond swiftly to changing circumstances, which is why the pretence that it can *predict* changing circumstances is laughable. It is dumb because there is no pay-off to taking risks—but, there is a considerable downside, because a civil servant can suffer if anyone is seen to benefit from her decision.

It is overworked, because there are too few of them. We have fewer cops, fewer diplomats, fewer government doctors, fewer regulators, fewer everything than any other country in the world, once you adjust properly for population. Our government is not too big. It is too intrusive, not too big. Let's not confuse the two concepts.

It is inefficient because it is overworked. And because there is no reason why it should be efficient. What incentives do public servants have to be efficient? The only thing keeping them going is integrity, or pride in their work—not pride in their position, but in their work—and who can have pride in a job if their fellow-citizens will assume that anyone doing the job is corrupt and inefficient?

There is a simple but incredibly hard solution: shut down the all-India services. The IAS has outlasted its utility. We no longer need a unifying 'steel frame'. Make bureaucrats truly accountable to politicians—after all, don't they already do what politicians say?

IAS independence hasn't exactly stopped corruption from happening or bad decisions from being taken. At least, if they lose their tenure, they might become more accountable.

If you can't shut down the all-India services, at the very least recruit new people massively. Not to the IAS, but nevertheless for real positions, with real power—not toothless officers on special duty or consultants. When this country was last uncomplicatedly optimistic, back when Nehru ran it, then it drew in talent from everywhere—and gave them things to run, and institutions to build. Homi Bhabha built the Indian nuclear establishment. Vikram Sarabhai created the Indian institutes of management. John Mathai wrote India's Budgets. And in Britain, where the IAS model was born, lateral entry at the highest level is now commonplace. That has to be the case here, too. After all, we need regulators and contract-drawers and people capable of out-thinking the private sector.

And so we need area experts and hands-on specialists, not smart exam-taking generalists—this is not a slow-moving agrarian empire any more, but a quick-moving modern democracy.

It is too easy to find examples of government incompetence, my bureaucratic friends will say. What about all the brilliant, smart stuff so many in it are doing? OK, let me find an example of the best and smartest bits of the Indian government being criminally stupid.

Here's one. It's madly annoying, and it's totally revealing: the Reserve Bank of India's feud with Uber.

Yes, that's right. The RBI—the awesome Indian central bank that is generally supposed to be one of the few institutions that work, and that is headed at the moment by Raghuram Rajan, whom we last heard from being incredibly smart about financial crises or oligarchies or something—in the summer of 2014 turned its attention from restoring Indian growth to shutting down a cellphone app that allows you to hail cabs.

Why, precisely, was Uber in Rajan's cross hairs? Well, the mobile phone app did a very simple thing: signed-up users were put in touch with taxi drivers in their vicinity, who came and picked them up. Once the ride was done, the rider swiped his phone, and his credit card was instantly charged. It's delightfully convenient for both rider and driver, which is no doubt why the app is worth $18 billion and is a hit in 44 countries. It has run into trouble in several of those countries, mainly because it may not screen the taxi drivers enough. But, in India, that was not the problem. It wasn't physical safety that we were worried about, no, that never keeps our government awake at night. No, India is the only country out of the aforementioned 44 in which it was Uber's payment mechanism that was the problem.

You see, the with-it tech geniuses at the RBI learned a few years ago that there was this new-fangled thing called 'the Internet' and people were 'buying things' on it with something called 'credit cards'. Naturally, they panicked. This looked to them suspiciously like consumers having fun. Which meant that they needed to be protected, i.e. prevented from having too much fun. And so the RBI enforced something called 'two-step authentication for card-not-present transactions'. Sorry, I just *had* to quote the lovely bureaucratese; I'll now tell you what that means. It means, that when you buy something online, putting in your card details isn't enough—you also need to put in a password. It may be a password you've previously agreed on with your bank, or it may be a new one-time password that your bank sends to your mobile phone every time you try to pay online. Either way, without the password, your purchase doesn't go through.

The only exception that was allowed was for foreign transactions. Now Uber, of course, is a foreign company; and when the rider swiped his phone, his credit card was charged somewhere abroad. And then the same amount was passed on to the driver's account. Uber, therefore, could operate in India legally, cheerfully, and with great success. With too much success, in fact. Its taxicab rivals, such as EasyCabs, were losing business. And so they wrote to the Reserve Bank, accusing Uber of violating the spirit of the law.

Now regulators, if they are smart, know that they should ignore a fat and happy domestic company if it complains that some foreign upstart, whom everyone is switching to, is breaking the rules. Sadly, the RBI is not that sort of regulator. They instead reproved Uber sternly. Some people, they said in a notification that was a masterpiece of passive-aggressive red tape, *some* people are 'camouflaging and flouting' the rules on two-step authentication.

I want you to pause to see exactly how colossally stupid this is. Remember one of the ways to authenticate payment? The bank sends you an SMS, with a password you then give the website as authentication. In other words, the source of the additional security is the card user's physical possession of her own phone. But—and this is the funny part—if you are paying Uber, or any other app, then you have your blasted phone with you anyway, don't you? So what additional security will sending it an SMS provide? Answer: none whatsoever. This is a regulation so completely bonkers that it should be confined to a padded cell and given dinner without cutlery. And yet Raghuram Rajan, a man smart enough to predict the financial crisis, defended this clinically insane policy in print. That, gentle readers, is what the Indian government does to you.

There is one way, though, to completely alter the nature of government: change the ministries around. Make them agencies.

Instead of a ministry of agriculture, have a set of departments and agencies focused on specific tasks. Many already exist—just make them the basic unit of organization instead of the ministry. Gillian Tett of the *Financial Times* tells the fascinating story of Syngenta, a $55-billion agricultural business from Switzerland. Syngenta, she says, has discovered that 'its internal structure was shaped by how the scientists inside the laboratories divided up the world, in their minds and lives'. So you had 'fertilizers' and 'fungicides' divisions. But its CEO, a few years ago, realized that you should set up organizations not for insiders, but for outsiders. So farmers, Syngenta's customers, don't say 'I need fungicide'; they say 'I want to protect my rice crop'. Syngenta reorganized into 'divisions defined by crops, not chemistry . . . you will see chirpy labels saying "rice", not "fungicide".'

So, says Tett, what if government services were organized 'according to the problems that voters faced, rather than the skills of bureaucrats, or historical precedents?'

Yes, big thought. But other people, such as former central banker Bimal Jalan, have made similar arguments. Reforming administration is also about reorganizing government. Make it face outwards, rather than upwards. Really, that is not too much to ask.

SEARCHING FOR SUITCASES

All very clever, you say, but the problem is that everyone is corrupt anyway, so all these super plans will falter because of that.

No.

Corruption is not what you think it is. For example, as we have already figured out, giving away natural resources to selected companies is not necessarily corrupt. Giving it to your friends may be immoral, but it's difficult to pin down as corruption if our laws not just permit it, but encourage it.

We are angry at corruption not because of the systems that underlie it, but because corrupt people seem to get away with it. And because corruption, we believe, can lead to bad decisions.

Corruption is not what you think it is. Corruption is not a moral collapse. Corruption is systems that do not build in accountability. That is all.

Anti-corruption crusaders, like Arvind Kejriwal, are wrong about a very great deal. But they are not wrong to fetishize decentralization and devolution as cures for 'corruption'. They are certainly cures for the anger we feel—because even if decentralization does not address corruption, it certainly addresses unaccountability.

Our bureaucrats are unaccountable, except to other unaccountable people like judges or policemen. The only people who *are* accountable are our politicians—and we feel they act with the most impunity, for they are answerable only to whoever heads their parties.

I agree. This must change. I do not condemn politicians, as most people do—having met several of them, I find them not unlike most businessmen or academics, and usually more honest than either. But, certainly, they can be made more accountable.

And here, again, I believe a well-intentioned law we passed in the now-distant past has done tremendous damage. Change it, and restore accountability.

The Tenth Schedule of the Constitution, added in 1985 and generally called 'the anti-defection law', was thought up by the same brilliant set of minds that imagined the Lokpal. It's the same complex of ideas, too—restrict the politician's field of behaviour, and he will behave better. After all, children, you may not believe this, but in the bad old days before the law was passed, politicians actually changed parties because they were *paid*! Now we know they still change parties—they just have to be paid more. But, in the process, we ensured that they can never question their party leader. According to the anti-defection law, if I am elected from a seat while being associated with a particular party, I have to do whatever the party tells me to do, or I will be thrown out of the legislature. Naturally, this means that our legislators have very little freedom of action. The one set of people we actually control, who are directly accountable to us, and we *reduced* their degree of accountability, replacing it with unquestioning loyalty to the unelected party boss! Utterly amazing. This is what happens when you try to legislate morality.

Make our politicians accountable again. Once that happens, the ripples will spread out through the system. It will then be in some legislators' interests to stand up against bad decisions taken by their own leaders, and for honesty and transparency—since that's what voters want. And party leaders, finally, will have some check on their behaviour.

Even more important, we need to recognize that corruption is born not because we have the wrong people in charge, but because we have the wrong systems, the wrong policies, the wrong incentives, and the wrong institutions. It is pointless to look for, or to demand, integrity in people placed in an environment where integrity means you do not survive.

I know it is difficult to admit. There was a time when corruption was simple. It involved large amounts of actual cash, and clear culpability. In the case that ruined Narasimha Rao's career, when he was accused of bribing legislators, the investigation turned on the crucial point of whether two big VIP-brand suitcases could, in fact, contain Rs 1 crore in 500-rupee notes. This is the kind of corruption we understand, the corruption of the petty clerk writ large, and so this is the kind of corruption we look for. This is the kind of guilt we expect and understand: personal, targeted, involving suitcases. We really need suitcases.

The modern economy, I am sorry to say, will not give us suitcases. It will instead give us conflicts of interest, dubious decisions, insider trading and offshore transactions. You can find scapegoats if you want. But in an economy and a government in which decision-making is necessarily collective, and where good intentions and deep dishonesty can only be told apart through well-timed wiretaps, a search for scapegoats is in itself dangerous. Move from a corruption that is individual, quantifiable, traceable to corruption that is imputed, systemic, and blurry, and you need to change your instincts, your intuitions as well.

We are a richer country, with rich-country corruption—corruption that can only be controlled, not eliminated; corruption that is a continuous battle, for it changes shape once it has been delineated; corruption that only exists once it has been discovered and defined, like all the most subtle of modern financial crimes. Can we please stop behaving like everything is about suitcases and Swiss accounts? That's so 1980s. Grow up.

THE MIRACLE CURE

Five paths we must retrace; five steps forward we must take; and three ways—judicial, administrative, and political—that our government itself must change.

Do that, and I think our growth will stun us. Our lives will be incalculably better, and the people we today struggle to help will help themselves.

Still, do you know the secret? The thing that would really turn our fortunes around? It's something that, since our Republic's first generation died, we have never imagined doing.

Social change.

Look, I've spent all this time talking about how policy should reform, how government should reform, blah blah blah. But the magic will happen most of all, really, when we reform ourselves.

A less hierarchical society, and we will have one where surprising collaborations are formed, that spark innovations and world-beating companies. A less class- and caste-conscious society, and more people will work with their hands, and manufacturing—the making of things—will receive greater attention. A less divided society, and we would create more liveable cities. A less stultified society, and we could put the best people in the best jobs for them, instead of the ones they inherited from their parents. We could be better entrepreneurs, better politicians, better lawyers, better carpenters, and most of all better actors.

The best sort of policy reform is that which engenders social progress. Primary education, of course, has always been the classic example of this. In India, the content of education is the most low-hanging fruit possible. We have pushed a large number of students into schools, but very few of them are learning the things they should. And not just from the point of view of employability. Instead of laughably regressive history textbooks, imagine if we focused on teaching kids the two building blocks for modern global citizens—statistics and the English language. (Yes, OK, I know the humanities are wonderful. But, seriously, statistics. Nothing teaches you critical thinking better than a course in statistics. Nothing warns you more against being dazzled by numbers, too.)

In so many ways, the Indian state could nudge its people towards becoming, well, better. We may not be terrible individuals, as individuals. But we so rarely are individuals! Most of the time, we are one group or another, most of which are at each other's throats. Constructing solidarity, creating citizenship, from this is not straightforward. But neither can it be completely ducked, the way the Indian state has chosen to do it.

This is, in fact, the biggest way in which we have rejected Gandhi. The Indian Republic is the heir of the British Raj and not Gandhi's nationalist movement because the Raj never sought to change India. It sought only to rule. After all, 1857's horrific violence had been caused, the British thought, by their unthinking imposition of their own cultural mores on Indians. Best to stop that. Instead of the intermingling that had become common among the East India's Company's nabobs, the sahibs of the Raj never thought that an Indian could be improved. At best, he could become a babu, an amusing caricature of modern man. (For them, as for today's crazy anti-globalization anarchists, modern=Western.)

The amazing thing is that when the babus took over the country, they chose to inherit this attitude. 'There is no point working to improve our subjects' problematic cultural practices; we have enough to do to keep them from each other's throats, and ours.' This is the thinking of the Raj in a nutshell, and it has also been the guiding philosophy of the Republic since 1950. Gandhi would have wanted us to make ourselves better, too; for him, that sort of self-government was as important as political *swaraj*, if not more. Not that Gandhi's ideas of better were necessarily the right ones. In fact, they *weren't* the right ones. But still.

At some point, this attitude has to change; for we are fast approaching the limits of our growth as a premodern society attempting postmodern economics.

Policy that creates solidarity is policy that promotes urbanization, for example. It breaks down the barriers of the past, and builds bonds over the ruins. Towns allow people to be what they want to be, to create what they dream of creating—to enter a profession barred to their fathers, to start a commercial enterprise that nobody in their village would have patronized. Urbanization means that people move around, and this mingling, this simple exposure to other ways of doing things, can help—as long as they do not form the ghettoes that we have allowed to spring up in our cities. Ghettoes are a symptom: our towns need shaping, not abandonment.

Indeed, migrants must not be seen as outsiders, as Mumbai's Senas would like, but as the building blocks of the town's own identity, as they are in Delhi. Towns need to be pushed towards being inclusive, and spaces that encourage cooperation rather than walls. Migrants, whom town planners despise and marginalize in India, are precisely those who are seen as vital indicators of a town's promise elsewhere. American towns like Portland and Charlotte have gone out of their way to lure young internal migrants, sparring with each other to be seen as the hottest destinations for potential workers. And not just high-end migrants either; the prosperity of America's Southwest— the 'Sun Belt'— in recent decades has been built on the arrival, in towns like Phoenix, of low-wage earners from the decaying industrial Midwest.

Once India's cities also become places that attract migrants, they must provide space for migrants to discover who they are, unaffected by the bonds and hates of the past. And they will discover they are, town-dwellers, ever so slightly different, and more liberal, than those they have left behind. Perhaps this transformation requires some faith; but, unlike most, this is a faith worth investing in.

Then there is policing. Better policing isn't just about ensuring that people will be able to sign contracts knowing that they will be enforced. It is not even just about each individual case of injustice. The change runs deeper. Ask yourself why, in troubled Uttar Pradesh, it was the party of Dalit power—and only the party of the Dalits—that worked to improve the provision of law and order. The provision of order and the rule of law is not thought of as being the cardinal duty of liberalism; but ours is a country aflame with local violence and private law—*privilege*, quite literally. Here, imposing law and order is a first step to upending the oppressions of the past. Here, imposing law and order is a first step to the bubbling up of creativity and innovation that happens when people are allowed to be themselves.

That bubbling up from below is really what sparks the most extraordinary expansions of growth, and the most progressive moments for societies. When people from groups that were previously excluded are allowed into the 'mainstream', everyone benefits. In India, many of us can't even find houses and schools, let alone jobs. Fix access to services, and ensure they're equal-opportunity. Are primary schools in poorer areas worse? Do our state health-care centres discriminate against Dalits? Does the man who represents the government to you today—a policeman investigating a crime, perhaps, or a public-sector banker offering you a loan—does he offer other people the same deal he offers you? Or is it better, or worse? Answer these questions, or better still, ensure they don't even need to be asked, and you will build a better state. You will build a state that earns people's trust.

Better states make better people. How do I know? Because I live in Delhi, an urban nightmare, where people travel long distances in a climate that is inhospitable for much of the year for work that pays too little to ever be able to give anyone a path to house-ownership, let alone affluence. This comes out in how we travel. Inside Delhi's badly driven buses, we shove and grope each other. On Delhi's overcrowded roads, we run each other down ruthlessly—and, worse, block the left lane.

But in the Delhi Metro, where the air is conditioned and the rides are smooth, we do not do that. In the Delhi Metro, everyone mostly is given a bit of personal space. In the Delhi Metro, we stand next to a daily-wage labourer, a Nepalese domestic worker, a Kannadiga engineer, and we don't care. In the Delhi Metro, we even try to queue.

Better people are possible to create, even in Delhi.

A SILVER BULLET

Yes, social change can make the biggest difference. And I have one pet example about how it can.

You got this far. You deserve the silver bullet. The one secret to hyper-growth.

Here it is. You ready?

Get women working.

No, seriously. The entry of a previously underemployed set of individuals into the workforce is the biggest possible boost to economic growth we can imagine. Don't underestimate the degree to which just throwing more labour into the mix can help an economy grow. As Alwyn Young and Paul Krugman have effectively demonstrated, the East Asian miracle—in spite of all the millions of words devoted to the policy changes that supposedly sparked it off—was almost all about more *things*: more capital, but crucially more labour. More women working, in other words.

In India, it isn't just that women are unsafe and discriminated against. Turns out that as we grow richer, women are less likely to work (except at the very top of the income distribution). What in other countries has pushed the economy towards faster growth, in our country slows it down.

I told you: social change. Change yourself. If you wanted a silver bullet, I've given one to you. I can't help it if it's not the kind you want.

CONCLUSION

THE NOISE OF BUILDING

India is unique.

This is something on which a lot of people agree. The less they know about any other place or any other time, the more strongly they agree.

I don't think India is unique. I do think it is large enough to contain a multitude of contradictions. Joan Robinson, the formidable economist who was Manmohan Singh's mentor at Cambridge, famously used to say that 'whatever you can rightly say about India, the opposite is also true'. (Put that together with 'India is unique', and you have a nice little logical paradox.)

Above all, governing India is about managing these contradictions. It is about finding a path through our multitude of differences.

Sometimes that path is a winding one indeed. So it has been for most of our history. We have been faced with countless dead ends. We have taken innumerable wrong turns—towards state control, towards 'services–led growth', towards 'private–public partnership', and so on.

My argument in this book has been that today, the path ahead is clear. It will be difficult, and it will be steep. But it is straight, not winding.

For once, there is a popular consensus that some sort of radical reform is necessary. There is a clear agenda, too, one on which agreement has been hammered out for decades, in a manner reminiscent of Narasimha Rao's claim in 1991 that 'the papers were ready'. All that is needed is to implement it.

If there is one way in which that agenda can be summarized, it is in this advice to the government: Do different things. Get out of manufacturers' faces, and stop tormenting them with Lime Registers and incredible tax demands and hundreds of incomprehensible and mutually contradictory regulations. Instead, transfer that energy to providing basic services: law and order, health care, skill education. Think different things: trust prices, don't manipulate them. Prices are the voice of the people; a democratic government should listen to them, not overrule them. Remember we are not as poor as we were, so stop trying to 'protect' people like farmers, and instead, allow them to be something else.

Be more democratic, by being more responsive. Respond to anger about corruption by increasing accountability. Respond to economic crisis by listening to what prices are telling you. We have taken growth for granted and it has failed us. Do not ever take democracy for granted.

And yes, in some ways we *are* unique. We are the grandest experiment in human history, and one that is halfway to succeeding. A country with deep and bitter divisions, too many divisions to count—in fact, a country whose most pervasive cultural characteristic is a fondness for division—is struggling towards some form of solidarity, and doing it democratically.

We are dealing with decades of building—of bridges, of power plants, of roads, of cities—in just a few years. We are dealing with

342

a people in transformation, as they judge their parents' attitudes and find their own. And we are dealing with 13 million young people joining the workforce every year. A new Kolkata joins the workforce every year. A new Greece.

Each individual problem is not unique, but it is possible that its scale is.

When problems are this vast, we have to trust the signals that democracy sends us. Democracy is not just a pressure valve for discontent. It is a crucial policymaking tool. Even when it comes to building infrastructure, as it happens. Yes, in India people would not accept the government taking away their savings, as happens in China. This has hurt growth. But much of China's savings went into investment that may prove to be unproductive. If India's leaders truly trust democracy, and trust prices, then we will not repeat that mistake. We will find a more wholesome path to growth.

We are a young country.

I remember returning to India, full of young people, and discovering that not only were they irritating, but also that the very word 'youth' was irritating. As I noticed then, it isn't just grossly overused—nobody is sure if they're using it correctly. Is it a collective noun? ('The youth vote for change.') A singular noun? ('This youth wants change.') An adjective? ('The youth vote is for change.') When do you put 'the' before it? If you are a youth, or a member of the youth, do you say 'd youth' instead of 'the youth'? And why must you, youth, talk like that when we now have predictive text on phones?

But there are so very many young people in India that it naturally changes how this country feels. We are mostly 25 years old—fifteen years younger than America, ten years younger than China. I actually think that's the most important fact about India today. It tells us why India today lacks all sense of proportion. It tells us why we want change immediately, why we are quick to anger. It tells us why we want to blame anyone but ourselves. It explains why every damn thing seems to us like the end of the world.

We are a young country, and so we have no perspective. Lessons from elsewhere or from the past, from theory and from history, are not exactly our favourite things. They happened to someone else; we are, of course, unique.

And yet, everywhere you look in the past, there are crucial lessons to be learned.

Look at Britain's rise to industrial power. That was centuries ago, in a different world—what does it matter to us? But it does. Because the lesson is that we need other countries to give us money to invest, even if we don't like them very much. Rising Britain, in the seventeenth and eighteenth centuries, didn't save and invest its way to becoming the first industrial nation while spitting in the teeth of all its enemies on the European continent. In fact, it was dependent on foreign investment to sustain its appetite for resources. Amazingly, its biggest investor was the Netherlands—which it was, simultaneously, trying to supplant as a mercantile power, and with which it was busy fighting wars, too. 'The devil shits Dutchmen,' Samuel Pepys recorded, as the acrid smoke from ships burned by the Dutch fleet spread across the rivers of 1680s England; but, over the century after he wrote that, the diabolical Dutch actually lent their rivals the money they used to rise to greatness.

Here is another lesson: a reminder of how dangerous it is to imagine that some energy sources are far more secure than others. Every major country, when expanding rapidly, has worried above all about fuel. As a result, countries that prided themselves on their power or their independence found they needed the outside world more than it needed them, just as we do today. Consider this: the expansion of intercontinental trade so essential to the West's industrialization came as sailing ships were replaced by coal-fired ships in the world's merchant fleets. But coal, unlike the wind, needed to be replenished. And so, the race to colonize the world gathered, well, steam—because every single trading economy wanted its own refuelling station. The fragile web of alliances and rivalries this rushed land-grab entailed meant that the First World War was inevitable. And, as the First World War broke out, Winston Churchill warned of the problems that coal posed for shipping and international politics, and suggested a shift to petroleum. Surely, he thought, nothing bad could come of that. Winston was wrong. He often was.

Here is yet another lesson, more recent. If there is any country that we resemble, and in which an Indian can feel instantly at home, it is Indonesia. Its syncretic culture, its youth (that blasted word again), its sense of urgency. And its traffic. OK, on that dimension Jakarta is worse even than any Indian city. Its roads are a perpetual, honking traffic jam. Luxury sedans jostle for space amid the abandoned pillars of an attempted elevated railway system. But that, like other urban transport projects, had to be abandoned. What happened? Well, money was scarce and so the Japanese were called in to fund it. But worries about extensive corruption led the Japanese to leave. The project had to be mothballed. We in India hope that Japanese money will help us overcome our infrastructure deficit. They are financing, after all, that grand bridge from Mumbai to the mainland. But are we ignoring lessons that Indonesia learned?

When you're young, you think your pain is yours alone. You do not look around and see how others suffer similarly. Nobody else could suffer like you do.

In India, we have an infrastructure deficit; so does Indonesia. In India, we have tough-to-remove fuel subsidies; so does Nigeria. In India, we have a problem in which the government is bankrupting itself subsidizing foodgrain production; so does Thailand. In India, we depend too much on mining, which has led to economic collapse;

so does South Africa. In India, we have old socialist-era protections that keep us from becoming competitive in manufacturing; so does Brazil. The Brazilians even have a phrase for it: the *custo Brasil*, or 'Brazil cost'. Like us, the Brazilians have tried to fix this. You know how? Through introducing a little technological fix, self-certification for small firms—just as the Modi government has done. It didn't work for them. Surely we should find out why?

Even our political crises have parallels, most of them designed, almost, to show us how lucky we are. Everywhere, governments are terrified of, or paralysed by, or cracking down on, middle-class protests: in Thailand, in Malaysia, in Brazil. In many of our fellow emerging markets—Thailand and Turkey, for example—the rural–urban divide in politics has turned into a perennial spat, with street fights and coups, about how the benefits of growth should be shared. Look at India's food inflation through this lens, and you realize how we have found a way around such destabilization.

Look at the world with a sense of proportion instead of youthful self-absorption, and you realize your problems are not unique. So many of our peers have them. All of us splurged back in the good years, when the West exported cheap money everywhere; and we're now having trouble cutting back. In the good years, all these countries could try buying off poor people with extensive welfare interventions; but, in tougher times, a newly powerful middle class has decided that all such democracies hand over too much of their money to other people. Oh, and infrastructure. What a mess everywhere. Besides China, the only place that's managing to keep infrastructure investment high is Malaysia—the most corrupt country in the world, according to recent business surveys, but also a place where the ruling elite tightly controls the media.

India's healthier path to growth will be one that incorporates lessons from all these places. It must allow for people to protest on the streets, and ensure our political and economic system stays flexible enough to deal with it. It must handle environmental activism and not alienate those who live closer to the land than most policymakers. It must keep in mind that redistribution and the consequent inflation is a fact of life, and isn't going away even if you are not yet a First World country. It has to be able to incorporate those big, radical decisions we have talked about: for example, giving up on coal.

If we somehow develop the wisdom to look around and learn; if we add a degree of respect for the signals that democracy sends us; and if we combine it with the audacity of youth, the willingness to take a leap forward into the unfamiliar; then we have a chance to stake out a path to prosperity that could be better than any we have trodden before.

When I first moved to the United States, I really couldn't figure out what was wrong with me. Something was missing. I would wander the streets, trying to work out what it was. Nothing as simple as Indian faces—there are enough of those in any university town.

Then, one day, three months in, I passed a construction site. And I sat down and stared at it in stupefaction. I had finally figured out what I had been missing.

Many parts of the West feel complete. Finished. There's nothing to add. In India, we are adding things at a tremendous rate. Now that I've moved back, I know the price of that frenetic activity. Within sight of any window in urban India, a house is being demolished, another is being built. The noise is incredible. It keeps you up at night. It fills your ears.

When things get built in the West, they put up screens to prevent the noise from bothering you. Any marble is cut indoors, or in workshops far away. Earth is not left to block up the street and delay traffic and inconvenience walkers. There is a lesson here, and a warning. When we account for growth, the building that was built goes in on the positive side of the ledger. But we do not account for the inconvenience caused. That inconvenience is valuable and quantifiable; in the West, I can value it in terms of what it costs to avoid it, such as the rent on a workshop elsewhere to cut marble. But here, we pretend that cost does not exist.

Economic growth is essential because it changes lives. It opens up horizons for all of us. If, that is, we do it right. If we account for it properly. Costs should not be ignored just because they're difficult to quantify.

Nor are we ever prepared, perfectly, for high growth. We now have more cars than we know what to do with—and certainly, we haven't become good drivers as quickly as we have become good buyers of cars. India has among the highest rate of road accidents in the world.

Even in the hinterland, in rural UP, people have come up to me and asked: Are you from Delhi? And when I have admitted to living there, they have assumed—as many people in villages still do—that I must have more power over their lives than they do. Tell Delhi, they said—waving at their brand-new rural road, perfectly metalled and winding through their fields—tell them in Delhi to put in some dashed speed breakers. This road is just too good. (True story.)

High growth has costs; we may not even know what they are, or be mentally prepared for them. But we know, now, that whatever they are, we will pay them. Because there are just too many of us who will live lives of desperation and anger, lives unfulfilled and truncated, if the Indian economy does not become the wonder of the world.

We are a democracy, and this anger, this anxiety, means there is a lot of noise. It, too, fills our ears. But we shouldn't fear it.

The noise that keeps us awake at night, the noise of building, is the sound of growth. It is the sound of a new path being fashioned. It is the sound of the future. It is the sound that is made when desperation becomes triumph.

AFTERWORD AND ACKNOWLEDGEMENTS

Every aspiring actor practises the gratitude-laced speech that he will give at the Oscars but, for some reason, few of those who want to write a book ever daydream about writing the acknowledgements section. This truth is sadly revealing. No book is ever written alone, but writers seem to pretend it is.

I have no such illusions and would thus like to start by profusely thanking whichever eighth-century Ethiopian discovered that the coffee bean had certain wonderful properties. Without the selfless service of that nameless genius, this book would never have been written.

Seriously, though, there are many people without whom this book would have been impossible to conceive of or write. First among them is my editor at *Business Standard*, A.K. Bhattacharya, who ensured that I had the time, space, and encouragement I needed. In addition, a vast number of the opinions and concerns expressed in it were sparked by things that he has said. It has been a privilege to work for him—and for T.N. Ninan, chairman of *Business Standard* and this country's greatest economic commentator. Mr Ninan is that exceptional sort of person who is constantly full of ideas both novel and sensible; from him I continue to try to learn the art of communicating complex concepts with respect for evidence, for data—and also for simplicity.

Many of the problems—and solutions—in *Restart* first occurred to me when they were discussed threadbare at the Monday morning editorial meetings at the *Business Standard* office. Thus I am grateful to Subir Gokarn, Shankar Acharya, Laveesh Bhandari, Kanika Datta, Rahul Jacob, Surinder Sud, Shubhashis Gangopadhyay, Shyam Saran, Deepak Lal, T.C.A. Srinivasa Raghavan, and Devangshu Datta—the people who make that meeting the best place to learn about how India really works.

That I am writing a book at all is thanks to those who first got me to write for a living. I was encouraged, early on, to think for myself through the issues we've discussed in *Restart* mainly because Shekhar Gupta, who edited the *Indian Express* when I worked there, has always pushed young journalists to write more and write better. So many of us owe our careers and our confidence to him. In many ways I think he has been the most influential Indian journalist of the past two decades, and this country has been the better for that fact. Thanks are due also to Raj Kamal Jha of the *Express*, a person more bubbling with ideas than any other I have known, and whose apparently unending energy made that newspaper a remarkably exciting place to work.

Books like this one are prone to all forms of error, exaggeration, and downright idiocy. This one is perhaps not quite as bad as it might have been because many of the ideas in it have been bounced off, borrowed from, or blatantly stolen from various people over the years. Not all of these people agree with me, but that only makes me more grateful to them—Amulya Gopalakrishnan, that means you. For those ideas, for that criticism, and for much feedback, I am indebted to Dhiraj Nayyar, Rukmini Shrinivasan, Pavan

Ahluwalia, Samir Patil, Amitabh Dubey, Saubhik Chakrabarti, Aruna Urs, Nandan Nilekani, Sunil Jain, Sadanand Dhume, Milan Vaishnav, Jonathan Shainin, James Crabtree, Mini Kapoor, Basharat Peer, Vivek Dehejia, Patrick French, Ajay Shah, Ila Patnaik, Vinay Sitapati, and Madhav Khosla. All of them have, over the years, shaped the ideas that have gone into this book.

I've also benefited from the discussions I've had, over long lunches or quick coffees, with Sushant Singh, Shashi Shekhar, Alok Kshirsagar, Dhruva Jaishankar, Mukul Kesavan, Milan Vaishnav, Ashok Malik, and Ashutosh Varshney—people whose work I read and admire.

That I have some of the tools needed to take on a task of this nature is thanks to the education that I was fortunate to receive. And I received it above all, from Bhaskar Dutta, who, eighteen years ago, gave me a paper to read on declining industries and political power—after which I understood, for the first time, that economic theory could explain why reform was tough, as well as why reform was essential. My other teachers at the Indian Statistical Institute— Bharat Ramaswami, Arunava Sen, and Shubhashis in particular— helped that realization along. That I am not an academic economist now is not because their example lacked the power to inspire, but because I am just bad at it—as evidenced by my ill-fated attempt at a doctoral degree.

Still, in the course of a long and ignominious exit from my PhD programme, I learned a great deal. That my time in graduate school was not a total loss is thanks to the superhuman efforts made by Abhijit Banerjee, Dani Rodrik, and Devesh Kapur in particular—and also Bob Bates, Ken Shepsle, Thomas Scanlon, Amartya Sen, Drew Fudenberg, Jeffrey Sachs, Esther Duflo, and Michael Kremer. Altogether, they ensured that I left graduate school far better informed and marginally more thoughtful than I was when I entered it. I still feel bad that I failed to live up to the high expectations that some of them had of me, and I hope this book goes part-way in showing them that the time they spent on me wasn't a complete waste.

Much of the value of those years in graduate school came from the people I talked to daily, the smartest set of individuals I can ever imagine knowing—Saugato Datta, Antara Dutta, Marius Hentea, Neeraja Poddar, Jimmy McMenamin, Charles Cohen, Karna Basu, Sanmay Das, Paula Bustos, Zaki Wahhaj, David Molin, Alex Wagner, Eric Werker, Radu Iovita, Emir Kamenica, Janmejay Singh, Karthik Muralidharan, Emmanuel Farhi, and Elsa Artadi. That was both the most stimulating and the most wearying time of my life, and I couldn't have survived without these friends and colleagues.

When I was finally thrown out into the outer darkness, where there is weeping and gnashing of teeth and, most importantly, an absence of doctoral degrees, the best advice I received on how and why to return to India was from Ramachandra Guha and Pratap Bhanu Mehta—for which I will be forever grateful. Pratap has continued to be an indispensable guide, as has Bibek Debroy, and I cannot thank them enough for their kindness.

I have lived in Delhi since 2008, and I am convinced that there is no more policy-obsessed city in the world. The journalists I work with, and the ones I have a drink with, can talk about Acts and Bills and Rules the way that, in other places, well-paid lawyers would. For the constant disagreements, frequent lectures—and occasional gentle advice—that have kept me honest over the years, I'm indebted to Mitali Saran, Shivam Vij, Raghu Karnad, Gargi Rawat, Aman Sethi, Nishita Jha, Sruthijith K.K., Abhimanyu Singh, C. Raja Mohan, Samanth Subramanian, Sarah Jacob, Ravish Tiwari, Kushan Mitra, Mehboob Jeelani, Pranab Dhal Samanta, Supriya Nair, Sonal Shah, Alex Blasdel, Cordelia Jenkins, Harsh Sethi, Chinki Sinha, Samrat, Nikhil Pahwa, Shruti Ravindran, Aletta

Andre, Rrishi Raote, James Fontanella-Khan, and Alia Allana. (That's a pretty impressive set of people to have in any profession. Delhi journalism's doing fine, thanks for asking.) This is in addition to those at *Business Standard*—Shailesh Dobhal, Bhupesh Bhandari, Aditi Phadnis, N. Sundaresha Subramanian, Jyoti Mukul, Shivam Saini, and Veenu Sandhu among them—whose work I admire, and from whom I have much to learn.

But, as I said, Delhi is special—it isn't just journalists. Most of my friends over the past six years in this town have, at some point, been not just friends—they have also been discussion partners, and have told a story or shared an idea that has affected this book. They are anthropologists and digital marketers, money managers and artists, advertising executives and lawyers—but, perhaps because they are Dilli-walas, they're all also policy experts in some way. (Some are actually Policy Experts, as in they're paid for it. Odd, since the rest of us do it for free.) So thanks, then, to Aarti Sethi, Shuddhabrata Sengupta, Kranti Saran, Gautam Bhan, Avi Singh, Biba and Brian Saxton, Yamini Aiyar and Adarsh Sinha, Santanam Swaminadhan and Aarthi Rajan, Shomikho Raha and Ferzina Banaji, Trisha Gupta and Anuj Bhuwania, Meenakshi Reddy Madhavan and Kian Ganz, Samit Basu and Sarnath Banerjee, Malvika and Tejbir Singh, Trupthi and Shruthi Basavaraj, Reetika Khera, Sunalini Kumar, Chiki Sarkar, Anand Vaidya, Aditi Saraf, Abhijit Iyer-Mitra, Amrita Ibrahim, Karuna Nundy, Nikhil Mehra, Nick Robinson, Ankur Bhardwaj, Venetia Aranha, Nilanjana Roy, and Ashok Mathew. You're all great people, and I owe you each a drink.

Restart got named, commissioned, written, and published because of the tyrannical and talented Meru Gokhale, who, I discovered to my dismay, was capable of chivvying me along even over the phone from London. She fed me home-made Japanese food, sent me home with leftovers, called me to gossip and to remind me to keep it readable, and what more can one ask for from an editor?

Thanks to her, and to all at Penguin Random House, especially Arpita Basu, for an exceptional job copy-editing—speaking as a copy-editor—and to Caroline Newbury for getting the word out, to Vedanti Sikka for the striking cover design and to R. Ajith Kumar who typeset the book.

But, truthfully, I must admit I wrote this book essentially because it seemed to me author photos on book jackets are always flattering, and I hadn't had a flattering photo taken of me since 2003. If, somehow, you judge the photo on this book to indeed be flattering, then that is due to the immense talents of Kavi Bhansali, who took it, and to Rishi Majumder and Pragya Tiwari, who stood around behind him proffering mostly useless advice and very useful whisky. I thank them for that, and for any number of memorable conversations.

Again, my parents. I can at least be sure that, even if nobody else reads this book all through, my mother will. For giving me that vital confidence, and for being so lovingly patient with a child who is naturally surly and uncommunicative, I owe her more than most kids do a parent. Thanks, Mum. And thanks, Dad, for always being more analytical than me and for convincing me that you have to write things down in order to truly understand them. I miss you.

And finally, I owe more than I can comfortably express to Snigdha Poonam, whom I rely on for advice and support and companionship; for on-point criticism and uncommon perspective; and for, every day, the best and most interesting stories I've ever heard.

Oh, and thank *you*, reader. Your surprise at actually managing to finish reading a book on the Indian economy is nothing when compared to my astonishment that I somehow finished writing it.

November, 2014
New Delhi

NOTES

1   These estimates are from a paper written by T.S. Papola and P.P. Sahu: 'Growth and Structure of Long-term Employment in India', Indian Council of Social Science Research, March 2012.

2   I just want to emphasize that I AM NOT MAKING ANY OF THIS UP.

3   *'Maang hai, lekin aakanksha nahin.'*

4   World Bank study, 2010, quoted by my colleague Aman Sethi in 'India Skilling the Willing', *Business Standard*, June 2, 2014.

5   According to two reports submitted by the consulting groups MaCS and Aon Hewitt to the National Skill Development Corporation in 2011.

6   S. Nihal Singh's obituary of Dhirubhai, 'The Phenomenon Called Dhirubhai', in the *Tribune*, July 13, 2002: 'There were reputable business houses—the Tatas above all—who symbolized excellence and ethical practices but they ran a predictable course. In Dhirubhai's case, not only did he cut corners to survive in India's business climate, but he converted a whole nation to the virtues of capitalism's heart, in the trading of shares and the stock exchange.'

7   It's actually 'Not all the world's armies can stop an idea . . .'

8   Back then, Indian finance ministers presented the Budget at 5.30 in the evening—a quaint colonial tradition, begun when the budget of the Government of India had to be presented at exactly the same time as the British Parliament settled in to hear that country's budget, at noon

Greenwich Mean Time. About fifty years after Independence, someone got around to changing this, a fair indication of the speed at which the Government of India usually works.

9 Exactly the kind of detail that the Rajiv hagiographies resolutely ignore. This particular detail has only recently come to light, thanks to dogged research by T.C.A. Srinivasa Raghavan—which he details in 'Two PMs and a Countdown to Financial Crisis', *The Hindu*, April 2013.

10 Mostly derision.

11 Although, according to his multitude of critics, it didn't happen quite enough.

12 With one exception: Manmohan Singh in 2012, when he decided to push on past Mamata Banerjee's departure from the alliance over whether India should allow foreigners to set up big retail chains.

13 Political writing in India has little in common with your average Homeric epic, except for the use of epithets. Just as Achilles was 'swift-footed', so Manmohan Singh is 'silent', Narendra Modi 'divisive', Rajiv Gandhi 'dynamic', Mamata Banerjee 'unpredictable'—and George Fernandes 'a firebrand'.

14 Said by Shourie to *The Economist*. Quoted by Rob Jenkins—the political economist who invented the indispensable phrase 'reform by stealth'—in his essay on the NDA and reforms in the excellent collection *Coalition Politics and Hindu Nationalism*, Routledge, 2005.

15 This was in an interview to Shekhar Gupta in 2004.

16 Caste and Creed No Bar, Wheatish Complexion Only, No Divorcees Please.

17 The American worker may still expect a lot, but the fact that suddenly energy is a lot cheaper in the US, thanks to shale gas, means that he may actually be paid that much. Decades on, 'Made in USA' might begin to be a thing again. For a succinct description of American manufacturing, what ails it, and how to fix it, see Ed Luce's excellent *Time to Start Thinking*. The parallels to aspects of India's re-industrialization problem are considerable.

18 Shame on you. When are you going to quit?

19 By the Homeric rule I mentioned earlier, Congress regional leaders are *always* called 'satraps'. This allows writers about Indian politics to

imagine that they are sounding distant, refined, and European.

It is dangerous to delve into the various etymological ironies of such usage, but here goes. The word 'satrap' is a Hellenized version of the title that the Persian Empire assigned to men who governed a largish area on behalf of emperors usually named Cyrus or Xerxes or Darius. That originated in an Old Persian word that had the same root as the Sanskrit word *kshetra*, or area. Thus, in India, large parts of the country were at various points ruled by dynasties that called themselves and their empires *kshatraps*—a word that has come down to us in various ways, including (probably) *chhatrapati*, the chosen title of Maratha rulers, and also (possibly) the corrupted form *khap*, generally associated with angry Jat caste panchayats. For additional amusement, note that Dara, among the proudest of Jat names, is an Indianized version of Darius. Next time someone says khap panchayats are 'Indian culture', suggest gently to them that khaps are about as Indian as Ayatollah Khomeini, and see what happens.

20 Zakir Hussain's Homeric epithet: 'scholar'. President Hussain was a mild-mannered man whose greatest contribution to Indian politics is that he was the target of the Hindu right's first successful rumour-mongering campaign, a method that they have now perfected. Even today, it is possible to meet people who remain convinced of the truth of the rumour that Hussain built a large mosque inside Rashtrapati Bhavan.

21 Whatever else Indira Gandhi was, she was very well brought up.

22 Who was later to be Narasimha Rao's first choice for finance minister in 1991. Only when Patel turned it down did Rao ask Manmohan Singh.

This is another one of those What Ifs that Indian economists love. If Patel had accepted instead of Dr Singh, what would have been different? Would Patel have persuaded Rao of changes that Dr Singh couldn't? Patel definitely wrote at length about the need to preserve manufacturing: 'It would be suicidal to let our capital goods industries wither away out of neglect, inefficiency and abject surrender to competition from abroad.' And here he is on reforming capital and labour markets: 'Exit has everything to do with big business also, it means that no one is going to say that nobody can take over the Tatas and Birlas or anything like that and that they must be there forever. Then you are not talking of exit policy. You are talking of the same things for which you are blaming labour.' For these quotes and more, pick up the volume of Patel's essays edited by Deena Khatkhate and Y.V. Reddy.

23 The development of Bombay's working class is, fortunately, overstudied. This is because, as with the Bengal Renaissance of the 1840s, it has the Indian history trifecta. First, there's a clear Western parallel, so your peers Over There understand what you're talking about. Second, many Indian historians are of the right ethnicity to read archives in the local language. Finally, the researcher can live comfortably in a big city while working on his history.

However, the best thing to read on the subject remains Raj Chandravarkar's *Origins of Industrial Capitalism in India*, published in 2004.

24 Krishna Menon's Homeric epithet: 'Machiavellian' or 'saturnine'. Much of Menon's reputation, one must conclude, came from judgement of his appearance. Ralph McGill—an American columnist and publisher who became a liberal icon in the 1950s and 1960s as the rare white southerner who took a strong progressive position on civil rights—made this explicit in a column from 1962 that quoted a 'reporter', most probably McGill himself: 'Menon is the only man in international politics whose appearance matches his reputation for evil and wicked machinations. He looks permanently made up to walk on stage and play Mephistopheles.' McGill went on, about Menon's 'sinister appearance': 'His posture and surly personality make one imagine the smell of burning sulphur each time he passes.' The column was headlined 'Sinister Minister', in a triumph of the headliner's undervalued art.

25 Nowhere are the causes and consequences of this murder better explained than in Gyan Prakash's *Mumbai Fables*, especially the superb sixth chapter, an inspiration for much of this section.

26 Luke 12:27.

27 For the sad, sad, story of Navi Mumbai, the ultimate disappointment, Annapurna Shaw's *The Making of Navi Bombay*; or Chapter 7 of Gyan Prakash's *Mumbai Fables*.

28 Also known as the floor area ratio or the floor space ratio. The fact that one number can be called three different things just to confuse you is how you know the property market is full of people trying to defraud you.

29 Bowling alleys, uncool in the US since the 1950s, are still extremely cool in India. I suspect this also explains our hairstyles and the cut of our trousers.

30 The battle between the two Maharashtra infrastructure agencies, and the political wrangling behind it, was the subject of much infuriated press coverage. One good article with which to start is 'Rift between Cong–NCP Ministers Slows Down Mumbai Infra Projects', by Manasi Phadke, *Indian Express*, July 5, 2013.

31 Jairam's Homeric epithet: 'crafty'. Or 'smooth'. Or 'suave'. Or 'witty'.

32 Common logical fallacy: If two sets of people who normally disagree with each other both accuse you of something, this does not mean that you are necessarily 'doing something right'.

33 In this case, be uncharitable.

34 Incredibly, the notification which included the gymnasium section was sold by Jairam Ramesh to the press as an *improvement*. Homeric epithet: 'Silvertongue'.

35 Most of these were brought to light by a superb series of articles by the *Business Standard* environment reporter Nitin Sethi.

36 'See, Mom, it's not my fault!'

37 Not you, of course. You're awesome.

38 At some point, economists must study the Business Family Wedding Gift Economy. It is an extraordinary, closed bubble. What happens is this: a woman marries into a conservative Indian business family. She may well be energetic and bright, but there's no place for her at work, nor can she work elsewhere. So, instead, she's urged to 'take up something'. Scented candles, usually. Sometimes kurta design. Or necklaces, or faux-Rajasthani coffee tables. She then becomes a 'success', because every other woman in the family buys her candles as wedding presents, at hideously inflated prices. In return, she buys their kurtas as wedding presents. Eventually, everyone is buying everyone else's hideous creations at hideously high prices, and nobody can ever tell anyone else their stuff

sucks, and that nobody really likes the smell of lavender anyway.

The most amazing thing is, this is not a very different economy from the one their husbands are in.

39 The news about JSW's controversial demand that a fee be paid to its chairman's wife for the brand name 'JSW', was broken by my colleague N. Sundaresha Subramanian in *Business Standard* on July 29, 2014. The article quoted an official report from a well-known shareholder advisory service that said it was an 'abusive' transaction. That service's head added: 'We do not understand the logic behind the JSW brand being owned by a company that is nearly 100 per cent owned by Sangita Jindal, wife of Sajjan Jindal. SES is of the opinion that ownership of the brand, which develops over a period of time along with growth of the business, cannot belong to a separate company promoted by the promoters of the company.'

40 I collect unnecessary bureaucratic acronyms. The United States Food and Drug Administration's report on Ranbaxy is totally the motherlode. Did you know the FDA uses the phrase 'too numerous to count' so often, it abbreviates it 'TNTC' without explanation? The TNTCs are TNTC.

41 In what is a total complete utter coincidence, spending on R&D helps you minimize your taxes.

42 These team names are simply insane. I can at least understand the Bangalore Royal Challengers; they semi-illegally advertise the whisky brand, Royal Challenge, that's paying their salaries. But the Super Kings? Are they a cigarette size? A mattress size? Did they just get named after the Kings XI Punjab and were feeling childish? Oh, and how about the Mumbai Indians? Is there any other nationality of people from Mumbai I don't know about? At least when the Red Sox were called the Boston Americans it was 1890 or something and they were all Americans—the 'Indians' are full of Australians.

Don't even get me started on the Kolkata Knight Riders.

43 Fortunately, the questions of conflict of interest raised by the Srinivasan case appeared so very egregious that they attracted the attention even of the Supreme Court. The court, it was reported in December 2014, had declared that the onus was on Srinivasan to show that there was

no conflict of interest in how he had run the BCCI. In the words of a *Hindustan Times* report, the 'Supreme Court has made scathing comments on the issue of conflict of interest in the case of both Dhoni and Srinivasan'.

44 i.e., dead inside.

45 India is a big whisky-drinking country. As a sting operation in the early 2000s confirmed, when you want to pay a bribe to get a major defence deal, you take along a bottle of Blue Label just to make the point. It used to be said, in the fine old days of import controls and bell-bottoms and villains who drank Vat 69, that more Scotch was drunk in India than produced in Scotland.

Of course, the most important thing to know about Indian whisky is that it is not, in fact, whisky. It is rum. This tells you more about India than any single fact should.

You see, whisky is made from malt—from fermented, mashed-up grain. Most Indian whisky is made from molasses. So it isn't whisky; it is rum, bleached, coloured and flavoured to taste like whisky.

At some point in the 1980s, the Scots decided enough was enough and Indian whiskies couldn't go around claiming to be whiskies. Indian whisky makers, such as Mallya, were shocked—shocked!—that anyone would imagine that their product could in any way be mistaken for Scotch whisky. The fact that Indian whisky-flavoured rums were named things like McDowell's and Bagpiper was, of course, strictly a coincidence.

The Scotch whisky guys were, however, particularly incensed by the only brand of Indian whisky that is, in fact, whisky: Peter Scot, made by Bangalore's venerable Khoday distillers. Peter Scot is indeed a malt whisky. And Scot is right there in the name. Back in 1986, the Scotch-wallahs demanded Peter Scot change its name, and took to the legal system to ensure it did.

In 2008—yes, twenty-two years later, amazingly quick work by Indian standards—the Supreme Court said Peter Scot didn't need to have its name changed. They came to the conclusion that it should be plainly obvious to absolutely anyone who tasted Peter Scot that it wasn't, in fact, Scottish. Seriously. Here's the lawyer Soli Sorabjee, writing on the verdict in the *Indian Express*: 'The Court concluded that it was concerned with the class of buyers who are supposed to know the value of money, the quality and content of Scotch whisky and the difference in the process of manufacture, the place of manufacture and their origin . . . One wonders whether ordinary consumers of Scotch whisky, including judges who are not teetotallers, are really aware of these factors.'

46 If you're over 30, you know that good times *never* come back.

47 Almost everyone agrees manufacturing is what we need. This book is, by and large, convinced of it too. But I do want to issue a warning as well. There are good reasons to think that time is running out for India to build a manufacturing sector as a ladder to middle-class prosperity. One that I particularly worry about is 3D printing—something that, just a few years ago, was science fiction. 3D printers are just like ordinary printers, except that instead of ink, they jet out plastic or plaster or even metals. Give it a blueprint, and waste plastic or metals, and it can print out the perfect auto component. And today they're getting to be cheaper than an iPhone. So what happens to our manufacturing revolution if cheap little plastic stuff, the basics of small-scale manufacturing, can be printed out at a local 3D-printerwala cum mobile top-up guy cum Xerox shop? Suppose, for example, that the mobile covers that we complain are imported from China are made in the future not in some little factory in a UP industrial park, as we dream, but by me downloading a blueprint onto a USB and walking round the corner to my local printerwala? This could completely upend everything we hope for.

In general, 3D printing is a symbol of a larger problem we might have to deal with. The world economy has become ever more unequal as technology has improved, and more and more money goes to the people and economies that are top-end innovators, owners of intellectual property, those who perform services only they can. If this process speeds up, even in manufacturing, are we doomed to be poor forever? Perhaps not. But our task will become even harder.